Fydell Edmund Garrett, E. J. Edwards

The Story of an African Crisis

The Truth About the Jameson Raid and Johannesburg Revolt of 1896

Fydell Edmund Garrett, E. J. Edwards

The Story of an African Crisis
The Truth About the Jameson Raid and Johannesburg Revolt of 1896

ISBN/EAN: 9783744753104

Printed in Europe, USA, Canada, Australia, Japan

Cover: Foto ©ninafisch / pixelio.de

More available books at **www.hansebooks.com**

THE STORY OF AN AFRICAN CRISIS

BEING THE TRUTH ABOUT THE JAMESON RAID
AND JOHANNESBURG REVOLT OF 1896
TOLD WITH THE ASSISTANCE
OF THE LEADING ACTORS
IN THE DRAMA

BY
EDMUND GARRETT
EDITOR OF
THE "CAPE TIMES," AUTHOR OF "IN AFRIKANDERLAND," ETC

AND

E. J. EDWARDS
ASSISTANT EDITOR OF THE "CAPE TIMES," SPECIAL
CORRESPONDENT AT JOHANNESBURG
DEC. 1895 AND JAN. 1896

WESTMINSTER
ARCHIBALD CONSTABLE AND CO
2 WHITEHALL GARDENS
1897

Preface to the Present Edition

STORY OF AN AFRICAN CRISIS

THE part of this little book which deals with the House of Commons Inquiry is new. The part which tells the Story of the Raid and Revolt is also new to the English public, and has been in the hands of the South African public not many weeks.

"The Story of a Crisis," published as the 1896 Christmas Number of the *Cape Times*, was intended for both these audiences; but the whole edition was exhausted by Cape Town, or at least by Cape Colony, eleven thousand copies being bought on the day of publication. Thus England was left practically unsupplied, though the reviewers have written very kind things already on the strength of the few copies that were accessible. By permission of the proprietors of the *Cape Times*, I have therefore arranged with Messrs. Archibald Constable & Co. that they should issue the Story in its present form, adding, besides some documentary Appendices which I hope will be found useful for reference, an Introduction dealing with the immediate developments of the hour.

As to the division of authorship, I am indebted to my friend and colleague, Mr. E. J. Edwards, for the most part of Chapters ix., xii., xiv., xv., the idea throughout being to make the narrative as far as possible first-hand.

F. E.

Preface to the African Edition

"WHAT an interesting story it would all make, if one could only get at the truth about it!" has been a common expression ever since the South African Crisis of last New Year first electrified the world.

For a long time the truth was difficult to get at, and on some points impossible to publish; but the psychological moment now seems to have come for telling the story.

The Jameson trial is over; the Reform trials are over; the Cape Select Committee has published its Report; the British Government has published Blue-books, and the Transvaal Government Green-books; the English Inquiry, by common consent, has little left to discover, and cannot well report till that little has become ancient history.

We are far enough removed now from these astonishing events for the story to be no longer *sub judice*; we are near enough to them still for memories to be fresh and first-hand evidence accessible.

The exact meaning of our phrase, "with the assistance of leading actors," is simply that the narrator has talked over crucial points, or secured communication, with almost every single man who could be so described; and he believes that the result takes fairly into account all the conflicting versions, as between the Reformers and the Imperial Government, the Reformers and the Raiders, the Raiders and the Boers; as to the relations between Rhodes and Jameson, and the other vexed questions. Most of these have been winnowed through the columns of the *Cape Times* during this stirring year, and the truth about some of them was first published in those columns. But many interesting details appear here for the first time, especially as to that political and personal side of the Crisis, the scenes of which were Cape Town and Pretoria rather than Johannesburg or Doornkop.

The story, dictated in the intervals of other work, makes no literary pretentions. The teller had to consider two classes of reader: those in South Africa, and those in England. As "The Princess" has it,—

> "And I, betwixt them both, to please them both,
> And yet to give the Story as it rose,
> I moved as in a strange diagonal,
> And maybe neither pleased myself nor them."

The attempt has been to make the story readable and intelligible. If that much has been attained, the defects incident to haste, a late change of plan, and the unresting wheel of a daily paper, may perhaps be overlooked.

Contents

CHAP.		PAGE
	INTRODUCTION	xi
	THE PRELUDE TO A CRISIS, AS TOLD BY MR. CHAMBERLAIN	1
I.	"ON THE MOST FRIENDLY FOOTING"	7
II.	"CLIVE WOULD HAVE DONE IT"	28
III.	THE PERVERSION OF MR. RHODES	33
IV.	THE PLOT THICKENS	42
V.	THE ARMING OF JOHANNESBURG	53
VI.	CONSPIRACY BY TELEGRAPH	60
VII.	A HITCH, AND A FALSE START	78
VIII.	THE GREAT FIASCO	87
IX.	JOHANNESBURG TAKES ITS COAT OFF	123
X.	THE IRENE MYSTERY AND THE NACHTMAAL SURPRISE	142
XI.	A PREMIER'S "APPLE-CART"	147
XII.	A BOOM IN REVOLUTIONS	161
XIII.	THE STORY OF THE PROCLAMATION	184
XIV.	A "SLUMP" IN REVOLUTIONS	201
XV.	JOHANNESBURG PUTS ITS COAT ON AGAIN	214
XVI.	SCENES AT PRETORIA, CAPE TOWN, AND ELSEWHERE	233
XVII.	PICKING UP THE BROKEN CROCKERY	252

APPENDICES :—

I.	THE "LETTER OF INVITATION"	271
II.	THE NATIONAL UNION MANIFESTO	273
III.	STATEMENT OF THE REFORM LEADERS AT THE TRIAL	287
IV.	THE CONVENTION OF LONDON (1884). (CRITICAL CLAUSES)	292
V.	CECIL RHODES AND HIS POLICY	296

Introduction

WITH SPECIAL REFERENCE TO THE HOUSE OF COMMONS INQUIRY

SINCE the Story set out in the following pages was written, a distinct change has come, not over the facts themselves, of course, nor even over the facts so far as known to the writer and here set out, but over the face and public colour of the Inquiry which is now beginning. In this Introduction I propose to deal with the history of this change, and with the true inwardness of the new issues which it raises.

The Situation of the Moment.

The centre of gravity has changed from Cape Town to London, and it has come to seem, for the moment, as if the man who must stand or fall by the Committee were not Mr. Cecil Rhodes any longer, but rather Mr. Joseph Chamberlain.

Around Mr. Rhodes' figure the air has cleared. In spite of the obstinate, year-long silence that he has kept, it is beginning to be fairly understood what his relationship to Dr. Jameson's venture was, and also what it was not. The whole episode is seen more in relation to the rest of Mr. Rhodes' extraordinary career, and to the permanent factors in South African politics. In South Africa men have already made up their minds about Mr. Rhodes' action, and, sensibly or insensibly, taken sides upon it. I do not think this Inquiry is likely to touch his position there, either for good or evil, except transiently.

Mr. Rhodes' Position.

Very different is the case with Mr. Chamberlain. If the rumour now revived were made good, and the strongest of Colonial Secretaries, equally with the strongest of Colonial Premiers, proved to be "in it up to his neck," he would be "in" a deep slough indeed. What matters more, what matters incalculably, he would have carried England "in" with him.

Mr. Chamberlain's Position.

In the game of cards that is playing between Mr. Kruger and Mr. Chamberlain, there are two trumps yet unplayed.

The Chamberlain trump card would be the conviction of the President of complicity in the Berlin intrigue begun by his State Secretary and rashly signalized by the Kaiser's telegram.

The Kruger trump card would be the conviction of the Colonial Secretary of complicity in the Jameson Raid.

And this, if we are to believe the gossip which has now circulated to every corner of the world, is the card which is about to be put into Mr. Kruger's hand by a Select Committee of the British House of Commons!

After Mr. Chamberlain's despatches, if not before, it is quite impossible to conceive anything more crushing to his personal reputation, or more damaging to *perfide Albion* on the Continent, to "the Imperial Factor" in South Africa.

The history of this gossip so far is as follows.

The first emergence of the rumour at the time of the Crisis is duly chronicled in the Story. Up to December, 1895, there was no idea abroad in South Africa at large of any change in the traditionally "correct" attitude of the Colonial Office to the *Uitlander* agitation in the Transvaal. The action taken on the Drifts Question[1] seemed to be strictly within the four corners of the London Convention, and was not taken as promising any interference with the Transvaal internally.

The Biography of a Rumour.

At the time of the Crisis, however, there was undoubtedly a

---

[1] Chap. i., pp. 22, 23.

firm impression among those who were "in the secret," or even on the outer fringes of the secret, alike at Cape Town and at Johannesburg, that Chamberlain was behind Rhodes, just as Rhodes was behind Jameson; in short, that "Chamberlain," as it was commonly put, was "in it up to his neck." It was but a whisper that had been passed round, till the "prompt and vigorous action," so much applauded by Mr. Chamberlain's colleagues and countrymen, provoked the less discreet confederates to babble.[1]

In those first days the public mind was not familiarized with the distinction between what Dr. Jameson actually did and what Mr. Rhodes had been ready to sanction his doing. The first murmurs at Johannesburg seemed to blame Mr. Chamberlain for "deserting" a blunder which even Mr. Rhodes had to disavow.

By the Transvaal Boers it was assumed, as a matter of course, with or without any rumours to fan the ever-ready Boer suspicion, that Jameson's policemen embodied a Suspicions. British official plot. Krugersdorp was to them another Laing's Nek, and Doornkop the second Majuba. Hence the cry that Oom Paul should tear up the Convention; and there was a juncture at which a very ugly situation might easily have arisen, but for the credit which Sir Hercules Robinson commanded with Afrikander leaders. That one fact entitles Lord Rosmead to our gratitude.[2] Has it ever struck the reader what the position would have been if (for instance) Mr. Hofmeyr and the Acting President of the Free State had suddenly joined President Kruger in an appeal from the perfidy of the British Government to the united moral sense of Europe? When Englishmen are facing a world in arms, they do like to be able to think they are in the right.

Thanks to Sir Hercules' private influence and the uncompromising correctness of Mr. Chamberlain's public action

[1] Chap. xii., p. 167.   [2] Chap. xiii., p. 182.

The Rumour killed in South Africa. against, not the Raiders only, but Mr. Rhodes and the Chartered Company, all this gossip soon died a natural death in South Africa, despite some efforts of the Pretoria Government's Reptile Press to keep it alive. A Colonial Minister (Sir James Sivewright), in the course of the debate on the Charter in the Cape Assembly, made a rather mischievous reference to what has been called the clairvoyance of 'Mr. Fairfield;[1] but nobody took much notice. The very complete telegraphic finds of the Transvaal Government compromised no Imperial official, save one Bechuanaland magistrate, and the anxiety of some members of the Cape Select Committee to drag in the Imperial Secretary (Sir Graham Bower) ended in disappointment. Meanwhile, the rumour which died a natural death in South Africa was being galvanized into artificial life in England.

For the numerous political enemies of Mr. Chamberlain there were obvious temptations, and equally for the friends of **Revived in England by the Raiders.** Mr. Rhodes; but those who first succumbed fall strictly under neither of these designations. It was reserved for those who commanded (so far as anybody did command) in the Raid itself—those British officers, or ex-officers, at whom already "all the world wondered," not quite in the Balaclavan sense—it was reserved for these strategists to show what kind of a hand they could make in *la haute politique*, by first giving body to the nine days' gossip of Johannesburg.

The impression which had got round among the plotters before the Crisis as to Imperial backing prevailed among the confederates at Pitsani, as well as at Johannesburg and Cape Town.

It was in the mind of Major "Bobby" White, no doubt, as he pulled on his riding gloves and called out to Inspector Fuller of the Cape Police, "It's all right, old chap; you can do what you like: the wires are cut!" It was the idea

---

[1] For probable explanation see chap. vi., p. 62.

which Dr. Jameson and Sir John Willoughby, in perfect good faith, conveyed to officers and men alike, as they "ga'ed o'er the border"; and it is just conceivable that it survived even the delivery to each several officer of a several note, from the High Commissioner, bidding him to stop, "on pain of rendering yourself liable to severe penalities."[1] It is just conceivable, I say, that Sir John Willoughby and his officers dismissed this explicit warning at all parts of the game. It is quite possible to admire them for deciding, since they had got so far, that they must now go through with it, and trust to success to cover up a splendid indiscipline. That one can understand. What puzzles is why, if all this was to be part of the game, it should not be equally part of the game to pay the forfeit of failure smiling. "Victory or Westminster Abbey" was Nelson's word; Jameson's men might, at least, have accepted the alternative, "Johannesburg or Holloway!" But that was not the view of all of them.

"Cast off by everybody, on they went, a fair mark for every Boer rifle. Careers and commissions they threw to the winds." So I remember writing of them in their darkest hour,—a little rhetorically, no doubt, for we were all a good deal moved. But, lo! it turns out that to throw careers and commissions to the wind was the last thing that some of these gentlemen, or their friends, and advisers, and spokesmen, contemplated.

The Officers' Position.

In the Pretoria gaol, the first cell occupied by the four Johannesburg leaders was one just vacated by the Raid officers; and they found scribbled on the vermin-haunted wall the Essex-Elizabeth couplet:

"I fain would climb, but I fear to fall;
If thy heart fail thee, climb not at all."

The controversy between Raiders and Reformers—idle, indeed, where there were so many mistakes on both sides—has

---

[1] Bluebook, c. 7933, Nos. 5, 7, 8, 10, and 220 § 16-18. See also Story, p. 91.

happily ended without any public laundry of soiled linen. But that mural taunt does suggest one odious comparison. In the matter of the alleged Imperial complicity, as in others, the " cowards " held their tongues and took their beating: it was the " heroes " who peached!

No doubt, to plead that they *thought* certain things is not exactly the same as pleading that certain things were so; but for all practical purposes it was impossible for the Raiders to shelter themselves or each other in any way under the *magni nominis umbra* of Mr. Chamberlain, without embarrassing their country in exact proportion as the plea availed to save themselves.

Yet it was actually proposed by some of their advisers that they should make the plea at their trial under the Foreign Enlistment Act. Dr. Jameson put his foot down on this, but the line of thought betrayed itself more than once during the proceedings, and no doubt accounted for the indeterminate muddle which the defence, with all its galaxy of legal talent, somehow gave the effect of. It is said, by the way, and I believe truly, that on the evidence Major Raleigh Grey and one of the others ought to have got clear off. That, however, is common fortune of law. They being convicted with the rest, the War Office could but retire them with the rest.

<small>Line at the Trail.</small>

The next step was to try the effect on the War Office of the plea which had almost come into open court. Sir John Willoughby made the plea confidentially, on behalf of the others. For himself, he said, he did not greatly care whether he was retired or not. He had large financial interests to attend to, but he felt bound to declare as Commanding Officer that he had given certain assurances to those under his orders. He believed at the time that he had Imperial warrant for his proceedings, and he told the others so. The chain of communication suggested is Chamberlain—Rhodes—Jameson—Willoughby.

<small>Plea to the War Office.</small>

This statement of Sir John Willoughby was backed by

Dr. Jameson in so far as it referred to himself. Rightly or wrongly, he *had* believed himself able to give the assurances which Sir John Willoughby passed on to the officers.

<small>Dr. Jameson.</small>

Confronted by a plea of this kind, what ought the War Office to have done? What Lord Lansdowne did was simple and obvious. To Mr. Chamberlain the whole story traced back: to Mr. Chamberlain he referred it. The Colonial Secretary was absent from England at the time. Lord Lansdowne communicated with him, told him the story, and asked plainly whether there was anything in it. Mr. Chamberlain replied by telegram, with equal plainness, that there was absolutely nothing in it whatever.

<small>Action of the War Office.</small>

The officers were retired accordingly, and forthwith friends and relatives and admirers and solicitors began to buzz it about that they had been monstrously hardly dealt with.

Hardship there was, undoubtedly. The gaol was a horribly dull experience. Enforced farewell to the army was still more serious. Few of these gentlemen, probably, are well equipped for making a living in any other profession. But if it was bad for them, it was, at least, as bad for Colonel Rhodes, who shared the same fate for the part he played at Johannesburg, to say nothing of a £25,000 fine, and twenty-four hours passed under sentence of hanging. Colonel Rhodes has seen service, and won the D.S.O. He had some sort of a military career to lose. And he said nothing.

"A monstrous hardship!" My mind goes back to one dismal day when the Colony realised that these gentlemen, who had ridden across the Border, had surrendered to President Kruger, that they were at the mercy of his burghers. We admired their pluck—the first accounts, indeed, were heroic. We respected their motives. We felt that in deciding their fate their Boer captors were deciding whether the Englishman in South Africa should or should not feel a quiet life worth living on the morrow. And we made haste to frame petitions and send up one united voice from British South Africa to the

Queen's representative that he should put the lives of these men before any franchises or diplomacies in the world. It was not Holloway that we thought of then. It was hanging, rather. What a bathos, if we had been asked to commiserate the probable loss of their commissions!

Apparently, the contention of the officers' friends and spokesmen was that the War Office ought to have held a sort of full-dress rehearsal of the present Inquiry—to decide the question, one might say, whether the Raiders should have to retire from the army, or the Colonial Secretary should have to retire from public life.

One zealous lawyer carried on a correspondence with Mr. Chamberlain which almost took on a tone of threatening. Mr. Chamberlain is a bad man to bully, and he broke the correspondence off after what he indignantly described as "a blackmailing letter."

Meanwhile, the air was thick with hint and innuendo. Never was more done in the way of "pronouncing of some doubtful phrase, as, *Well, well, we know*; or, *We could, an if we would*; or, *If we list to speak*; or, *There be, an if they might*." At last, we in South Africa were astonished to learn by cable of an actual newspaper discussion on the question whether the War Office had not done a flagrant injustice to British officers by dismissing, without full inquiry, an allegation that they thought they had Imperial warrant for raiding the Transvaal.

During most of this time the officers themselves were in Holloway, where two of them are still completing their sentences. It would be pleasant to be assured that they had no kind of responsibility for all this. I, for my part, am most willing and anxious to believe that, after the first indiscretion of the leading Raiders in presenting the plea, the exploitation of it has lain at other doors. And I wish to make it clear beyond possibility of misconception that I am not charging these gentlemen with misstatement. The whole point of my commentary is precisely

If there really were a Secret.

the opposite. What they say about their own belief at the time is true past a doubt. I shall discuss, in a moment, what there was to lend colour to the belief. But assume, for the argument, that it was in fact a true belief, justified up to the hilt. Assume that all apparent veto upon the Raid was neutralised by a nod or a wink, so to speak, from Downing Street. Assume that these officers were the secret agents of a Machiavellian British policy, playing a sinister game such as Russian officers have played in the Balkans, or such as intriguing kings and cardinals in Dumas are always sending adventurers to play. Then I say if that was the game, if they took that to be the game, why not play it according to the rules? On those Dumas adventures, he who succeeded was enriched and decorated, indeed; but he who was unlucky enough to fail was always cheerfully disowned. And he was expected not to render up his secret though torn to pieces by wild horses before the Queen-Mother with a Duchess of Guise, dressed as a page boy, among the sightseers, laying her finger on her lip. Perhaps Sir John Willoughby found himself torn to pieces by wild asses, and the strain became insupportable. At any rate, it seems to me that the best and only defence of soldiers who disclose a State secret is the one which I set up —to wit, that there was not really any State secret to disclose. And now, what *was* the allegation?

What does the suggested chain of communication—Chamberlain, Rhodes, Jameson, Willoughby—amount to? The question brings us to the next step in this Bio-

Mr. Stead's Publication.

graphy of a Rumour: Mr. Stead's " History of the Mystery," which, in the form in which it finally met the public eye of England, might rather have been called, "The Mystery of a History," but which has probably made the most that ever will be made of "the skeleton in Blastus's cupboard."

As to the mischievousness of that publication there seems to have been an almost universal consensus. Unfortunately, a similar consensus sometimes has greeted audacities of Mr.

Stead's that were in their essence brave, useful, and patriotic. Nobody who has once worked under that Dr. Stockmann of English journalists—an experience which is a liberal education in itself—can ever again feel quite happy on finding himself in a majority. Personally, nothing would be more to my liking than to stand beside Mr. Stead in a minority of two. But an offence is not necessarily Socratic because the whole city prescribes hemlock for it; a bad argument is not made good even by crucifixion; and in this case I must repeat, even though everybody agrees with me, the opinion that Mr. Stead's "History" of "the Skeleton in Blastus's Cupboard," as heralded and projected, was from every point of view (save, perhaps, Dr. Leyds') a most mistaken and unfortunate effort.

One thing, and one thing only, can turn the tables on Mr. Stead's critics. He started from certain postulates about the Inquiry and its coming disclosures. If he was right about the disclosures, he was unquestionably right also in thinking that there was not a day to lose for any apologist who meant to try putting a good face on them. Well, the Select Committee is sitting. Its composition is a guarantee that there will be no mawkish anxiety to suppress any disclosures. Its proceedings will decide, perhaps almost as soon as this is in the reader's hands, whether it is Mr. Stead or *nous autres* who must look foolish.

The serious thing about all this "Blastus" business was the inference naturally drawn as to the attitude and intentions of Mr. Cecil Rhodes. Anything which rests on Mr. Rhodes' word is apt to be found true and to become rather important. Mr. Stead was known to be a great friend of his; Mr. Hawksley, who was evidently behind, was the Chartered Company's solicitor; it was whispered, among those who were likely to know, that we had here another outcome of the headstrong inspiration of "Dr. Jim" himself. In reality, Mr. Rhodes was away on the veld or in the Matoppos, living in the saddle, sleeping in the air, discoursing to rebel indunas, declining (in his own way and Mr. Parnell's) to open a letter; and none but a clairvoyant could say what his attitude and intentions might be. Mr. Hawksley is a very clever lawyer, but he was hopelessly wrong... Dr. Jameson is a man who, throughout the great country which he helped to add to the Empire, is beloved with a kind of fond extravagance; but here he was ending 1896 with a blunder only second to the one with which he began it.

As for Dr. Harris, the other putative father of the rumour, he it was, it seems, whose protests compelled Mr. Stead to the extraordinary course by which, at the last moment, he made his "Mystery" literally blacker still, and so attained—in perfect good faith—the maximum of suggestion with the minimum of plain statement. The "blotting out" of "State secrets" was at that stage the only alternative to complete suppression; but I can recall nothing in the unexpurgated text, as I saw it, that was as bad as the blots.

Happily, however, in the meantime the cat was out of the bag, and proved to be only a cat after all. Mr. Stead had been corresponding with me about the plan and plot of his Story, and had borne with exemplary good humour my continued protests against it. On the eve of publication he favoured me with advance proofs, humorously remarking that I now knew the worst, and could proceed to "slate" him. I did proceed to slate him. On the day when the History was published in London, the *Cape Times* quoted what seemed to be the gist of it in Cape Town, reviewing it with a judicious mixture of sorrow and anger. And, by a misunderstanding the blame of which (if any) was wholly mine (but how could one have guessed that incredible "blacking-out" expedient?) the very chapter quoted in Cape Town was the one "blacked out" on the machine in London!

South Africa—and later London—was thus apprised that what the whole Mystery amounted to was simply that Mr. Rhodes, and through him others, had been led to form an exaggerated view of the extent of Mr. Chamberlain's cognisance and approval of their plans, owing to the terms in which friends or agents in London

<small>What it all came to.</small>

reported the tenour of conversations at the Colonial Office, mainly or partly in connection with the negotiations for transfer of the Protectorate, and of the duty of policing the Protectorate, to the Chartered Company.

I think that will be accepted as a fair summary: a fair prose translation of Mr. Stead's ingenious and poetical fantasy about the Cable-Serpent, which drags its slow length through the Atlantic ooze, and tempts the denizens of a political Eden by repeating broken whispers and condensed perversions of each other's thoughts.

"Is *that* all?" was the universal remark of the Cape Town reader. For Mr. Stead's oceanic "Serpent" had been carrying us a great many echoes of the trumpets preliminary.

I stated then, in reviewing this suggestion of compromising cables, and I repeat my belief now, that I have known for nearly a year the tenour of these much-talked-of cables, and that they are not really compromising enough to "hang a dog." By this I mean that they are susceptible on the face of them of a perfectly innocent and proper explanation; like so many other expressions or actions on the eve of the Transvaal Crisis, which, seen after the event, in the distorting search-light thrown by the event, got quite a sinister look. Any one who, like myself, has had to study the history of this affair at all closely, could mention some absurd illustrations of this phenomenon. The Transvaal Government put into a greenbook a telegram of my own, which to this day (in all probability) they firmly believe to implicate the Imperial Government. *They*, no doubt, will display all the inductive certainty of Sergeant Buzfuz if somebody should prove to have cabled "chops and tomato sauce."

What any body *did* cable we shall all know soon; for the Committee will order the Cable Company to produce the documents. The Company's rule, I believe, is to destroy copies of messages after one year; but Sir William Harcourt, like a sleuthhound on the promising scent, sent round a warning some time ago, and saved any "good copy" which may be going.

INTRODUCTION   xxiii

But for this certainty that the whole matter must needs come to light in a few days, and that the time of rumour and the poring dark is at an end, I should not have said so much unless I had leave to say all. I wish I had leave. But the few who know the exact truth are of two classes. There are those who hold their tongues for obvious and proper reasons; but there are also some who cry "Hush!" because they have already, in an indignant phrase of Mr. Chamberlain's own, "worked the thing for all it was worth." *Omne ignotum pro terribili.*

What I believe the inquiry will show to be the truth about the affair is set out partly in the Narrative, and shall now be stated explicitly.

What is the Truth? Much has been conjectured as to the part played in the communications by Dr. Harris—the Dr. Cactus of Mr. Stead's pages—who was South African Secretary of the Chartered Company, and confidential secretary of Mr. Rhodes, and was in London during much of the territorial negotiations with the Colonial Office which went on between August and November, 1895. The reader will notice passages in the following narrative—especially in chapters iv. and vi.— written before the present discussion arose, which bear on this point. I have not been favoured by Dr. Harris with his version. But it seems to be forgotten, by those who expect tremendous cable finds, that Dr. Harris left England and returned to Cape Town in the middle of December, well before the crisis; so that if Mr. Chamberlain really had a mania for sending compromising messages through Dr. Harris at that time, he might just as well have sent them by word of mouth. The way in which the minor confederates in South Africa telegraphed about to each other has astonished the world; but a British Colonial Secretary, if he took to conspiracy, could hardly do it quite like that.

"Reference to possible developments, however discreet, was bound to be made during those prolonged negotiations about the Border territory," it is pointed out in chapter iv. I have ascertained that the prospect at *Johannesburg* (not the *Jameson* part) was much better known beforehand by certain high officials of the Transvaal—by one high official, at any rate—than by sympathetic journalists, politicians, Cape folk, and well-informed South Africans generally. I think it will be found that the Colonial Office's Intelligence Bureau was in the same position as these high officials of the Transvaal. One sees at once, therefore, the temptation to an audacious and sanguine confederate in the Jameson part of the arrangements, who felt himself and his friends to be about to do so much better for England than she had ever done for herself, to stray tentatively at the Colonial Office off the legitimate ground into that where no Imperial official may tread.

It will be found, I think, that Dr. Harris did once begin to do so.

Mr. Chamberlain is a very unconventional official, and he was new to his work; but he certainly is no fool.

He checked the indiscreet discussion, and Dr. Harris, who is also no fool, dared not return to it; but he was not quite sure how far he had carried Mr. Chamberlain along with him.

Now, those who have once tested the matter know well that no two men ever have just the same identical memory of a conversation. So much, in all talk, depends on the ellipses. Thenceforward even a chance-dropped phrase in conversation where other parties where present—conversation, perhaps, on quite another subject—came to be scrutinized in this light. How much did the Colonial Secretary know? How much would he consent to? Would he give Mr. Rhodes and Dr. Jameson *carte blanche*?

Not Dr. Harris only—the Story casts him altogether too much for the villain, or if you like the hero, of the piece—not Dr. Harris only, but all kinds of insiders and outsiders who had an inkling: the harmful necessary journalist, the sympathetic irresponsible who really cannot compromise anybody but himself: became the means of conveying to Mr. Rhodes or to Johannesburg, or to some one or other of the revolutionary sympathisers in South Africa, the impression that the Colonial Office really did know a great deal—as in fact it did, and was ready to allow all—as in fact it was not.

In short, it came to pass in this way that Mr. Cecil Rhodes became convinced that here was a new and "pushful" Minister for the Empire, burning to let off fireworks and distinguish himself, and relying on Mr. Rhodes' resource and ingenuity to enable him to do so without compromising the Imperial factor.

What Mr. Rhodes Thought.

This fitted in excellently with Mr. Rhodes' own dreams, the Johannesburg temptation, and the course of events; and no doubt it contributed to the fine recklessness with which he took on himself other responsibilities that in his wildest moments he never supposed Mr. Chamberlain cognisant of— such as the arming beforehand of the very revolution which was to form the pretext of action.

Meanwhile, the impatient, in search of a bald, bold Aye or Nay, may be asking, "Why not say at once that Mr. Chamberlain knew nothing, and that it's all a disgraceful lie, and that people who 'thought' had no business to think, and so on, or else leave it alone?" The answer is, that when you really go into this matter, you soon leave the region of bald, bold Aye or Nay behind. It is so with most questions where more than two or three human beings are concerned. It took Browning—how many thousand lines to "whitewash" Pompilia? Yet he did whitewash her. It is easy to say that to know anything at all was to know too much. Perhaps it was. Perhaps Mr. Chamberlain will be censured for not telling President Kruger all that his Intelligence Bureau had collected or surmised as to the state of mind of President Kruger's own aggrieved subjects; just as Mr. Chamberlain once said [1] that the President's Government "ought to have communicated their suspicions or information" (as to troops on the border) to the High Com-

A Case of Nuances.

[1] C. 7933, Dispatch 220.

missioner. I can only say that the situation was one in which to know just exactly the right amount was a feat like the schoolman's, of balancing so many angels on the point of a needle.

Downing Street stood to be blamed after the event in any case, either for culpable indiscretion or for culpable ignorance. I do not suppose for a moment that any one concerned will escape blame altogether. But to show how utterly inapplicable are crude generalisations in this matter, and how easy it must have been for misunderstandings to arise in perfect good faith, one has only to sit down and try to draw up definitions of the various attitudes. Here is *my* attempt, after a year's puzzling :—

1. *What Lord Ripon presumably sanctioned, and Lord Loch did, in* 1894 :—

Upon signs of a rising in the Transvaal, to assemble British Bechuanaland Police quietly on the border with a view to their being ordered in by the High Commissioner to protect life and property at Johannesburg.

2. *What Mr. Chamberlain was probably prepared to sanction in* 1895 :—

Upon report of a probable rising in the Transvaal at a definite time (the end of December) to allow the British South Africa Company's police (including the ex-B.B.P.)—a force subject, but not quite so directly subject, to the High Commissioner's orders—to be assembled in the same way and for the same purpose as above; the possibility of such measures being called for being indirectly[1] recognised in territorial arrangements some time beforehand.

3. *What Mr. Rhodes was probably prepared to sanction*:—

Upon advices from Johannesburg leaders to Jameson (who should help to arm them, largely at Mr. Rhodes' expense) that the rising would be on a certain day; and upon a distinct statement from these leaders that they called upon the Com-

---

[1] I believe that Mr. Chamberlain flatly denies that it was *directly* recognised.

pany's troops to come in and "protect life and property" at the moment of the upheaval; to allow the use of the police, assembled as above, almost simultaneously with the action within the Transvaal, Mr. Rhodes to secure High Commissioner's assent as best he could.

4. *What Jameson actually did:*—

To act on the concert just described, and about the time first fixed upon, although the concert had been broken off and the day countermanded, Mr. Rhodes accordingly joining with the Johannesburg leaders in forbidding the use of the police.

Now, it will be seen at once that between 3 and 4 there is a gulf. But between 1, 2 and 3 there is really only a sheet of paper, if we put aside one feature. That one feature is Mr. Rhodes' assistance to the Johannesburg revolution beforehand. Had Mr. Rhodes resigned his Premiership and Charter Directorship before, instead of after: the affair of the arms would have been hailed as exhibiting all those qualities which Johannesburg has been reproached for lacking. For this is covered by "the sacred rights of revolution"; the question of raids, which have not yet established any "sacred rights," is quite apart from it. And, leaving aside this one point, as I say, it is possible to state the positions of Mr. Rhodes, Mr. Chamberlain, and Sir Henry Loch, so that there shall seem to be only a sheet of paper between them.

The difference between going in to help a revolution, and going in to "restore order," or "prevent a riot," or "protect life and property," is one which in practice it would have required superhuman ingenuity to maintain.

The question, just how much should happen before the border might decently be crossed, is another point which must always have been left to circumstances. When the Johannesburg leaders took the responsibility of the provisional appeal to Jameson, they took also the responsibility of a signal.

The High Commissioner's mediation, backed by material

support if necessary, was also a feature common to all four positions or policies. Though Sir Hercules Robinson never dreamed, of course, of the use which was made of the understanding in reassuring timid Reformers at Johannesburg, I have no doubt that he had fully arranged to go up and mediate, and that it was only the compromising of the situation by Jameson's act which made him so slow to offer his services when the time came.

Such action by the High Commissioner, upon any such long-expected crisis arising, had been a Downing Street South African axiom for years. Sir Hercules Robinson's appointment was defended in the Press on the ground of his special fitness for such a task. I remember a conversation with Lord Ripon at the Colonial Office at that time in which this was made clear; and if it had been a few months later, and I a confederate in the "complot," I might have rushed away and telegraphed that "Ripon is in it up to his neck." Yet (let me hasten to add) the late Colonial Secretary said no single word to which Dr. Leyds or Baron Marschall von Bieberstein, notebook in hand, could have taken exception.

Given this general prearrangement for a crisis; given Sir Hercules Robinson's particular consent to it beforehand; given the foreknowledge of Mr. Chamberlain's Intelligence Bureau that a crisis was brewing for this particular time—the end of December—for that much I am sure he will boast with some departmental pride; given the precedent of Lord Loch's assembling of the police to lend moral or material support, and the provision of Mr. Chamberlain, when the police were passing out of direct Imperial control, to facilitate any similar assembling of them under altered conditions in the future: given all these things, it will be seen at once how easy it would be to *make Mr. Chamberlain seem to have been* "up to his neck," if Mr. Rhodes tried to shelter himself (as some of his friends would have him do) behind the Colonial Office. I am able to say that he will do nothing of the kind. "How can he," asks somebody, "if, as you say, there's nothing in it?"

INTRODUCTION xxix

He could very easily, as I have shown, if he set himself to emphasize and enlarge on all the ambiguous little things that went to form or bear out the impressions which I have described. It would be very unpatriotic, and very selfish; and no doubt exploring party men on the Select Committee can do a great deal of mischief yet by pressing such ambiguous points, which, when pressed at all, require pages of explanation to clear up their suspiciousness.

Mr. Rhodes has the gift of silence. But I believe I have rightly represented what his impression was in December, 1895. I am also in a position to affirm, from personal assurance, that Lord Rosmead was not responsible for that impression, and that Mr. Chamberlain was not responsible. I have here tried to account for the divergence, and though the enquiry drag on for months I believe this is the conclusion it will have to come to. Mr. Rhodes did not plan or foresee *the* Raid. But he was willing for Johannesburg to engage Jameson for *a* "raid" of a certain kind. Mr. Chamberlain was also willing to arrange for *a* "raid," something between Lord Loch's and Mr. Rhodes'. *The* raid he never dreamed of. The "sheet of paper" may not be thick enough to please some swashbuckling polemists, to make Mr. Rhodes a criminal or Mr. Chamberlain a model of what I might call unctuous correctitude; but it suffices, unless one or both of two high servants of the Queen have lied as English gentlemen do not lie, to keep clear in a situation of unique difficulty the honour and good faith of England—never more indispensable as an element in the South Africa hurly-burly than they are to-day.

This Introduction is not concerned with the position of Mr. Rhodes. For that the reader is referred to the pages that follow. In them I have done his position, if anything, a little less than even justice. As an incurable English Radical, and in other capacities, I have had and shall have many occasions to differ from Mr. Rhodes, and to criticise him with, I hope, plenty of zest and vigour. But this is not the place or the moment for such

Cecil Rhodes.

criticism, and, I would add, England is not the country. Afrikanders of Republican sympathies have a good right to challenge him—those who have ever worked with him in the Colony—on the connection between the wild venture of 1895-6 and the British flag. His only answer to them is the *plébiscite*;[1] his "treachery to the Republic" consisted in bargaining that its future relation to a United South Africa under the British flag should be put to the vote of all its white inhabitants. But if it be true of Mr. Rhodes' day-dreams that they turned upon something grander than merely "substituting President Barnato for President Kruger," in his own phrase, at least it is not for Englishmen to make that a reproach. "What will you do if you have to go to prison?" I asked Mr. Rhodes on his way to England on the *Dunvegan Castle*. "If I have to go to prison? Well, I once read eight hours a day for my degree. I haven't had much time to read since then: I think I'd take on a course of reading." That is exactly what Wools Sampson has done in Pretoria *tronk*. I hope Mr. Rhodes' answers to the Committee—they are likely to be frank even to brutality, for he never conceives that anything he has done can be wrong—will not lead to that "course of reading." *Ruat cælum*, of course; but even the hungry exultation of Hollanders and Germans and Boers will hardly compensate us for the sullen feelings which we should have to rouse throughout British South Africa. At any rate, while Dutchmen denounce the raid as privateering for the Union Jack, it seems a little squalid that some Englishmen should be denouncing it as "a stock-jobbing speculation." There are still many who believe that "Rhodes sent Jameson in": there are not a few who hug the notion that what he sent him in for was to seize, in some unexplained and inexplicable way, the auriferous conglomerate of the Rand, or to merge with the Boer Republic the land which he has toiled for nearly twenty years to add to the Empire. Well! Shrewd judges estimate that the Raid

[1] Chap. iii., p. 34; see also chap. vii.

and his friends' part in it cost Mr. Rhodes a quarter of a million, first to last; and a good part of the rest of his fortune is locked up in Rhodesia, the future of which, as a factor in Africa, will be the romance or the tragedy of one man's life-work. I demur to that Continental sneer about "unctuous rectitude," but I do sometimes wish that my countrymen, and especially my fellow Liberals, had a little more *imagination*.

F. EDMUND GARRETT.

LONDON, *February*, 1897.

The Prelude to a Crisis

AS TOLD BY MR. CHAMBERLAIN

(Extract from the Dispatch of Feb. 4, 1896)

FOR a proper apprehension of the events which have led up to the Crisis, I must go back to the period immediately succeeding the conclusion of the Convention of Pretoria in 1881.

At that period, and for some time afterwards, the population of the South African Republic was comparatively small, and composed almost entirely of burghers and their families. The British element in it was made up of traders, a handful of farmers or landowners, and a small, and not very thriving, body of gold-miners, living chiefly in the neighbourhood of Lydenburg. The revenue was meagre, and hardly sufficient for the barest needs of Government.

About ten years ago the discovery of gold deposits at the De Kaap Fields gave indications of a new state of things, and a little later came the discoveries of gold at the Witwatersrand, which worked a complete revolution in the situation of the Republic, both financial and political. The discovery of the Reefs at the Rand gave rise to the inevitable gold fever, followed by the usual reaction. From such reaction the industry was saved by the foresight and financial courage of certain of the capitalists most interested, and since 1890 the progress has been uninterrupted and rapid.

Owing to peculiarities of temperament and circumstance, participation in the new industry had no attraction for the burgher population. It remained almost entirely in the hands of new-comers, commonly known as " Uitlanders," and a sharp line of cleavage was thus created within the Republic—the Uitlanders being chiefly resident in the industrial and mining centres, whilst the burgher population remained absorbed in its pastoral avocations and dispersed widely through the country districts. It is very difficult to arrive at any exact idea of the numbers of these two classes of inhabitants. But I conceive that I am well within the mark in estimating the white population along the Rand at something like 110,000, and it may safely be said that the aliens (the large majority of whom are British subjects) at the present time outnumber the citizens of the Republic.

The political situation resulting from these conditions is an anomalous one. The new-comers are men who were accustomed to the fullest exercise of political rights. In other communities, where immigration has played an important part in building up the population, it has been the policy of the Legislatures to make liberal provision for admitting all new-comers who are desirous of naturalization, after a comparatively brief period of probation, to the rights and duties of citizenship—a policy which, so far as national interests were concerned, has been fully justified by the event, for experience shows that the naturalized alien soon vies with—if he does not outstrip—the natural-born citizen in the fervour of his patriotism.

In the South African Republic, however, different counsels have prevailed with those who were the depositories of power. More than one law has been enacted, rendering more difficult the requirements imposed on those desiring naturalization, the effect being, so far as I can find, that whereas in 1882 an Uitlander could obtain full rights of citizenship after a residence of five years, he can now never hope to attain those rights *in full*; and their partial enjoyment is only conceded after a term of probation so prolonged as to amount, for most men, to a practical denial of the claim.

If he omits to obtain any kind of naturalization for himself, his children, though born on the soil, remain aliens like himself.

By this course of legislation the whole political direction of affairs and the whole right of taxation are made the monopoly of what is becoming a decreasing minority of the population, composed almost entirely of men engaged in pastoral and agricultural pursuits; whilst the great majority of all those engaged in the other avocations of civilization—the men, in fact, who have by their exertions in a few years raised the revenues of the country from some £75,000 to an amount which cannot now be less than £2,000,000, and who find eighteen or nineteen twentieths of the total revenue—are denied any voice in the conduct of the most important class of affairs, and have not succeeded in obtaining any redress for what seems a formidable array of grievances which, it is alleged, hamper and injure them at every step of their lives. The feelings of intense irritation which have been aroused by this state of things have not been lessened by the manner in which remonstrances have been met.

Whatever may be the truth as to the occurrences of the first few weeks of 1896, the Uitlander leaders had previously kept within the limits of constitutional agitation, but their success in this direction was not encouraging. It is true that hopes have been held out to them by persons of high position and influence in the South African Republic, and they have at times obtained what they regarded as promises, but these have not been practically fulfilled, and when they have remonstrated they have occasionally been met with jeers and insult—none the less irritating to strangers because, as I hope is a fact, they emanated only from a minority of the ruling class. Thus, in May, 1894, a petition for the extension of the franchise, signed by 13,000 inhabitants, is credibly reported to have been rejected by the Volksraad amid scornful laughter, and in April, 1895, a similar petition, signed by upwards of 32,500 inhabitants, is stated to have met a similar fate—one member of the Volksraad so far forgetting himself as to challenge the Uitlanders to take up arms and fight.

At a meeting of the National Union at Johannesburg in 1894, the grievances and the demands of the Uitlanders were set forth in a formal and elaborate manner, and it was then emphatically stated that no resort to violence was contemplated; although one of the principal speakers warned the Government that, if their policy were persisted in, blood would be shed in the streets of Johannesburg, and that the responsibility would lie at the doors of the Volksraad. At that time much was hoped from the coming elections, as it was anticipated that a "progressive" majority would be returned to the Raad, and that a more liberal policy would be pursued.

But those hopes were doomed to disappointment. The elections to the Raad did, indeed, result in the return of a majority of members who were commonly reckoned as "progressives," and the National Union, in view of the suggestion that reforms were hindered by the making of inflammatory speeches at Johannesburg, discontinued their agitation. Nothing, however, came of this change of policy.

On the 20th November, 1895, a speech was delivered by Mr. Lionel Phillips, the Chairman of the Chamber of Mines, which marks a reversion to the policy of active agitation. I note that on that occasion Mr. Phillips stated that the position had been endured, and it was likely to be endured still longer, and that he added that "nothing was further from his heart than a desire to see an upheaval, which would be disastrous from every point of view, and which would probably end in the most horrible of all possible endings—bloodshed." Finally came the manifesto issued by the National Union on the 27th December, in which their objects were stated to be the maintenance of the independence of the Republic, the securing of equal rights, and the redress of grievances. In that manifesto, although the complaints of the Uitlanders were set out in detail, and very plain language was used concerning the administration, no hint was given of an intention to resort to force.

I mention these matters because they seem to me to prove that, whatever may have been the secret schemes of individuals, the agitation, as the great majority of the Uitlanders understood it, and to which they gave their sympathy, was one proceeding on the only lines on which an agitation against an organized Government of military strength can proceed with any hope of success—that is to say, it was an open and above-board agitation, prosecuted without violence and within the lines of the Constitution.

It is needless to say that Her Majesty's Government had watched the progress of these events with careful attention. Apart from their legitimate concern for the interests of so large a body of British subjects, they could not but feel a keen anxiety lest the agitation should degenerate into a contest with the constituted authorities; but there was no ground for their active intervention. The Uitlanders and their organs had always deprecated the introduction into the dispute of what is called in South Africa the "Imperial factor." To have intervened uninvited seemed impracticable, and calculated only to be injurious to the prospects of a peaceful and satisfactory settlement.

There were, indeed, rumours from time to time that violent measures were in contemplation, but these rumours were continually falsified by the event, so that, in the long run, the opinion gained ground that the Uitlanders did not mean to risk a collision with the Government; and in the light of later occurrences it would seem evident that, so far as the Rand itself is concerned, that view was the correct one. Nor was it confined to Her Majesty's Government, for the Consul-General in London of the South African Republic, the Government at Pretoria, and the Press of South Africa as a whole, appear to have been of much the same way of thinking.

Such was the position of affairs when, on the 30th December, I learned the grave fact that Dr. Jameson had invaded the territory of the South African Republic at the head of a force of armed police.

The Story of an African Crisis

Chapter I

"ON THE MOST FRIENDLY FOOTING"

"DR. JAMESON entered the South African Republic at the head of over 500 mounted men and a strong force of Artillery . . . at a time when the relations between the Government of the South African Republic and those of the other States and Colonies of South Africa were on the most friendly footing." So the Select Committee of the Cape House of Assembly declares in the first section of its report on the Raid.

In the language of diplomacy all Powers not actually belligerent at the moment are supposed to be on "the most friendly footing," but to any one who remembers the extraordinary state of feeling at the close of 1895, the tension in the Transvaal and in South Africa at large, the words quoted must carry a more than diplomatic flavour.

Mr. Chamberlain's despatch which has served us as Introduction, gives a lucid sketch of the stages by which this tension of feeling had been brought about within the Transvaal itself. He does not say anything as to the Republic's external relations. It may be well to glance back over a few years, taking both together. Perfect peace and serenity cannot be said to have prevailed in the Transvaal at the time of the Raid, but perfect peace and serenity had not prevailed much in the Transvaal in any year since its foundation. Mr. Chamberlain's Raad member who "so far forgot himself as to challenge the

Uitlanders to fight for their rights," perhaps did not so much forget himself as he remembered the history of his country. A reader's first impression from that history might lead him to say that when the Transvaal Boers were not being raided themselves they were generally raiding other people, north, south, east or west, and that before the Uitlanders' revolutionary movement came to birth the burghers supplied the deficiency by civil war amongst themselves, covert or overt.

The early history of the Transvaal in the fifties resolves itself into a struggle on the part of Pretorius, the Boer leader, whose "South African Republic" only covered a small part of the Transvaal, to swallow up the independent republics of Lydenburg (originally the centre of Government), Zoutpansberg, and the Free State.

As far as the two former republics were concerned, the party of Pretorius eventually succeeded, but not without a long series of military and semi-military movements in which the Pope of Rome and the Pope of Avignon liberally excommunicated each other, each side proclaiming the other as "rebels."

These struggles actually reached the point of civil bloodshed, though more often one party of farmers carrying firearms would retire when another party appeared in greater force.

In the course of these obscure civil brawls, S. J. P. Kruger flits across the scene generally as a stormy petrel. We find him on the side of certain Boer revolutionaries or reformers, upholding them in their action and protesting against their being saddled with fines when the action failed. On two separate occasions we find him marching on Pretoria to drive out the head of a rival party. We even find him joining in a kind of raid across the border of the friendly Free State and issuing a twenty-four hours' ultimatum to its Government, and by an odd coincidence actually figuring as the man who carried the flag of truce which averted actual fighting when the rival commandoes were drawn up facing each other.

During these transformation scenes young Kruger is sometimes on the side of Pretorius and sometimes against him, but he is always exceedingly ready to take up arms, and exhibits all the traditional contempt of the South African Boer for what is called constitutional agitation.

In one of his speeches or conversations after the Jameson Raid President Kruger spoke, rather in sorrow than in anger, in that tone which he so well knows how to assume, of the perfidy involved in taking up arms against a peaceful neighbour, a

COLONEL FRANCIS RHODES.
From a Photograph by Messrs. ELLIOTT & FRY.

perfidy, the darkest side of which was the story then current that the assistance of native chiefs had actually been invoked by the raiders, thus setting black against white, in South Africa the unforgivable sin.

President Kruger has a keen memory, but it may be described as rather selective than retentive. Paul Kruger the President has undoubtedly forgotten how Paul Kruger the Raider once gave the Government of the Free State twenty-four hours in which to set free its imprisoned reformer rebels.

Even the stirring up of natives, a story now thoroughly discredited, and indeed at no time supported by a shred of proof, might recall to his memory the advances made by Pretorius to the military Moshesh against the Free State, advances which President Boshof, in his opening speech to the next Session of the Free State Raad, gave Moshesh credit for declining.

But, it may be said, all this is ancient history; like the Boer raids into British Bechuanaland in the eighties which we spare recalling. In the presence of the stranger it may be thought burghers of the Transvaal have sunk all differences. On the contrary, within two years the Transvaal burghers of to-day have twice come close to civil war among themselves. A civil war with which the Uitlander had nothing to do except in so far as his presence exercised a deterrent effect. So that in each case the crisis blew over. In 1892–3 the last Presidential election contest was fought between S. J. P. Kruger and Piet Joubert, the present Commandant-General. It was a close fight. Joubert was supposed to represent the progressives, that is to say, burghers who were inclined to conciliate the Uitlander population by the extension of some modest instalment of rights. Kruger, of course, represented what he represents to-day—the opposite. He won, but not by much. Joubert's supporters alleged that corrupt practices, impersonation, and dual voting had flourished rankly on the Kruger side. They demanded a scrutiny, at which the supporters of each candidate should be represented. The Executive Council, being a Krugerite body, refused this, and undertook the scrutiny itself. Three times the votes were counted, and three times different results were announced, the final version giving Kruger 7,854 against Joubert's 7,009. Although the Joubert party finally accepted this finding there was intensely bitter feeling for some months, and persons in a position to judge believe that there was more than mere threatening in the talk indulged in among the Joubert adherents of resorting to the traditional Transvaal method of redressing what they considered their wrongs : that is, by a demonstration in arms. The General himself, in a conversation which the writer once had with him, though of course talking like a book about the impropriety of resorting to arms against countrymen under any provocation, distinctly took credit to himself for having resisted the temptation.

More recently the most dangerous feeling was aroused in an unintelligible squabble between the Hervormde and the Gereformeerde branches of the Dutch Reformed Church, one of which, again, is allied with the narrower "dopper" sect of Oom Paul himself. Theologically, it would take a Scotsman to distinguish between them; and for that reason, need it be said, the schism is excessively sharp and keen. Matters came to a head over a decision of the Court transferring *en bloc* a quantity of Church property from one sect to the other. It is not quite settled yet what the upshot will be, the religious division being complicated by political and family cross-divisions and feuds impossible for an outsider to trace; but here, again, persons on the spot and closely acquainted with the character and drift of the people, believe that an acute crisis over the Church dispute has only been averted by the Uitlander and Jameson crisis, which swamped all else.

Turning to the Uitlander issue in itself, there have been three or four distinct occasions, before any Jameson complication was heard of, in which a street scuffle or a random shot might have precipitated bloodshed.

Once, in 1891, on his way to confer with the High Commissioner on various questions, President Kruger passed through Johannesburg and was besieged in the Landdrost's house by a mob, which uproariously demanded a speech, groaned, broke in the railings, and actually hauled down the Transvaal flag and trampled it under foot to the strains of "Rule Britannia." There was a similar scene in 1894 at the time of the Commandeering Incident, when men who were denied with contempt every other right of citizenship were favoured with a requisition to go to the front and fight for the Republic in one of its native wars. Let Lord Loch (then Sir

Henry and High Commissioner) tell the story in his own words :—

"On my arrival at Pretoria I was met at the station by President Kruger, accompanied by many of his Executive. There was a great crowd at the station, and it was with the greatest difficulty that President Kruger was enabled to have the way cleared for himself and myself going to his carriage. The crowd was a very excited crowd. They removed the President's coachman from the box and took out his horses. Two men clambered on the box with Union Jacks, and in this way we were conducted to Pretoria, a distance of from a quarter to half a mile. On our arrival at the hotel where rooms had been prepared for me, there was a great crowd assembled in the streets wishing to present addresses. I reminded those who were anxious to present addresses to me that I was the guest of a friendly Power, and I refused to receive any address unless proper consideration was paid to the President, to his Government, and to the people of the South African Republic. There was much excitement at Johannesburg at this period."

There was indeed. So much that Mr. Kruger personally wrote to Sir Henry begging him not to visit Johannesburg, "lest a collision should arise." "It would be very agreeable to me, personally, and would be regarded by my Government as an act of international friendship, if you would give up your intended journey to Johannesburg." Accordingly Sir Henry received a deputation at Pretoria instead, and the conversation took place in which the possibility of Johannesburg being driven to defend itself by arms was mooted. According to a recent sensational statement in the *Temps*, the High Commissioner incited the deputation to this course. That, of course, is from the home of *canards*. But on his own showing he found the prospect so likely that he found it necessary to dissuade them from it. To quote again his House of Lords statement :

"To strengthen my position to the deputation I asked them what amount of arms they had at the time in Johannesburg. They told me they had a thousand rifles, and at the outside ten rounds of ammunition per rifle. I then pointed out to them, not as an encouragement to resist, but to show them what a futile measure it would be, if any action on their part brought about disturbances, and as a consequence an attack upon Johannesburg. I

Mr. CECIL J. RHODES

From a Photograph by Messrs. BASSANO, *Old Bond Street*

also pointed out to them that, if I went there, and they would admit it, there would be a danger of disturbance arising, and if disturbance arose the Government of the Transvaal would be justified, under all the circumstances, in putting it down with very stringent hands. . . . They saw the force of my reasons."

Sir Henry was quite prepared, by the way, for a kind of authorized raid from Bechuanaland, as well as a revolution in Johannesburg, on this occasion; but of that, more anon.

The strained relations of the Transvaal at the close of 1895 were external as well as internal. The Republic had become the one supreme obstacle to South African unity. The inter-state politics of South Africa are, and will remain until it becomes united, largely Customs politics and Railway politics. Ever since the failure of Lord Carnarvon's attempt to rush Federation, and especially since the failure and reversal of the Transvaal annexation, it is to a loose union of the States and Colonies as regards their fiscal and railway systems that most statesmen have looked forward when they used the formula of an United South Africa. That it was possible to link together a republic and a colony for friendly co-operation by this means was shown by the Customs Union which has existed between the Cape and the Free State since 1889. That Union, being based on a protective system made to please the farmers, while the Natal system is dominated by the importers, Natal could not join; but a still stronger reason was that the Transvaal would not join, and Natal lives on the Transvaal trade. Now, why would not the Transvaal join? Certainly not because it considered the interests of the Uitlander consumer class more than those of its pastoral burghers. The continued preference of the Transvaal for "splendid isolation" is at bottom due to the fact that those who govern it have never really given up the hope which is enshrined in the title of South African Republic. British statesmanship has long realized that it is not practicable politics to try and turn the Republics into Colonies; but Pretoria statesmanship has never quite given up the dream of turning the Colonies into Republics. At first the developments which the Rand gold led to seemed likely to revive the former hope and to Anglicise the Transvaal; but as President Kruger found by experience that he could hold the English-speaking population down, while the State was strengthened by their wealth, that development has tended in the opposite direction, and the hope of absorbing the Free State and eventually dominating all South Africa has once more inspired Transvaal policy. It has been assumed, and it cannot be denied that so far the assumption has worked, that the Englishman in Africa can be treated as a negligible quantity, save as a revenue producer. Accordingly, to unite upon such terms as are practicable—*i.e.*, upon Customs and Railways and the like—has become, in South Africa, a British formula; while it has become the Transvaal formula, or at any rate guiding spirit, to decline union upon such half measures at all. Thus it comes about that Mr. Rhodes has consistently worked for a united South Africa of some kind, while "closer union with the Free State" is the nearest aspiration of the sort attributable to his great rival. Mr. Rhodes' policy was for years directed to redressing the balance, to neutralizing the Transvaal superiority of wealth, to keeping open way to the North as against Transvaal raiders, to surrounding and embracing the Republic with territory which, like it, should contain great gold-fields and great populations, and should go into the British side of the balance when the hegemony of South Africa comes to waver between the two.

So far Mr. Rhodes as the opener of the North. Meanwhile, Mr. Rhodes, as the Premier of the Cape, was set upon these minor measures of union which have been described; and it was after a stormy interview with President Kruger late in 1894 on the Cape-Transvaal relations that he finally made up his mind that it was hopeless ever to look for the conversion of the present rulers of the Transvaal to any such modest programme of South African co-operation.

They had often coquetted with the idea of joining a Customs Union, but had always treated it as a favour to the Imperial

Government, a favour which must be bargained for by giving Swaziland, or a way to the sea, or some other advantage. It is a striking proof, by the way, of the purely South African motives of Great Britain's policy in South Africa that a Customs Union, under which British trade would be handicapped by high tariffs, should be treated as a goal of British diplomacy. In this sense it was treated for in one abortive Convention about Swaziland, which, however, was rejected by the Raad. Eventually Swaziland was bargained away for another consideration, and then Oom Paul used the same bait, the idea of the Transvaal entering a Customs Union, in order to obtain the littoral beyond Swaziland, and there make his own Port. In the interval, however, a maladroit speech of his on the Kaiser's birthday had focussed attention on his policy (disapproved in every other South African country) of bartering trade advantages for political support from Germany, with the result that Great Britain in the course of 1895 declared a Protectorate, and blocked his right of way to the littoral in question. At an interview with which Oom Paul favoured the present writer in 1889 His Honour drew an idyllic picture of the general South African amity and Customs Union which would follow when he was given Swaziland. At another interview in 1895 he took the line that Swaziland in itself had never been of any importance ; what he wanted was the littoral beyond, from which he had then just been headed off. To the interviewer it seemed only a following out of the previous British policy to take him at his word, and give him his territory, his Port, or rather the somewhat otiose permission to get a Port out of a spit of sand if he could, and to get in return Customs and Railway Union both for a substantial term of years, only insisting in this case on " cash down "—that is, immediate fulfilment of the bargain. The way in which this policy, as sketched, was received in 1895, first by Oom Paul, and secondly by Mr. Rhodes, is perhaps, in the light of after events, significant of the lines on which their minds were developing. Oom Paul lost his temper, and was for breaking off the interview when he was pressed

C

for a straightforward disavowal of any intention of bringing in the German factor in the way which has been described, while Mr. Rhodes abruptly treated the whole spirit of the bargain proposed as one out of date and impossible. It was universally assumed that the sudden blocking of the Transvaal's way to the sea was done upon Mr. Rhodes' prompting, and that it marked the end of the policy of sops to the Transvaal. It remains to add that the Transvaal is the only one of the States and Colonies which has persistently declined even to be represented at a Customs Conference, and that one of Oom Paul's worst blunders, from his own point of view, has been the illiberal treatment in this regard with which he has rewarded the support of Cape Afrikander farmers in 1881, a support which had more than anything else to do with Great Britain's decision to restore the Republic's independence.

It was Railway politics, however, rather than Customs politics, which brought about the strained relations at the close of 1895, and led to the almost war measure, as it was considered, of the Closing of the Drifts.

The essence of the Railway Question is simple. Kimberley was once, Bulawayo may become some time, the magnet which attracts the iron rails, but at present, and for the last six years, the great loadstone is the Rand. The Transvaal Boer does not belong to the railway epoch. Left to himself he would not have had a yard of railway in his Republic to-day, but the Uitlander came in and developed the mines and created a community which could not be fed or served by ox-wagon. For some time the Government compelled it to make shift with the ox-wagon as best it could. A railway which should touch the sea at Delagoa Bay, the natural port of the country, had been a dream of President Burgers. The fact that it need not touch British territory, though it must cross that of another European power, made it a dream dear to the heart of President Kruger, but the national prejudice against the iron horse, aided by incompetence and apathy, had prevented the dream coming much nearer to accomplishment till the time when Cape Colony forced the Government's hand by thrusting up its own railway through the Free State to the very border of the Republic, only fifty miles from the mines. Mr. Rhodes was then Prime Minister. Despite having got the Free State as partner, thus securing Republican backing, the enterprising railway management of the Colony found itself blocked at the Vaal by Presi-

LORD ROSMEAD.
(FORMERLY SIR HERCULES ROBINSON.)
From a Photograph by Messrs. ELLIOTT & FRY.

dent Kruger's declared determination to allow no other railway into the country until, in process of years, the Delagoa Bay line were completed to Pretoria. Drought, which struck at the transport by oxen, threatened famine in Johannesburg literally as well as industrially, and at a moment when revolution, or at any rate riot, seemed imminent, the hand of the Government was forced by the agitations from outside and inside, and the British Colony saw its enterprise rewarded by the completion of railway communication from Table Bay to Johannesburg.

The result was, of course, tremendous traffic, the industrial salvation of Johannesburg, and the filling of the Cape Treasury and that of the Free State, its partner, out of the carrying trade to the largest goldfields in the world. Three years later the Delagoa Bay line was completed; and later that of Natal. The Johannesburg importer had thus the choice of three lines offering various advantages. On the first glance at the map it would seem impossible for the others to compete with the Delagoa line, which is much the shortest.

Natal is handicapped by steep gradients; Delagoa Bay by malarial fever, necessitating double staffs, and by the Portuguese; while the Cape Ports, though further from Johannesburg by land, are some days nearer England by sea. The adjustment of the shares which each line should eventually carry would, no doubt, have been settled by simple competition at cutting rates if the rival companies had been simply companies and not States. In the case of Natal and the Cape, however, the railways are a Government concern, and the aid which they at present give to the Treasury, thus lightening taxation, represents the chief way in which the colonies are able to share in nature's bounty to the inland Republic. The Free State was then in the position of a sleeping partner, the Cape Colony providing the capital, taking the risks and working the line, but it, too, is now taking over its railway to work on its own account. The Transvaal railway is a State railway with a difference. The Republic is essentially the home of concessions, and of course it gave a concession for the railway. The entire railway communication of the State is in the hands of a company domiciled in Amsterdam, and working upon such terms that its interest is to swell its profits by all possible means, looking only to the present in order to get bought out by the State at a fancy price when its yoke has become intolerable. The railway is one of the chief fortresses of Hollander officialdom in the Transvaal, and thus again it falls in with President Kruger's idea of filling all those offices in the State household which Transvaal burghers are not competent to take with Continental Dutch speakers instead of with English-speaking Afrikanders. This Hollanderism of the Netherlands South Africa Railway Company adds an embittering factor to the situation, as it makes it a most powerful engine of Dr. Leyds' policy of setting the Transvaal and the neighbouring States by the ears while looking for support to Continental Europe. It was found, when all the railways began working together, that the Cape line still held its own, and that the devolution of traffic was extraordinarily slow. For the first few months the Cape carried 83 per cent. It was undoubtedly a disgrace to the Portuguese and the Netherlanders alike that their geographical advantages should have been so slow in making themselves felt. Failing fair competition, they proposed to bring the Colony to a suitable mind for Convention purposes by throttling the Colonial line by means of the clutch upon its throat afforded by their position. The Cape-Free State line to the Vaal is carried to Johannesburg by a Netherlands line only fifty miles long. The first act of the Netherlands Company was to pile up the rates for this short length so high as to frighten away traffic to the Natal and Delagoa lines; it increased its rates over this piece of line from 1*s.* to 1*s.* 8*d.* per hundred pounds. Experience, economy in working, the slowness of trade in transferring itself, and the urgent need for quick delivery in the stage of industrial development in which Johannesburg was, enabled the Cape to lower its rates and keep the traffic, while still retaining a margin of profit; but to such a pitch did the Netherlands handicap attain that it actually paid to unload goods at the Vaal River and send them the rest of the way by the old, traditional ox-wagon. The strip of veld between the terminus of the Cape-Free State line and the consuming centres of the Rand became the only spot on the surface of the earth, probably, which witnessed an actual competition between the ox and the steam locomotive. Such was the state of affairs when the Transvaal summoned a Railway Conference at Pretoria for October, 1895, and if the Cape was to be brought to its knees some more extreme expedient must be thought of.

It was actually determined to invoke the power of the Republic to close the two drifts by which the wagons crossed the Vaal against the importation of goods which the Cape Government Railway dumped down on the further bank. In August the Transvaal published a proclamation in the *Staats Courant* notifying that these drifts would be closed against over-sea traffic on the first of October. The distinction between over-sea traffic and other was meant to square the Free State farmer, who would have used very strong language against the neighbour Republic if he had found his produce shut out of the Johannesburg market. It was supposed that he would not so much object to the remoter injury of bleeding the Free State Railway returns. The proclamation made a sensation throughout South Africa, for, when it was issued, the incompetence of the Netherlands Railway to cope with the traffic they already had, to say nothing of monopolising the rest, was causing a tremendous railway block on the border, and something like a paralysis of trade was threatened. As the day for closing the drifts drew near, agitation grew more and more intense, the Rand Chamber of Commerce used strong language to the Government from the consumer's and importer's point of view, while the indignation of the Cape Colony from the point of view of the railway carrier and forwarding agent was echoed from Bloemfontein. A deputation of the Chamber of Commerce of the Free State capital waited on President Reitz to protest against the neighbour Republic's action, and President Reitz, though he shrugged his shoulders and asked what he could do, publicly stated that he shared the views of the deputation. The Free State had telegraphed to the Transvaal Government expressing regret, and remarking that they had not been consulted or recognised at all, and had not even got a reply. But President Kruger and his advisers stopped their ears. " You fellows have had enough of the Johannesburg trade," the President had declared to Dr. Smuts, an Afrikander member of the Cape House of Assembly, who told the story to the *Cape Times*. " I have made up my mind that the Delagoa

DR. L. S. JAMESON.
From a Portrait by PROFESSOR HERKOMER, 1895.

Bay line shall have the lion's share, and what there is to spare I shall give to Natal. You Cape Colonists must be content with the crumbs which fall from the Natal table."

The drifts were closed, and the block was piled up worse than ever. Firms at Johannesburg were in despair. Truckloads of goods accumulated undistributed. There was only one hope, since the commercial and industrial community had no say in the Government of the Transvaal, while the burghers were about the only class of people in South Africa unaffected. The one hope was the London Convention. In giving back the independence of the Transvaal, while the Republic was allowed the fullest liberty internally, one or two small guarantees were kept against extremes of action prejudicial to the rest of South Africa. Those guarantees of the Convention of Pretoria were reduced in 1884 in the Convention of London, but Article 13 of the latter instrument did give a certain security against preferential measures taken to handicap British or Colonial trade. The relevant part of Article 13 runs as follows: " Nor will any prohibition be maintained or imposed on the importation into the South African Republic of any article coming from any part of Her Majesty's dominions which shall not equally extend to like articles from any other country or place." The closing of the drifts was dead against the spirit of the Convention; the question was, did it luckily happen to be provided against by the letter of this Article? Thanks to the word "over-sea" it did. The Cape Attorney-General, Mr. Schreiner, then Mr. Rhodes' right-hand man, but an Afrikander whose prejudices were all against anything like unnecessary Imperial interference in South African affairs, decided that it did, and Sir Hercules Robinson, at the request of the Cape Government, drew the attention of the Transvaal Government to the Article. The question was referred to the Law Officers of the Crown at Home. Meantime, the date appointed for the Railway Conference at Pretoria drew near, and the Transvaal Government having shown that it could put on the screw, announced the re-opening of the drifts as a temporary measure on the 30th of October. To facilitate friendly discussion at the Conference, they were to be opened on the 5th of November and to be closed on the 15th. It was clear that the Government saw it had gone too far, and hoped to make the Cape accept the Netherlands terms at the Conference by simply holding the drifts *in terrorem*. But the issue was to be taken out of its hands. On the very day of the meeting of the Conference, as it happened, a sensation was caused throughout South Africa by the announcement that Her Majesty's Government had informed that of the South African Republic that the Proclamation closing the drifts violated the Convention, and that it was not competent for them, after the 15th of November, to close the drifts again, which must be allowed to remain open for all time. The interventions of the Imperial Government are so rare as regards the actions of the Transvaal, and the tone of them usually so different from that of this peremptory insistance on a Treaty obligation, that President Kruger and his advisers were dumbfounded. Speculation turned eagerly on what answer they would make, but it was soon announced that they had accepted the situation with a wry face, and undertaken "never to close the drifts in future without first consulting Her Majesty's Government."

The Conference broke up without having arrived at any basis of agreement, but the key of the railway situation was no longer in the pocket of the Netherlands Company. The prestige of the President had suffered a severe shock, and although the ultra-republican Press muttered threats of resistance and gnashed its teeth over the vigorous resurrection of the Imperial factor, these mutterings were drowned in the Colonial and Uitlander jubilation, and South Africa as a whole hailed with relief and gratitude the termination of a dangerous deadlock.

It will thus be seen that it was the action of the Transvaal itself, under the direct incitation of its Hollander advisers, which first made acute the question both of inter-state relationships and of Uitlander grievances in the closing months of 1895.

It is not suggested that there was any direct connection between the drifts incident of October and November and the conspiracy during the same months which was being promoted by certain movements of troops on the western border of the Republic. What the events just described did do was to foment the angry state of public disquietude, and to prepare insensibly for what followed. We find meetings of the Chamber of Commerce, the Chamber of Mines, and the Mercantile Association, protesting in the most determined tone against the Government treating the Rand community with contempt, and thanking the Cape Government for its efforts. Such a meeting was presided over by one of the four Reformers on whom a death sentence was afterwards passed. The link is significant.

Throughout South Africa papers freely discussed the remedy of force as one certain to be resorted to in the long run by a community whose industry was being threatened.

When in the following month Johannesburg capitalists began openly to talk sedition, and when a manifesto of revolutionary tone was issued by the National Union, nobody was at all surprised. There was a feeling that matters were coming to a climax, and the only question was not how far the Rand was justified, but how far it was competent.

NOTE.—Since the above was written Mr. Stead has made known (under guise of fiction) a more striking illustration of the extent to which the Transvaal had alienated Afrikander feeling at the time of the Drifts incident. It seems that Mr. Chamberlain made sure of the support of Cape Colony before issuing his ultimatum, and that Mr. Rhodes' Ministry secretly pledged itself not only to carry free over the colonial railway any troops with which the Imperial Government might have to follow the ultimatum up, but actually to share the expense of any such measures! I think the Ministry would have had a rather lively time with its Dutch supporters when the Colonial Parliament came to consider this item. Happily the drifts were opened peacefully. But the agreement, assented to by such a Republican sympathizer and "full-blooded Afrikander" as Mr. W. P. Schreiner, is an eloquent fact.

Chapter II

"CLIVE WOULD HAVE DONE IT"

A NOVELIST would begin this Story of a Crisis from the following incident which, be it premised, is absolutely authentic, and comes from one who was present.

One day, long before the very earliest hint of a beginning of the "complot" as shown by any evidence which is before the world, a man sat on the stoep of Government House, Bulawayo, smoking cigarettes and reading a Life of Clive. A rather short man (the novelist would tell us) whose head, growing a little bald, was noticeably broad and rather too noticeably squat; what is called a bullet-headed man in short, with a firm jaw, firm chin, short nose and moustache, keen eyes, and a general air of good-natured, forcible abruptness.

This, of course, was Dr. Jim, officially known as His Honour Leander Starr Jameson, M.D., C.B., Administrator of Matabeleland.

It was about the time of one of those excitements which kept convulsing South Africa, as we saw in the last chapter, over some special display of autocratic insolence on the part of the Pretoria Government towards its Uitlanders and its neighbours. The papers were all loud with it, and a great deal of ineffectual froth was being poured out.

Suddenly Jameson looked up from his book and exclaimed, "I have a jolly good mind to march straight down off the plateau with the men I have here and settle the thing out of hand. The idea of South Africa going on being trodden upon by this Pretoria gang is absurd. I have a good mind to get the fellows together and start to-morrow, *viâ* Tati."

Now the men to whom Jameson referred were only about a couple of hundred M.M.P., and the time that it would take them to carry out this airy programme, marching down off the plateau, would be two or three weeks, during which the national and international situation would be rather peculiar, the disbanding of the forces by cable, not to say the cancelling of the Company's Charter, being probable incidents of the march.

Dr. Jim's interlocutor somewhat drily pointed this out, and a little argument ensued.

"Well," said Jameson at last, banging down the book on his knee, "you may say what you like, but Clive would have done it."

I remember in the early days after the raid talking to Mr. Hofmeyr one day, when he said, "Rhodes flattered himself he was going to be a kind of Clive and Warren Hastings rolled into one." What actually Rhodes did flatter himself is a difficult question, but the above incident shows that the Clive inspiration was actually working long before the raid in the mind of another chief actor.

Does the germ of the whole inscrutable business lie between the leaves of Jameson's "Life of Clive"?

*　　*　　*　　*　　*

Dr. Jameson, like Mr. Rhodes, like two members of the present Cape Ministry, and many other prominent South Africans, went to South Africa for his health. He had been a brilliant London medical student. He reached the head of his profession in South Africa, having special repute as a surgeon. Settled at Kimberley, he was one of the most intimate personal friends of Cecil Rhodes, and the confidant of his large Imperial schemes at a time when the outside world only knew Mr. Rhodes as a young man speculating in diamonds, with a genius for finance and amalgamation, and a curious fad of sending himself to Oxford and going backwards and forwards between the hum of the washing gear at Kimberley and the silence of the courts of Oriel. Jameson knew more than that, and, like so many doctors who have come to Africa, he determined to play a part as a man of action, and play it in his friend's schemes.

A trait in Jameson's character was shown in a half-forgotten incident of his life as a Kimberley doctor. A disease broke out among the natives working in the mines. Was it small-pox, or was it a comparatively harmless malady which on black skins was known to counterfeit small-pox? Other doctors diagnosed the former, Jameson the latter. Most men would have hesitated, and given the public safety the benefit of the doubt; but Jameson stuck to his own opinion in the teeth of everybody, declaring that where the thing was so perfectly clear it was absurd to dislocate the mining industry by a panic quarantine. This element in the affair—the fact that scepticism as to the small-pox suited the book of the great capitalists—embittered the controversy, for it made Jameson's obstinacy take on a flavour of too little scruple as well as too little caution. But to appreciate the doggedness of the thing, and its value as a present illustration, it need only be added that Jameson's opinion turned out to be absolutely wrong. After the risk of spreading the infection through the colony had been incurred it was proved beyond doubt that the disease was small-pox.

But such an incident as this was soon to be overlaid by a series of achievements in which boldness was so well mixed with foresight as to make the idea that Jameson could act recklessly, foolishly, and obstinately become incredible.

The chance of the medico to turn man of action came when Mr. Rhodes occupied the Transvaal hinterland in the name of British South Africa. Jameson turned out to be an Administrator with an extraordinary gift for dealing with men and attracting their enthusiastic loyalty. I remember, at the time of Jameson's sentence, a groom at a stable asking me eagerly for news. I said, "You seem interested in Dr. Jim." "Interested?" said he; "whatever 'quod' he gets I'd gladly do half of it for him. That I would." This groom had once broken his leg in a race at Kimberley, and the Doctor had attended him in the hospital. That was all. But it is the same with all sorts and conditions of men whom "Dr. Jim" has come in contact with in other ways. This gift is as useful to an Administrator as to a doctor. At the time of the Matabele War Jameson was able to add yet a third *rôle*. The credit of the campaign rests with his military advisers; still Jameson had an intoxicating taste of the great war-game, and civilian as he was, it was he who galloped across country to effect a junction between the two columns so admirably timed to meet each other. It was he, too, who precipitated the war. The Company meant peace till the Matabele made development impossible, and gave the Mashonaland settlers "the jumps," in the Doctor's phrase, by raiding into their very streets; whereupon the Company, or rather the Doctor for them, determined that the golden occasion should be seized An impi was driven headlong, war preparations hurried forward, and war became inevitable. The war itself, waged against the most formidable military tribe left unbroken, was the most rapid and brilliant in the history of South African native wars. The heroic death of Wilson's patrol, on a daring quest which was more due to Jameson's inspiration than to that of Major Forbes, might have taught a lesson. But then the daring was so nearly rewarded by success (and *what* success!)—that the lesson may well have missed its mark. Intimates declare that "Rhodes was really more cut up than Jameson."

It was Jameson, too, who met and stopped the "trek" of Boers who had the audacity to dispute the Company's title. He met them with a few police troopers, just as they were about to cross the Limpopo. He was authorized to try persuasion, failing that not to hesitate to shoot. They knew that he would not hesitate to shoot; and he persuaded so well that he turned them back peacefully.

Up to December, 1895, Jameson's career was one unbroken success. He had tasted the stern joy of extreme responsibility; had held in his hand the issues of peace and war; had found it easy to carry through dangerous decisions; to foresee and even to command events almost equally with men ; to exact implicit confidence and to justify it. He was as one clothed in the strength of his own will. He had come to believe in his star, and his friend, the Managing Director, and all South Africa, and a good part of England, had come to believe in it also. Such was the man who had cast for himself, or for whom others had cast, the leading part in the strangest adventure of the century. However the plot originated, a matter which perhaps even the actors in it would find it hard to determine exactly, it became irrevocable when once it was committed into the hands of a man of this temper and these antecedents. Dogged inflexibility, reckless of life, moving with intense force in a narrow groove not broad enough to take in scruples, which to him would seem mere infirmity, unsparing of himself and having an irresistible grip on his confederates: such a man, thrust by fate into the right epoch at the right turn of affairs, might make a dint in the world's history, and go down to posterity as a Carlylean hero. Here were all the materials for a great achievement in action—or a greater failure.

Chapter III

THE PERVERSION OF MR. RHODES

THE Johannesburg Capitalists, who were capitalists first and politicians afterwards, thought twice and thrice before they could bring themselves to call in the aid of that dangerous political Pict, Cecil Rhodes.

This, like some other things equally foreign to the Government's purpose, was well illustrated as the result of its raid on the private correspondence between Mr. Lionel Phillips and the heads in London of the great firm of Wernher, Beit & Co.

Even the excerpts picked and paraded by the Government show clearly that it was only the hopelessness of Reform which ever drove these rich Johannesburgers to coquette with Revolution. For years it was the reproach of the National Union against them that they, the natural leaders of the industry, would not come into line, preferring to take their chances under the system of autocracy tempered by corruption, rather than run the risks incidental to any political upheaval.

The Phillips letters of 1894 exhibit the transition from this attitude to that of being driven into politics, by the Government becoming a distinct menace to the industry, in which men and masters were alike concerned.

"The old man is in no case a friend to the industry," he writes in June to "my dear Beit." "He has the most perverted ideas of political economy, suspects that we are working in concert with his old opponent C.J.R., sees imaginary combinations looming in the distance and the country bought up by Rhodes." "I don't of course want to meddle in politics, and as to the franchise, do not think many people care a fig about it." So an English capitalist and employer would have written about his men's aspirations during the Reform Agitation in England. However, Mr. Phillips was probably right in assuming that a yearning for citizenship would never enter the head of the Johannesburgers as a whole, if they could get the treatment they wanted from Government without voting, particularly without voting on the arduous terms on which alone there seemed any chance of the franchise being extended to them. "If events fulfil appearances," he writes in another letter :—

"It means ultimate frightful loss to the industry or revolution. Now of course our mission is to avoid both. The Gold-fields people urged me to go down to Cape Town and talk over matters with Rhodes. I felt inclined to do this, but two considerations deter me. 1stly: If it were for a moment conjectured that I had approached Rhodes, I should incur the most virulent revenge from the Government, and perhaps justly; and 2ndly, should I be wise to trust Rhodes' advice?"

"If you trust Rhodes, and cable 'see Rhodes,' I will run down." And again, later :—

"It seems that the British Government means to have a say here, and it is about time. What I fear is that they may put the brake on one thing, and we may be more oppressed by some devilment of the Government in another direction. The Government is absolutely rotten, and we must have reform. The alternative is revolution or English interference. Kruger seems beyond himself, and imagines he is guided by Divine will."

In July, "My dear Beit . . . Politics. Just got your cable reading 'Don't see Rhodes,' etc., of which I am rather glad. Things are quieter, but I think a good many men are buying rifles in case of contingencies." The same letter contains a sigh of regret that the mining companies do not possess the Government advantage of a secret service fund. The letters also contain hints of corruption affecting both the legislature and the judiciary, but these are not to our present purpose. In August he writes :—

"I will also see whether it is not possible, without creating unnecessary alarm here, or active steps in Pretoria, to get the Companies to possess themselves of a few rifles, etc. One thing is certain. The Boer prowess is much overrated since they licked our troops, and in the Malaboch campaign they distinguished themselves by making the Pretoria contingent do any of the risky business, and appear generally to have behaved badly. If they knew there were 3,000 or so well-armed men here, there would be less talk—anyhow less real danger—of wiping out Johannesburg upon occasions like the recent incident. In addition to that we can never tell when some complication with England may arise, and this place ought to be prepared to hold its own for a few days at least. If the spending of money does not bring reform, the only alternative is force, and that will come in time."

While Johannesburg leaders were thus screwing up their courage for the plunge from finance into politics, as understood at Groote Schuur, what was Mr. Rhodes' attitude towards them? Mr. Hofmeyr has put it on record that during all his intimacy with Mr. Rhodes he never heard him drop one word of sympathy with the rights of the Uitlanders. Certain it is that Mr. Rhodes is neither a radical nor a democrat. He accepts government by the people as he accepts any other part of the great British system spread over the world, but it was a well-known belief of his that all this is only an outer cloak for the inner reality of government by a few. There are only a certain number of people in the world who matter, and in any given part of the world one or two of these can pull the rest almost any way if they only pull together. That is his faith. He accepts the present phase of democracy just as he accepts the present phase of competitive capitalism, as being the latest arrangements evolved by humankind for so shaking up the great mass that these few who matter can conveniently come to the top. His sympathy for English miners held under at Johannesburg by a minority of Boers was certainly more for the Englishmen than for the miners. Even with friends much less intimate than Mr. Hofmeyr then was he would discuss, for years past, the impossibility of a majority of such men, whether or not they "cared a fig for the franchise" *per se*, being permanently governed by a Boer oligarchy. The whole thing presented itself to him as a matter of power, of the fitness of things, of conformity to the working theory of the British Empire, rather than as a matter of abstract right-high sentiments, "liberty, equality, and fraternity."

In the muddle of South African politics, it has been a common saying that two men at least knew their own minds, Cecil Rhodes and Paul Kruger. Mr. Chamberlain remarked lately that had these two men agreed together they could have settled the immediate future of South Africa with the most happy results. And in those unifying measures, discussed in a previous chapter, Mr. Rhodes long hoped to get his great rival to work with him. A stormy interview towards the close of 1894 between the two men has been mentioned already as the turning-point. After that he gave up Paul Kruger as hopeless.

From that time he seems to have begun to make his account, not with the Government of to-day, but with the Revolutionary Government of to-morrow. Capitalist, and in a sense Johannesburger, as he was, many of his sympathies were rather with the old than with the new population. Conservative and protectionist by habit of mind, it was as a leader of the Old Colonists rather than the new that he had gained at the Cape the ascendency which was to give him a leading voice, he hoped, in piecing together the fragments when the Transvaal crash should come. Perhaps it was distrust of the new population at Johannesburg, as much as sympathy with it, that led him eventually to venture all in their cause. If the power passed in a day from the hands of the old burghers into those of the Rand cosmopolites, how would it be used? What if the new *régime*, flushed with victory, and confident from the great wealth lying at its feet, chose to take up as domineering, as separatist, as anti-Cape and anti-British a policy as the old? The finger of Johannesburg might well prove thicker than Pretoria's loins. Had Mr. Rhodes' career been cast in the Transvaal instead of in the Colony he would have thrown himself into the cause, no doubt, trusting to keep the direction of the new order after throwing off the old. His plan would have been to utilise the commanding position of the Transvaal to squeeze all the rest of South Africa into union. The task would have been comparatively easy if the future United States of South Africa were to be separated from the British Empire. As it happened his dream was the opposite, and the base he had to work from was the Cape. Of course if the Johannesburgers should make good their revolution with the Union Jack flying over it, and confront the rest of South Africa with the *fait accompli*, that might be one solution of the problem. But could Johannesburg? And, if it could, did it want to? No man could tell what the revolution would bring forth! If it succeeded too easily, it might go to extremes hardly less dangerous than its failure. In short, Kruger was forcing things not only out of his own control, but out of that of Cecil Rhodes, who had come to think himself indispensable to the destinies of South Africa. The conclusion was, in plain language, that, at all hazards, he must have a finger in the pie.

The Johannesburg leaders wanted mainly four things for their movement, two within the Transvaal and two outside, In Johannesburg they wanted arms and they wanted enthusiasm. Outside they wanted some colour at least of armed support should it come to a tussle, and they wanted an influence which would gain over, or at least neutralize, Afrikander sympathies in Cape Colony. One of these things, the enthusiasm, Mr. Rhodes could not supply. He could tell the Johannesburg owners and managers that if they wanted their men to be as solid with them as his men were at Kimberley, they must take as much interest in them, their housing, and their well-being generally, as he had done. The white miners of Kimberley live in a model village. But apparently the idea in Johannesburg was that a revolution, like everything else, could be ordered for money. They tried to close the ranks too late. When Mr. Rhodes' brother, in November, proposed to the employés of one of the companies most under Mr. Rhodes' control a plan based something on the Kimberley model the men were quick to catch at motives behind. The plan fell through owing to the frank opposition of the men. But while Mr. Rhodes could not supply this one prime necessity, the enthusiasm of the masses in Johannesburg, he could supply all the other three wants—the arms within, the armed support without, and the spiking of the Afrikander gun in Cape Colony, and some months before the end of 1895 he had pledged himself to do so.

The plot, concisely stated, was this: Johannesburg was to formulate an ultimatum. On its being treated with contempt the revolutionary party was to take possession of Johannesburg one fine night, declare itself the provisional Government of the country, and the same night pay a surprise visit to Pretoria, seize the State arsenal and the seat of Government, and issue an appeal to South Africa and the world proposing to submit its acts and grievances, and the future of the Transvaal, to a *plébiscite* of the entire white population of the country. It was calculated that with proper organization the *coup* could be accomplished almost without firing a shot, and the great point then would be to prevent the burghers rushing to arms all over the country. For this the conspirators relied partly on the breathless surprise of the *fait accompli*, the sympathies of a large part of the burghers, which would rather be attracted than alienated by the proof that these new-comers were really in earnest about their rights, and the moderation of the appeal which the provisional Government would make to Uitlander and Boer population alike, but most of all they relied on a diversion from the border.

For a year or two years past the Johannesburg leaders had been sounding the Colonial Office at home as to what it would do, in the event of this or that happening on the Rand, and for many reasons they had always got the same answer, which was a discouraging one. Alternately with intimations that no Downing Street interference was wanted by Johannesburgers, who could look after themselves, some at least of the leaders had given Downing Street to understand that not a finger could be raised or would be raised without the assurance of some backing. Downing Street always shook its head, having learnt something in South Africa from past blunders. It always told the sounders that it could not interfere in the internal affairs of the Transvaal on their behalf, and that if they accordingly took

MR. LIONEL PHILLIPS.
From a Photograph by DUFFUS BROS., *Johannesburg.*

steps to win their rights for themselves, Great Britain could only interfere by way of keeping the peace in South Africa, and not at a time or in a way which could be construed as assisting them to break it. To the leaders thus repulsed, and to Rhodes and Jameson, the machinery of the British South Africa Company, which had already served once to make short work of international red tape in the case of the Portuguese in East Africa, offered an excellent means of doing for Great Britain what Great Britain declined to do for herself. From nowhere could external support, moral or actual, be better rendered than from the Company's new territory touching the western border. The moment uproar began, and life and property were in danger, a plausible excuse would be created for the interposition of any organized British force which was within two days of striking distance. The pretext for its action would be the jeopardy of British lives, property and interests, the interregnum in the country, the necessity for the preservation of order, and an emergency of a kind to justify acting first and asking leave afterwards. The exact method and moment of such action were never clearly fixed, but the idea was that Jameson would be there, and that Jameson was Jameson, and that a diversion of some kind, with a vague background of support from the Company's other forces farther north, might at least serve to secure to the revolutionary *camarilla* a pause and a breathing space before the burghers closed in upon them. That breathing space meant everything. Civil war would be imminent, and for that very reason the hand of the British Government, it was calculated, would be forced. Intervene they must to part the combatants, and to avert chaos. The moment these events took place South Africa would be plunged from end to end into a maelstrom of conflicting sympathies, and much would turn on the attitude of the Cape Government. Here came in Mr. Rhodes' part. Sticking like glue to his Premiership he was to fling all his official and unofficial advantages into the scale. His personality was to make the Government weather the storm long enough for him to advise the High Commissioner, who is also the Governor of the Cape, to proceed at once to the Transvaal as mediator, accompanied by Mr. Rhodes himself. The rest of the programme is easily imagined. Thus the man who was at once

Premier of the Cape, and uncrowned king of John Bull's modern "John Company," besides being head of some great capitalist amalgamations, proposed to add the *rôles* of arming a revolution, of succouring it with troops from the border, of "facing the music" when the crash came, and governing the extraordinary situation which would ensue as the one man who could mediate between Dutch and English Cape Colony, and between England and the Transvaal. Upon this hazard he staked the most brilliant and promising career boasted by any contemporary politician in the British Empire.

On the obvious weaknesses of this amazing scheme, considered simply on a balance of probability, it is unnecessary to dilate here. Events have done that. The question which forces itself upon us is; how on earth could a man of the caution, the patience, and the foresight of Cecil Rhodes have made up his mind to shut his eyes to them? The answer of the present Premier is a simple one. All those months when the plot was brewing Mr. Rhodes was miserable with the well-known nervous *sequelæ* of influenza. "He was not himself," Sir Gordon Sprigg declares. "Whatever part he took in the thing was simply due to the influenza." A solution which has all the charm of simplicity.

Chapter IV

THE PLOT THICKENS

AS the Uitlander demands made themselves more and more vocal at the time of the Drifts incident, the Government made it clear that it was providing itself with the last argument of kings. For weeks it brought offensive arms to bear on Johannesburg. The Uitlander saw contracts entered into for building, with his money, forts on the latest pattern of scientific destructiveness, which could be aimed only at himself: a fort at Pretoria at £25,000, and site chosen for another openly commanding Johannesburg. A Mr. Van Zwieten, one of Oom Paul's Hollanders, was sent to Europe, as it was understood, with credentials to the military authorities of Germany, and instructions to engage expert tuition for the shooting of Uitlanders on the latest European methods. While the conspirators were smuggling up Maxims in oil tanks, the Government was laying in two for every one of theirs by Delagoa Bay. Orders for heavy artillery and quick-firing guns were placed with the German firm, Krupp, and a battery of quick-firers was established on the Hospital Hill, directly overlooking the streets of Johannesburg. Ever since the raid these aggressive military preparations have been spoken of as a painful necessity to be numbered among its consequences, but in strict chronology it was the Government which armed itself first, while the Uitlanders, as a body, were still on constitutional lines, and when the Government, by its own account, had not the slightest knowledge of the plot in which a few of them afterwards proved to have been engaged. It became clear to the leaders that if Pretoria was to be taken by surprise, it must be taken quickly.

At the same time events were forcing on that transfer of the Protectorate which was destined to put the British South Africa Company in charge of the western border. In its 1895 Session the Cape Parliament had closed a bargain with the Imperial Government for the southern part of Bechuanaland—the Crown Colony. The reversion of the northern part of Bechuanaland, the Protectorate, had long been promised to the great Company which to north of it already spread away across the Zambesi to Lake Tanganyika, and which was pushing on the railway which could alone make Bechuanaland productive. The claims of certain native chiefs, Khama and others, had at the same time to be safeguarded. Mr. Chamberlain settled with them in September and October, and on 7th November the rest of the Protectorate was transferred to the Company.[1] Already in October the Company had come to terms with the two smaller chiefs, Montsioa and Ikanning, and had accordingly got its administration of their territory proclaimed (18th October). These two petty chiefs owned a part of Bechuanaland, close to the railway extension on the one hand, and on the other in contact with the Transvaal border. It was here that the conspirators chose the swooping point for the raid; and everything fitted in so conveniently that, when the swoop came, and before the Imperial Government had spoken, no wonder that many jumped to the conclusion that the British Government was a party to the preparations. The truth about this appears to be quite simple. To understand it the first thing is to put out of one's mind what actually did happen and to imagine what observant people fully expected to see happen at the time of the events already described. In handing over the territory the Imperial Government disbanded the troops; but had it retained them, and if the High Commissioner had held them in readiness to intervene in case of a kind of Alexandria riot suddenly supervening in Johannesburg, he would only have been doing exactly what his predecessor did at the

[1] The transference was not completed when the crisis came, and has not been carried out now.

critical period in 1894. What that was let Lord Loch himself describe:—

"My lords, I may perhaps be permitted to add a few words to what I have already said. In consideration of the excited state of the city of Johannesburg at that time, with the probability—the near possibility at one time—of an insurrection arising in Johannesburg, I felt it to be my duty, in the position I filled as Her Majesty's High Commissioner, to take steps, if necessary, to protect the lives of the British subjects and property of the British subjects in Johannesburg (cheers). The steps I adopted were in connection with an assembly at certain points of the British and Imperial Bechuanaland police. My intention was that, if disturbances had arisen in Johannesburg—disturbances resulting from the administration extended by the Republic towards the 'Uitlanders' in that city—it would have been my duty, I considered, to have informed President Kruger that he would be held responsible for the safety of the lives and property of British subjects in the country. I further conceived it to be my duty to inform President Kruger that, if he had failed to provide the necessary protection for the lives and property of British subjects, I should have felt myself at liberty to have taken such steps as I may have felt expedient to give that protection which he failed to give. I think it will be admitted that a statement of that kind, coming from me as High Commissioner representing Her Majesty's Government, was a very different act from the unfortunate action which has recently taken place, and which has brought about so much sorrow and trouble on the whole of South Africa" (cheers).

In this connection there is a notable passage in Mr. Chamberlain's speech on the Address when Parliament met after the raid:—

"My hon. friend opposite (Mr. Buxton) will bear me out that in July, 1894, there was a disturbance in Johannesburg, and an outbreak was expected at any moment. What happened? The British Bechuanaland police were collected and concentrated at Mafeking, and other forces were under orders to move. Was this wrong? Of course this was done by the High Commissioner; but was it wrong? Certainly not. In my opinion it was absolutely right and justified by the circumstances. When your neighbour's house is on fire you are quite right to get out your apparatus in order to extinguish it, and nobody can accuse you, unless they can prove that you are bringing it out not with the object of stopping mischief, of preventing damage, of interfering with general consent, but with the deliberate intention of promoting the mischief that you profess a desire to prevent."

In this sense, it would seem, Mr. Chamberlain spoke, not only in the House of Commons after the raid, but also to agents of Mr. Rhodes and of the British South Africa Company before the raid, when the negotiations were proceeding between the Company and chief Khama. These negotiations were made more difficult by what is called in South Africa an "Exeter Hall outcry" for specially generous terms to the chief. Khama was encouraged to hold out for high terms. There was long higgling at the Colonial Office; and agents as clever as those who represented Mr. Rhodes, urged on as they were by impatient cables from Cape Town to get the bargain struck quickly, were not likely to overlook so useful an argument towards expediting matters as was supplied by the disturbed situation just across the border. Troops and territory both changing hands, and a prolonged state of unsettled jurisdiction as between the British Government and the British Company were obviously undesirable at a time when it might at any moment become necessary to repeat the precautions taken a year before by Lord Loch. Reference of some sort to possible developments, however discreet, was bound to be made during these prolonged negotiations about the border territory; and it was only in conformity with the principle habitually acted on for years by the Colonial Office in dealing with the Transvaal and native neighbours, when the Company induced Mr. Chamberlain to make it "Warden of the Marches," and to arrange that, whatever territory Khama got, the Company should secure for its railway, and for the purposes of its ward upon the border, the strip of country fringing the Transvaal.

To the conspirators, however, these convenient arrangements for the fire-extinguishing apparatus, to adopt Mr. Chamberlain's metaphor, were pleasantly indistinguishable from their own plans of "promoting" (to quote him again) "the mischief that you profess a desire to prevent,"—or at least running the most reckless risk of promoting it. They were in high feather. The bargain was struck, and the "Wardens of the Marches" proceeded to take advantage of it with all their energy: a legend gradually growing up among conspirators—who had a hint from So-and-so who had a wink from Such-and-such—that "Chamberlain was in it up to his neck." There were painful surprises in store for these gentlemen.

To the High Commissioner the sole reason given for forming a police camp at Pitsani Pothlugo was the need for protecting the railway works. To him not a word was ventured about the Border Watch.

The High Commissioner found the arrangement a most natural one, and Sir Sidney Shippard, the Administrator under the Imperial Government, then about to be supplanted by the Company's Administrator, was enjoined to facilitate arrangements with Montsioa and Ikanning. Sir Sidney inspected a site "for a camp and a seat of Magistracy" in Colonel Rhodes' company, and wrote for Major "Bobby" White a letter of introduction to "Ikanning, Chief of the Bamalite." The farm eventually taken was not this one, but another near Pitsani Pothlugo in Montsioa's territory, but here again Sir Sidney's aid was invoked. "Saw Silas Molema, nephew to the Chief Montsioa," says "Bobby" White's day book, October 30th; "This man gives us the farm 'Maliete' near Pitsani, in exchange for two farms which will be given to him under promise from Sir S. Shippard." It was just these official routine transactions which to Transvaal eyes after the raid seemed confirmation strong as Holy Writ of Imperial complicity.

The camp being fixed, then came the gradual and quiet moving down of the troops into it. From the 20th to the 29th the Company's force, the Mashonaland Mounted Police, were being drafted from Bulawayo to Pitsani, in all 250 men, 293 horses, 168 mules, 6 Maxims, and 2 field guns. On 15th November the Imperial Government in handing over the Protectorate to the Company, was to disband the Bechuanaland Border Police, a force of rather better stuff than the Company's and numbering a few hundred. It was indispensable that these troopers should be got to re-enlist in the Company's force, and so swell it. On the day before the disbandment, Jameson had the satisfaction of hearing from Major White that "majority B.B.P. will be pleased to join."

From the middle of November, Mafeking was lively with the passing through of recruits, all *en route* to the Pitsani camp. Sir John Willoughby writes to Major White, November 18th, from Bulawayo, chafing that "he" (the Doctor) "will not let me move yet." "Mind you and Harry drill the men inside, outposts, and advanced guards, skirmishing, etc." On the 18th November Jameson arrived at Mafeking from Bulawayo, inspected the new camp, talked over matters, and hurried down to Cape Town. Thence he wired that he was sending up equipments and all that was needed, and estimated that "we shall have 600 men and 700 horses."

The Doctor not only sent up equipments, but also a certain number of picked men from the Colonial Volunteers (D.E.O.V.R.) at Cape Town.

From Cape Town he hurried up to Johannesburg to settle the details of the plot with the leaders there, and arrange a signal.

It was agreed that Jameson should move in response to a written appeal prepared beforehand as soon as the appeal was confirmed by telegram. As to the written appeal, Jameson's argument was that he must have something to read to the men when asking them to volunteer for so hazardous an expedition, while at the same time it was obvious that such a document would be his only possible answer to the astonished questions of the directors and shareholders whose troops he was to use, and to all and sundry who might suspect him of dashing into the Transvaal on a mere annexation project of his own. So one day, during his visit to Johannesburg, Jameson set Mr. Charles Leonard, President of the National Union, down at a table with pen, ink, and paper, and the result was the famous Letter of Invitation in which Johannesburg, on the eve of a mortal struggle, in which it was not made clear whether they were the threateners or the threatened, sent forth a cry to the nearest British troops not to desert them in their extremity, and made use of the phrase about rescuing women and children which it is impossible to quote now without wincing. "We guarantee any expense," the letter concludes, "that may reasonably be incurred by you in helping us, and ask you to believe that nothing but the sternest necessity prompted this appeal." The letter put the basis of co-operation in black and white once and for all, and though Jameson probably had no very fixed plan in his own mind as to what use to make of it, he regarded it as a great stroke to have secured it.

The next afternoon Mr. Charles Leonard went round to the Doctor to ask for the letter back, as on second thoughts he had concluded that it was a mistake.

"Awfully sorry, old man," said the Doctor drily, "but it has gone down to Cape Town by the last train."

Mr. Leonard protested and hesitated, but the Doctor took him by the arm, gave vent to his usual interjection—an abbreviation of the word balderdash—and managed the Chairman of the National Union in his usual style.

The signatures to this letter give us the ringleaders in Johannesburg.

Mr. Charles Leonard, a successful and well-known solicitor, born a Cape Colonist, had succeeded his brother, Mr. Jim Leonard, Q.C., as President of the National Union, the body which for some years had carried on all the political work that had been done on behalf of the Uitlander cause, the holding of meetings, the printing of pamphlets, and working of petitions to the Raad. Mr. Leonard comes of a stock noted in South Africa for great abilities, great amenities, but not equal strength of character; he was, however, very sincerely liked and respected as a good fellow and an honest, clever, professional man. And as an Afrikander (a Cape Dutch word originally used to imply an African native, then a half caste, then a South African white of Dutch speech and sympathies, and now becoming enlarged to mean any South African-born white) he was a suitable figure-head for the constitutional Uitlander movement. A less apt man to cast for the part of President by force of arms of an insurrectionary Republic, it would be hard to find.

Mr. Lionel Phillips is a financier born. He is of the great financial race. He has been through the mill, first at Kimberley and then at Johannesburg, and has come out of it with a large fortune. He is a prop of the great "Corner House" of Eckstein, Johannesburg, and of Wernher & Beit, London. A shrewd, clever, organizing man, full of go and of spirit, he admirably represents the better type of Johannesburg money maker. Politics came to him as a late ambition; revolutionary leadership as a still later one.

John Hays Hammond represents the American mining expert. It is a successful South African type, and he has been the most successful of them all. His retainer as Consulting Engineer of the Goldfields of South Africa (Limited) is alone a President's salary. A man of simple and attractive character, he also was a popular Johannesburger, and is trusted to an extent which, for an expert, is quite extraordinary. His health and his nerves were not made for stormy times, but there is a background of American grit.

George Farrar came of Yorkshire stock, and spent his youth in Cape Colony. As a youth he was a great athlete, he and his brother winning many triumphs on the running path. A wiry, sharp, determined-looking man, he is, as Managing Director of various large companies, the largest direct employer of labour on the Rand, and in far more direct touch than any of the others with the miners who were expected to play a part in the revolution. With them, despite the rooted local suspicion of capitalists, he is popular, being referred to commonly as "George." He has the temper and the tenacity for a tough fight.

Colonel Francis Rhodes, late 1st Dragoons, is the best known of Mr. Rhodes' brothers in the army. He has over twenty-three years' service, and has smelt plenty of powder. He was in the

Soudan and Nile expeditions, was at El Teb and Tamai, and at Abu Klea; had several horses shot under him, got several clasps and mentions in despatches, and in 1891 the Distinguished Service Order. As to Civil appointments, he was with Sir Gerald Portal in Uganda, on Lord Harris's Staff in Bombay, and served a term as Acting Administrator in Mashonaland, where he was much liked. It is easy to imagine things so turning out at Johannesburg as to put him into his right *métier*, but Fate was unkind, or he was not quite equal to her. The "best of good fellows" and one of the most popular officers in the service, he is competent in his own calling—which is not that of a revolutionary.

It may be convenient to add here, though it does not appear among the signatories whom the Letter of Invitation well nigh hanged, the name of Mr. Percy Fitzpatrick, who acted as Secretary of the Reform Committee.

Percy Fitzpatrick was a Barberton miner before he came to the more placid camp at Johannesburg. He is younger than the others, or seems so by reason of his impulsiveness and enthusiasm, and less the Capitalist and more the Politician demanding his vote. He is not always discreet, a virtue cheap at Johannesburg, but he is loyal and plucky.

Such were the ringleaders in Johannesburg, and though, when their names appeared, it was murmured that there was too much flavour of Rhodes about the list, it makes, take it all round, a good representative selection.

So the plot thickened. We have seen the preparations for the troops. In the next chapter we shall see the arming of Johannesburg. Let this one conclude with the arrangements connecting the two points. For a dash across country it would be convenient to be able to dispense with commissariat. On the pretext of establishing a coach service between Mafeking and Johannesburg a line of stores at intervals of a few hours' ride were built and stocked with food and forage all the way from Mafeking to Krugersdorp. One Dr. Wolff, another old Kimberley doctor, was told off by Jameson for this work, and figured for the purpose as the Rand Produce and Trading Syndicate. No part of the plot seems at the first blush cooler and more barefaced than this elaborate collection of stores for the baiting of men and horses along the whole line of invasion. The road, however, was becoming a frequented one. The pretext was plausible enough, and it was only certain Boers who noticed the presence of "bully beef" among the so-called produce stored in these sheds, whose suspicions began to be aroused. Under the same pretext Dr. Wolff bought up some hundreds of horses for remounts from the well-known Johannesburg coaching firm of Heys, and these horses were stationed midway on the intended line of march upon a farm which actually belongs to a member of the Transvaal Volksraad. In all, Dr. Wolff's part of the business cost over £18,500.

The best index to show the point to which Jameson brought things upon his Johannesburg visit when he obtained the Leonard letter is afforded by the following letter, in which he assures "Bobby" White that the almost certain date will be 26th December :—

"[Private.]   "JOHANNESBURG,
                    "*Nov.* 19*th*, 1895.

"DEAR BOBBY,—

"Hope by the time you get this you will have our men in camp—also about a hundred from Stevens and I shall get a couple from Grey when I arrive in about a fortnight or a little longer. The almost certain date will be 26th Dec. From Willoughby's wire to me there ought to be 150 complete equipments on the way down—you better find out from him when they are likely to arrive; but I have wired to Willoughby that he is not to send down any men or anything further, as those people up there have been blabbing and here they are still getting letters on the subject—therefore I wired to Willoughby to stop all drilling—give out all the horses, etc. W. himself must not come down till much later, though I know he does not like it. Now you see the force ought to be about six—if short of saddles after finding out all Grey has in reserve, then tell Stevens and he must get them below. I don't see that you can want any more uniforms or horses, but if required they would also have to come from Stevens. Of course efficiency and proper equipment are important, but what is much more important, in fact, vital, is that suspicion should not be raised in any way. I am going to the Cape on Friday, and shall be a week there before coming to Mafeking unless some unforeseen blabbing occurs when we might have to hurry things. Wolff will tell you rest.

"Yrs.,
"L. S. J.'

Soon after Jameson telegraphed up to Sir John Willoughby, his military adviser, whom he still kept chafing up at Bulawayo:—

"Caratulero carcaras prognare dijudicor egelatus squinanzia polyhedral Zegeling."

Which being translated is:—

"Date fixed is 28th of December to start from here, do not want small Lee-Metford Rifles."

Chapter V

THE ARMING OF JOHANNESBURG

WHILE matters on the border were thus pressed forward by Dr. Jameson and his officers, Col. Rhodes had been sent up to Johannesburg to assist in the organization at that end. Another soldier brother—Captain Ernest Rhodes—was just leaving the Rand after a term of directorship at the "Goldfields" offices. The Colonel took his place, and soon set to work to get in arms. October 20 is the date of his first draft on the B.S.A. Company for the "New Concessions Account," *alias* "New Concessions Syndicate," *alias* "Development Syndicate," and later "Relief Fund," which was drawn on as the War Chest of the Revolution. About the same date began the forwarding of arms under the Company's auspices to Kimberley and Mafeking, and the drafts and the forwarding went on busily during the next two months.

It is curious, by the way, that with all the crises and riotous "incidents" of several years past, Johannesburg men had done so little to arm themselves.[1] Many of them quite expected that some day a street brawl or a row with the police would end in shooting. That, though not a set revolution, was often in their minds. And a good number of men in offices must have lived in country districts, perhaps been born in country districts, where every grown man has his rifle or his gun as a matter of course, and where the accomplishment of guiding a horse across the veld, and carrying arms at the same time, is as a thing that comes by nature. One would have expected such men to have a gun for shooting birds, if not a rifle for buck; for even

[1] See passage in Phillips' letter, Chapter IV. near beginning.

the Johannesburg stockbroker goes shooting in the country sometimes.

The outside world had never supposed there would be any difficulty about arms at Johannesburg; it was assumed that arms would turn up all right when arms were wanted. Johannesburg leaders seemed to share the illusion. Months before the raid and revolution were being plotted, I remember talking to a couple of the leaders in what was then the constitutional movement, and their remarking in the most positive way that matters would come to an open breach with the Government eventually; whereupon I said, "If I were in your place, I should not take another step till a store of rifles had been got in": and they replied in a way and with an expression which made me drop the matter at once and assume copious underground arsenals.

Yet the crisis found Johannesburg without even a nucleus of men who could shoot and had weapons. How was this? The obvious expedient for giving force to a Rand agitation for a kind of Grattan Parliament, would have seemed to be to form a kind of Grattan Volunteers. There are Volunteers (Vrywillige) in Johannesburg, but they are a Government force, recruited largely from Germans and Hollanders, armed by the Government and paid in perquisites. The nearest thing to a Uitlander force was the Rand Rifle Association, which languished under the lack of enthusiasm and the difficulties with which the Government surrounded the procuring of permits for getting in a single rifle. And it must be remembered that the Afrikanders on the Rand were largely of the town-bred kind. A Cape Town Afrikander is no more a shooter than a Cape Town Englishman, lately a Cockney.

Be all this as it may, it is clear that Johannesburg leaders did not only appeal to Mr. Rhodes to support them from without: they appealed to him to arm them within.

Probably there were few Uitlander sympathisers in the Colony who would not have been glad to help Uitlander friends on the Rand to provide themselves with arms and ammunition.

Nobody could be surprised if Cecil Rhodes, the private individual, saw to it that a brother of his on the Rand should get a rifle before incensing by a Declaration of Right the armed Government and the rifle-carrying burghers.

For Mr. Rhodes, the Premier of Cape Colony, to take sides in the same way was another matter. He had his official position; and it is one of the propositions always assumed in this discussion that he could not have done what he did without that position.

As far as this refers to his position as Minister of the Colony, it is quite untrue. Rhodes the Premier helped Rhodes the Conspirator in no way.

Rhodes of the British South Africa Company, of De Beers, and of two large gold-mining properties at Johannesburg, was more indispensable.

But on reading the evidence of the casual, irresponsible way in which all sorts of people co-operated in forwarding arms and incurring expenses, one sees at once that what helped most of all was a certain idiosyncrasy of Cecil Rhodes the man.

The evidence shows that many conversations must have taken place something upon this model :—

"You are to go here, see this man, say that, and spend so-and-so." "By whose orders?" "Never mind. You won't be 'left'"—and an expressive look. The person instructed says to himself at once "Rhodes,"—and goes ahead with confidence. He requires no written guarantee. He has perfect confidence; he knows that even if there has been some misunderstanding, the man whose plans he thought he was facilitating will "see him through."

There are few millionaires who inspire this peculiar confidence, not only among their creatures, but in independent men of business. It has far more to do with the man than with his money. Take the case of more than one South African money-bag, much fatter than Mr. Rhodes, and try whether you can get business connections or underlings to commit themselves for sums of money and other responsibilities without security in black and white.

Rough-and-ready, non-legal informality, has been part of Mr. Rhodes' business methods throughout his career; it cannot be denied that the peculiarity, eccentricity almost, came in extremely handy when he turned conspirator.

Mr. F. F. Rutherfoord was examined by the Select Committee as to the way in which he signed cheques in Mr. Rhodes' name for the B.S.A. Company. Apparently, some years before, he had been told verbally that he could sign anything put before him by the officials of the Company, and initialled by one of them. The War Chest cheques to Colonel Rhodes he signed in this way, without asking questions.

"Do you make any inquiries as to the cheques you sign?—No, none whatever. I go over to the Company's office at two o'clock and sign the cheques put before me.

"Did you never communicate with anybody about those drafts of Colonel Francis Rhodes?—With not a soul.

"*Mr. Schreiner.*—Then Mr. Stevens, an estimable gentleman no doubt, could draw a cheque for £20,000 in his own interest and place it before you, and you, as representative of the managing director, would sign it without making any inquiry, and the next you might hear of him was that he had 'gone to Guam'?—If the cheques are initialled by Mr. Stevens or by Mr. Berry, I make no inquiries.

"Though you are the representative of the managing director?—When I see the stamp with Mr. Rhodes' names on the cheque I sign . . .

"*Mr. Jones.*—If a cheque for a hundred thousand pounds were presented to you, would you sign it without inquiry?—I signed a cheque for very nearly that amount the other day, and I did not ask any questions . . .

"Your signature purports to go through as the signature of the managing director, and you undertake a responsibility to the managing director by agreeing to give your signature to the cheques. Now what instructions did you receive relative to that from the managing director?—I have had none from the managing director.

"Who gave you the original instructions?—I was told——

"By whom?—I cannot tell you whether it was Dr. Harris, but I can tell you that it was not Mr. Rhodes; I had no communication with him at the time.

"Then if it was not Mr. Rhodes, who was it?—I cannot recall it.

It is some years ago. I went down to the Standard Bank and Mr. Michell told me that my signature would be recognised. I do not think I have any written authority, nor have I had any communication with Mr. Rhodes on the point."

But to the arms. The B.S.A. Company had been in the habit of importing arms freely ever since the first Matabele War.

There was nothing peculiar in cases of arms addressed to them, being cleared at Cape Town and forwarded to Mafeking, or housed in the De Beers stores *en route*, to be sent on as required.

Kimberley, therefore, was chosen as the centre from which to arm Johannesburg. During November, the hospitality of the great Diamond Company was freely drawn on by stuffing one of its store houses with rifles and ammunition, some of which came down the line from Mafeking, and some up the line from Cape Town.

The law in South Africa places restrictions on moving arms about the country. A statute, originally passed to check the forbidden but lucrative practice of supplying arms to native territories, requires a permit to be obtained before even a single rifle can be taken from one district of Cape Colony to another. With the purpose for which it was passed, this law had fallen into desuetude. Officials wink at evasion. After the raid, fines of £50 were imposed on the Manager of De Beers, and on Mr. Rutherfoord, a forwarding agent at Cape Town, for treating these particular arms just as they would have treated any others. It is clear, however, that no suspicion would have been aroused had permits been got for every rifle.

The trouble was only when it came to getting them into the Transvaal.

The leaders at Johannesburg put off the solution of this problem till rather late. Mr. Farrar, the last of the five leaders to be taken into the plot, was one of the largest employers of labour on the Rand, and in direct touch with the work of importing machinery. His adhesion soon removed the difficulty.

The arms were smuggled in as mining material in bulk. Some of them were sent direct from Kimberley to Johannesburg by rail under the rather flimsy pretext of De Beers supplying the Simmer and Jack mine with coke suddenly required. Five sheep-trucks were thus got through, in which 800 rifles were thinly heaped over with coke.

Other consignments were sent in oil-drums, each with a nice little tap oozing oil. The drums were sent from Kimberley to Port Elizabeth, and thence by a forwarding agent—as if they had come over sea—up to Johannesburg. They contained 3 Maxims, 125 cases of ammunition, and 1,800 rifles.

The oil-tank forwarding went on from November 6th, and Dr. Jameson had the satisfaction of seeing some of the trucks, when he was visiting Johannesburg during that month, standing innocently on the Simmer and Jack siding. He recalled the fact when Johannesburg leaders complained of being taken unprepared; but the fact is, they left the unloading of the trucks to the last minute, because of the risk of discovery in disposing the arms. Discovery of any single batch of the arms imported would have "blown on" the whole revolutionary design. That is why the arming was left so late.

The "coke-trucks" actually only arrived at Johannesburg on the 26th December, three days before Jameson crossed the border. The balance of the guns, the Maxims, and bulk of the ammunition only arrived on the Tuesday, two days after his crossing. A few arms came a day after the fair, and were seized by Government.

The smuggling was one of the few things which were really well done. "Everything seems to be going right," Dr. Jameson wrote from Kimberley, "especially Gardner Williams's part of it." "Holden" (one of the B.S.A. Company's officers) "is here, and is doing very good work. He is a capital chap." Captain Holden certainly knew how to hold his tongue. As an illustration of this part of the work, some evidence of Mr. Pickering, the Port Elizabeth forwarding agent, may be quoted here. The subject is the oil-tanks:—

"How did you become aware that the trucks were consigned to your firm?—A gentleman, named Holden, I think, waited upon me.

"And informed you of what?—That trucks with tanks of oil were consigned or were to be consigned to me.

"By De Beers?—He did not say De Beers.

"Did you ask him by what authority?—I did, and he asked me to ask him as few questions as possible.

"As a business man, did you not think it necessary to ask him where these trucks had come from?—I did not ask him.

"You did not know where they came from?—I am not prepared to say what I thought.

"But you knew that the consignment had relation to the disturbance at Johannesburg?—There was no disturbance at the time.

"Say the threatened movement, then?—I knew nothing of the movement.

"Did you not know that this consignment was going up in relation to that?—I knew that it was a consignment going up to the mines, and I thought things were in a very unsettled state.

"And that it might be necessary to pour oil on the troubled waters. You knew that those tanks did not contain oil?—I had a very strong suspicion.

"And that suspicion was awakened by what took place between you and Holden?—Yes.

"You had no communication, telegraphic or in writing, relative to this matter?—No.

"That is very unusual, is it not?—Not necessarily. I simply forwarded the stuff as a forwarding agent.

"Where did Holden come from when he came to you?—I had no idea.

"You did not inquire?—No.

"You had never seen him before?—He was most extraordinary. I have never found a man so silent before. He was like an oyster."

So the arming of Johannesburg went on apace.

Chapter VI

CONSPIRACY BY TELEGRAPH

"I THINK," wrote a well-known Englishwoman after the publication of the famous cipher telegrams, "that our English people have no gift for conspiracy. On the whole, I think I am rather glad that they have not." In one respect these particular conspirators did show some gift. Considering how many people were privy to the scheme, the secret was well kept. But meantime some of them were committing every detail of it to paper with the particularity of an office ledger. Was a compromising letter written? A copy was filed by the writer, and another by the recipient. Was a telegram loaded with secret meanings received? It was docketed and put away in a despatch box. Was the precaution used of writing in cipher? The cipher chosen was the Bedford McNeil Mining Code, a copy of which is to be found in every telegraph office in South Africa. Were names and other special matter confided to a more special code? Copies of the key were carefully secreted by the recipient along with his copies of the messages, as if the anxiety were far less for the secrecy of the plot than for the curiosity of the future historian or the legal exigencies of a prosecuting Government. Surely, except on the stage, where it is sometimes necessary for a situation that conspirators should walk about with their sinister designs neatly engrossed on vellum and sticking out of their pockets, never was plot plotted in the manner of this plot! It was a system of conspiracy by double entry.

Had it been merely the business men of Johannesburg who carried these admirably systematic methods from the counting-house to the revolutionary camarilla it would seem more natural; but it was in camp at Pitsani, not in offices at Johannesburg, that these things were done. The Johannesburgers destroyed nearly all their papers. The person whose name is dotted about the Green Books attached to almost every compromising document in the hands of Government was a more or less young Guardsman. "*Gevonden in de trommel van R. White*" is the foot-note painfully iterated through pages of discovery, "R. White" being the invariable "Bobby" of so many messages. He it was who, in an airy way, to oblige the Pretoria State Attorney signed an affidavit when in gaol after Doornkop certifying as genuine the copy (of course a copy was carefully taken to the field of battle) of the Leonard letter, which then proved the sole and the almost sufficient piece of evidence to hang its signatories. But this is anticipating. For the most part the mania exhibited by Major the Honourable R. White for keeping and filing everything, and carrying it about with him, seems to have been due simply to the conscientiousness of a not very brilliant officer, who felt that he must supplement his deficiencies by using double care in routine details. The code key which revealed to Pretoria most of the personal names used was Jameson's own. The Doctor tore up an important despatch on the field of battle so roughly that it was afterwards picked up and put together, and he supplied further finds by sending a despatch box round by train, labelled, apparently as if for the express convenience of the Government.

It would be ungrateful to complain of all this, for but for the quires of letters, telegrams, etc., which have come to light how could the Story of a Crisis be written? As it is, there is an *embarras de richesses* in the way of documents, and chief among these are the Cipher Telegrams.

As the time for action drew near, when Jameson had finished his flying visits to Johannesburg and Cape Town, and was waiting the signal at Pitsani like a dog straining at the leash, the telegraph wire became the medium of communication between the three foci of the plot. Johannesburg and Cape Town, Cape Town and Pitsani, wired to each other from day to day under the nose of the Government they were plotting against, in the thin disguise of an easily read code and a not very abstruse metaphor, in which political and military conceptions were translated into terms of company-promoting. Revolution became "flotation"; troops on the border were "foreign subscribers," and held "shareholders' meetings"; a manifesto was a "directors' circular," etc., etc. In these terms Johannesburg and Jameson corresponded, mostly *via* Cape Town through the Chartered Company's offices. More rarely Johannesburg and Jameson wired to one another direct across country. At the Cape Town end the communication was latterly in the hands of Dr. F. Rutherfoord Harris, Secretary in South Africa of the British South Africa Company, and like Dr. Jameson and Dr. Wolff, a Kimberley medico who had not stuck to his last, being both clever and ambitious. Dr. Harris was then a member of the Cape House of Assembly, and a whip of Mr. Rhodes' party there. As a whip he was very successful. He could generally, it is said, make a hesitating member agree with him, or believe that he agreed sufficiently for the division or the purposes of the moment. It was a defect of this quality, however, that the sanguine and persuasive diplomatist would sometimes come away convinced that the person he had talked to accepted his point of view, and that all was understood and settled between them, when nothing really was further from the case, the other man having been simply not ready enough or not determined enough to contradict. It is obvious that this was a drawback for the purposes of a go-between in delicate and important negotiations. In much of what Dr. Harris did, then and at other times, he was undoubtedly the perfect agent of his chief. But he was quite capable, at a critical period of South African history, of taking larger responsibilities and aspiring to a more commanding *rôle*. It was he, by the way, who negotiated with Mr. Chamberlain the Khama settlement.

The Stevens of the telegrams, whom the Cape Select Committee found a *non mi ricordo* witness of amazing powers of oblivion, is the confidential assistant in the Company's Cape Town Office, and acted as intermediary till Dr. Harris returned from England.

The telegrams which passed between the three points of the conspiratorial triangle for a week or two before the crisis have left a record day by day like that traced by the needle of some meteorological instrument. Their significance in some respects is still to be decided; for instance, as to the division of responsibility between Secretary and Managing Director. Their chief value for solving the evergreen enigma of immediate responsibility for the crossing of the border consists in the clear way in which they show Jameson forcing the hand alike of Rhodes and of Johannesburg.

As the date drew nearer which had been arranged on for action when Jameson was at Johannesburg the leaders there began to be sensible that the heaviest part of their work was still before them. They could not take the people into their confidence, and by mere vague phrases they could not rouse the necessary enthusiasm. Now was felt the want of the steady political work which should have been done in the past when capital was still "sitting on the fence." After years of easy-going agitation—a meeting here, a pamphlet there—you cannot rush a population to the white-heat point of revolt in a few weeks. Besides, the material organization was in arrears, and as little by little new men were taken into the plot the seeds of disunion and irresolution began to sprout.

On the 7th of December Colonel Rhodes wired from Johannesburg to Major White at Mafeking :—

"Tell Zahlbar (Jameson) the Polo Tournament here is postponed for one week, or it would clash with the race week."

"Polo tournament"—a sporting metaphor varying from the commercial one—evidently meant the same as "flotation" in subsequent messages Major White replied next day :—

"Hope [? no] delay, do not alter unless obliged according original understanding. Considerable suspicion already, therefore any delay would be most injurious."

A few days later "Zahlbar" himself wired to Stevens, Cape Town, to:

"Tell Mr. Rhodes everything is very satisfactory, also ready here. The entire journey occupies two and a half days."

On the 11th Colonel Rhodes again strikes the note of delay to Major White:—

"Inform Dr. Jameson, do not send any more heroes before January, no room for them. I am sending Captain R. M. Heyman to Graham's Town for next fourteen days."

For "heroes" some have conjectured horses. The context makes it more probable that the term was a code word for the picked men whom at that date the Doctor was recruiting in Cape Town and Kimberley—old soldiers and others—and sending up to Johannesburg, as well as to Pitsani. About 120 were so sent. The "eleven fine diamonds from De Beers" (Volunteer Corps?), whose sending Dr. Harris advised just before the crisis, were similarly metaphorical.

To which "Zahlbar" next day replies:—

"Have everything ready here. Hope your telegram received yesterday Bobby White does not imply any delay, because any delay would be most injurious. Dr. Wolff leaves to-morrow, will explain."

And at the same time Jameson sent a more urgent and plain message *via* Cape Town:—

"Send following message to Col. F. Rhodes: (begin) Grave suspicion has been aroused. Surely, in your estimation, do you consider that races is of the utmost importance compared to immense risks of discovery, daily expected, by which under these circumstances it will be necessary to act prematurely? Let J. H. Hammond inform weak partners [the] more delay [the] more danger. Dr. Wolff will explain fully reasons to anticipate rather than postpone action. Do all you can to hasten the completion of works."

What sort of suspicions those were that were aroused one

gathers from hints scattered through letters of earlier date: "So-and-so has been blabbing," "fellows have been stupidly talking," "it is more important to avoid exciting suspicion than to go on drilling," and other sentences to like effect. It is in evidence, also, that the presence of bully beef among the so-called "produce" at the stores between Mafeking and Krugersdorp had not escaped notice. But there were also other suspicions elsewhere, as we shall see. No wonder, with all this on his nerves, Jameson thought it a frivolous pretext to adjourn a revolution for a race-meeting. At Johannesburg, on the other hand, it was considered that to have the town swarming with the number and the kind of strangers always attracted by the races would be a most awkward complication. But it is incredible that any one of the various successive reasons assigned for delay would not have been brushed aside had Johannesburg been ready and united for the tremendous enterprise.

On the 13th Stevens duly passes Jameson's urgent message on, and adds:—

"The London *Times* also cables confidentially to that effect. Postponement of meeting would be a most unwise course."[1]

Here is a new element of mystery. What could happen in England to affect the matter? And what is the *Times* doing in that *galère*? Pressed before the Cape Select Committee Mr. Stevens could not recall knowing of any such *Times* message, and its seems likely that this particular message was dictated by Mr. Rhodes. The *Times* is evidently used loosely for somebody more or less connected with that journal, or using *Times* information. The paper itself denies having ever sent any such message; that is, presumably, the Editor denies that *he* ever sent or authorized it. Note that the thing sent is also very loosely indicated. Any news which, to the recipient in South Africa, bore on the question of delay, would satisfy

[1] From appearance of cipher it should be decoded "to effect that postponement," as in Dutch version.

the terms of this reference. The present writer has no doubt that the solution of this mystery, which has greatly fluttered the Fleet Street dovecots, is something as follows: A great paper like the *Times* has writers who make a speciality of colonial subjects, who stretch out tentacles touching Johannesburg, Cape Town, Rhodes, and on the other hand the Colonial Office, clubland, officialdom. In South Africa the gossip and guesses of the young troopers and officers at Mafeking and at Pitsani were beginning to make people talk. In London, especially in the Service clubs, letters were received in which the writers airily announced as undoubted facts that they were going to eat their Christmas dinner in Pretoria. Upon such talk Mr. Fairfield, of the Colonial Office (a Permanent Secretary whom one would enjoy seeing cross-examine some of the South Africans who talk about the "ignorance of Downing Street"), was moved to give that warning to his chief which set Mr. Chamberlain cabling anxiously to the High Commissioner just as Jameson was preparing to trot over the border. The *Times* Colonial Intelligence Bureau would soon note that people at the Colonial Office were in this frame of mind, and one or other of them, on friendly terms with Mr. Rhodes or Dr. Jameson, would send the "tip" by cable. It might be a very vague "tip," but to the conspirators in South Africa it would mean a threat of disbandment and the ruin of their schemes. The moment attention was called in England to the troops on the border, and to any rumours about their object, there was a risk of inquiries and prohibitions by cable, such as were actually sent while Jameson was, so to speak, in the act of starting. Apprised of such warnings as this (and of a similar one conveyed from a similar source to Johannesburg), Jameson quickly made up his mind that unless he soon started he would never get the chance of starting at all.

Dr. Wolff, however, found the prospect at Johannesburg better than was expected, and wired to Pitsani on the 18th, "there is not likely to be postponement," adding a request for surplus ammunition to be sent round (to Johannesburg) by way of Gardner Williams at Kimberley. But repetitions of Jameson's warning about the danger of delay continued to be sent on from Cape Town by the Secretary of the B.S.A. Company to Col. Rhodes, and by Mr. Beit (of Wernher, Beit & Co.) to his colleague, Mr. Phillips. Messrs. Beit and Harris had just arrived together from England, and they evidently shared Jameson's fears of awkward inquiries by cable. On the 18th Hammond had wired to Mr. Rhodes at Groote Schuur :—

"Cannot arrange respective interests without Beit, flotation must be delayed until his arrival. How soon can he come?"

The phrase "respective interests" has been caught at, like other company-promoting metaphors of the correspondence, to show that there was some stock-jobbing "deal" on hand. In reality, the division in question was not one of spoils, but one of expenses. Mr. Phillips wanted further authority as regards Mr. Beit's contributions to the War Chest, then swimming in tens of thousands. Mr. Beit replied (19th) to Mr. Phillips, not in code, but using a few private code words of the firm :—

"Cannot come at present owing to health. Wire where is the hitch. *Santrog* [= Jameson ?] very impatient, cannot *naturzug* [= give extension ?]. Our *schallhorn* [= foreign ?] supporters [1] urge immediate flotation."

Next day he again wired that he was worse, was in fact laid up and ordered to the seaside. He was too ill to be of any use, but—

"Most anxious that you should not delay flotation of new Company on my account a day longer than necessary. Immediate flotation is the thing most desired, as we never know what may hinder it, if now delayed."

Poor "Herr Beit!" as Mr. Labouchere will call him. He really was ill—at least, he looked it—and he really did recruit at Muizenberg. The cool nerve which had ruled markets and manœuvred huge financial operations was now undergoing a

[1] "Foreign supporters" elsewhere = the allies on the border, and once (to Jameson) the Johannesburgers.

new strain. But no one could suppose Mr. Beit, millionaire speculator as he is, to be devoid of the ambition to manœuvre men, as well as markets, who saw him during the first Matabele war, following every telegram and moving little paper flags or pointers over a map in his office on the Viaduct, as the forces of "John Company" Secundus pushed across the veld. Mr. Beit may not be a soldier, may not be a statesman; but he has been fairly caught up at the chariot wheels of Mr. Rhodes, with his grand political schemes.

Mr. Beit's telegram to Mr. Phillips was followed (21st) by another from Dr. Harris to Col. Rhodes, in code, drawing attention to it, and adding :—

"Reply when you can float in your opinion, so that I may advise Dr. Jameson."

At the same time Dr. Harris wired to Jameson, telling him what he and Beit had done to hurry up Johannesburg, promising to telegraph answer promptly, and adding, "Zoutpacht [Paul Kruger] is returning immediately to Pretoria."

But Colonel Rhodes was very far from being able to "name a day." The party of delay had just discovered reason for another hitch, and the Colonel had to cross Dr. Harris's request with the following :—

"Please inform C. J. Rhodes : it is stated that Chairman will not leave unless special letter inviting him. Definite assurance has been given by all of us, that on day of flotation you and he will leave ; there must absolutely be no departure from this, as many subscribers have agreed to take shares on this assurance ; if letter necessary, it can still be sent, but it was agreed documents left with J. A. Stevens was sufficient, and that you are responsible for Chairman's departure. It is very important to put this right ; reply to Lionel Phillips."

What did all this mean ? Who was "Chairman" ? It will be remembered, from the earliest sketch of the revolutionary plot, what stress was laid on the "breathing-space" to be secured by forcing the Imperial Government to intervene as mediator. Mr. Rhodes, as Cape Premier, was to advise Sir Hercules

Robinson to go up to the spot at once. The Johannesburg leaders were to appeal to his intervention if necessary (and eventually did); but Mr. Rhodes was relied on to see that the appeal was responded to. It was, of course, absolutely the right thing to do, and the High Commissioner eventually did it with the full approval of Mr. Hofmeyr; but his feelings may be imagined when he found long after how his action had been counted on and made capital of to assist in " floating " the revolution.

This particular reason or pretext for delay was soon cleared up, Harris telling Col. Rhodes (23rd) :—

"A. Beit telegraphed L. Phillips assuring him that Chairman starts immediately flotation takes place. No invite necessary."

Readers with a turn for puzzles may like to see the message from Beit referred to; it is in the private code to which the key has not been found.

"Have seen Saufinder mitzdruse to Schaffiger bleimass absolutely that Chairman hablohner on flotation no request or letter is hobelspane as anlegespan is ausgerodet as previously angelstern."

And now comes a strange thing. We have seen Harris on the 21st asking Colonel Rhodes to name a day for " floating." We have seen him on the 23rd, so far from getting the date he asked for, having to send a message of reassurance about another hitch. On the very same day, the 23rd, without any message from Johannesburg to go upon so far as the Pretoria Detective Department and the Cape Select Committee can tell us, is sent the following telegram, as if everything were settled :—

"From   " To
Harris, Cape Town   Jameson, Pitsani.
"Company will be floated next Saturday, 12 (twelve) o'clock at night : they are very anxious you must not start before 8 (eight) o'clock and secure telegraph office silence. We suspect Transvaal is getting aware slightly."

It is not clear whether 8 means 8 a.m. or 8 p.m. "Telegraph office silence" probably means cutting the wire to Pretoria, rather than that to the Colony. But where is the authority for these precise arrangements?

When the liberation of Sicily was hanging in the balance, the Sicilians were ready to fly to arms if Garibaldi landed, but Garibaldi, unlike Jameson, determined not to move till they gave proof that they were in earnest. Crispi invented a despatch from Sicily which gave Garibaldi his proof and started him on his road. It was not true, at that moment, that Sicily had risen; but it rose like one man the moment Garibaldi landed. The deadlock was forced. The cause was won. Sicily was liberated. Is it conceivable that Dr. Harris sent this message "off his own bat," consciously or unconsciously emulating the *splendide mendax* Italian statesman? Or was he, or one of the others, or Mr. Rhodes himself, simply bent on quieting Jameson and gaining time? Was this message meant, as others which followed it obviously were meant, to stop the firebrand on the border from despairing of his confederates and breaking away? People in writing to an impatient correspondent are apt to speak of things as already arranged which they are only arranging. Of course it must be remembered that as long ago as the 19th of December we had Jameson writing to "Bobby" White, "almost certain date will be 26th December," and soon after telegraphing to Sir John Willoughby, "date fixed is 28th of December, to start from here,"—the 28th being the very "Saturday" now named by Harris.[1]

Be this as it may, next day, the 24th, Harris returns to the charge and tries to prevent Jameson going off at a tangent upon Dr. Wolff's reports of Johannesburg vacillation :—

"You must not move before Saturday night: we are feeling confident it will take place Saturday night. Since Dr. Wolff left feeling our subscribers greatly improved."

While Cape Town was thus holding back Pitsani with one

[1] Who says he had it by word of mouth from ———, fresh from Johannesburg.

hand, it was trying with the other to bring Johannesburg into line with Pitsani. On the morning of the 26th Colonel Rhodes received the following from "Cactus," one of Dr. Harris's code names:—

"Dr. Jameson says he cannot give extension of refusal for flotation beyond December, as Transvaal Boers opposition shareholders hold meeting on Limpopo at Pitsani Mackluke."

The effect of this message was the opposite of what was intended. Now that the fatal day was almost upon them, with the terrible Doctor on the border straining at his leash, the party of delay at Johannesburg, which had made hitches already about "races," about "Chairman," and about Beit's authority, had just seized occasion, by raising the "Flag Question," which shall be entered into in another chapter, to make the last and the greatest "hitch" of all. A secret conclave was held on Christmas Day, which could agree upon nothing except to gain time. Two messengers—Holden and Heany, both Chartered Company officers—were sent across country, one by road and one by rail, to entreat Jameson to hold his hand. Other two messengers—Messrs. Leonard and Hamilton—were sent to Cape Town to entreat Mr. Rhodes to add his voice peremptorily to theirs. Finally, as the result of "Cactus's" message just quoted, the following decisive telegrams were despatched on the 26th December. The first from "Toad," Johannesburg (Toad being one of the code names for Colonel Rhodes, dating from a schoolboy perversion of his name at Eton), to Charter, Cape Town:—

"It is absolutely necessary to postpone flotation. Charles Leonard left last night for Cape Town."

The second from Jameson's brother at Johannesburg, S. W. Jameson, to Pitsani:—

"It is absolutely necessary to postpone flotation through unforeseen circumstances here altogether unexpected, and until we have C. J. Rhodes' absolute pledge that authority of Imperial Government will not be insisted on. Charles Leonard left last night to interview C. J. Rhodes. We will endeavour to meet your wishes as regards December, but you must not move until you have received instructions to. Please confirm."

In forwarding "Toad's" message to Jameson, Dr. Harris accepts the delay implicitly, however regretfully, adding :—

"Charles Leonard will therefore arrive Cape Town Saturday morning; so you must not move until you hear from us again. Too awful. Very sorry."

He telegraphs again next day :—

"*Re* Secheleland Concession shareholders' meeting postponed until 6th day of January; meanwhile, circular has been publicly issued and opinion of all interested will then be taken and then action decided upon. Charles Leonard arrives here to-morrow morning. We must wait patiently, and will do our very utmost, but am beginning to see our shareholders in Matabeleland concession were very different to those in Secheleland matter !"

"Secheleland Concession" is evidently our old friend "flotation." The circular publicly issued is the famous manifesto, signed Charles Leonard, Chairman of the National Union, which was published on the morning of the 27th calling a meeting for the 6th January. The melancholy last sentence of the telegram seems to institute a feeling comparison between the delays and vacillations at Johannesburg and the unity and promptitude which carried the first Matabele war to victory. Meanwhile, Mr. Rhodes' anxiety was all to prevent Jameson going off at a tangent; for on the heels of these regrets Dr. Harris sends another telegram beginning with the code formula for "Mr. Rhodes says," the idea of the message obviously being to show Jameson that he need not be in such fear of the rumours and suspicions which had been excited, as he has a perfectly good excuse to give for keeping the troops there if necessary till the Day of Judgment :—

"Mr. Rhodes says : Do not be alarmed at our having 600 men at Pitsani Mackluke ; we have the right to have them ; you know we are sorting the B.S.A. Company's Police for eventual distribution, and if people are so foolish as to think you are threatening Transvaal, we cannot help that.

[1] Mr. Rhodes's acquaintance with this course of telegrams was rather general than detailed.

B.S.A. Company's Police at Mafeking will cost half what they do in Matabeleland, and horses do not die. At the same time, as you know, we must keep up a certain B.S.A. Company Police force for the country as per our agreement with Imperial Government."

Thoroughly out of patience at all this, Jameson now determined to force the hands of his confederates both at Johannesburg and at Cape Town by a little judicious "bluff." We are now, it must be remembered, at Friday, the 27th, the eve of the very date originally fixed for the inroad, or at any rate for the revolution. Jameson begins by making out that his troopers had already taken an irrevocable step, so that it was too late to turn back, and he therefore calls on Cape Town and Johannesburg both to telegraph the signal.

To Harris he telegraphs at three o'clock :—

"I am afraid of Bechuanaland Police for cutting wire. They have now all gone forward, but will endeavour to put a stop to it. Therefore expect to receive telegram from you nine to-morrow morning authorizing movements. Surely Col. F. W. Rhodes advisable to come to terms at once. Give guarantee,[1] or you can telegraph before Charles Leonard arrives."

And again at five o'clock :—

"If I cannot, as I expect, communicate with Bechuanaland Border Police cutting, then we must carry into effect original plans. They have then two days for flotation. If they do not, we will make our own flotation with help of letter which I will publish. Inform John Hays Hammond, Dr. Wolff, A. L. Lawley, whom you may rely upon to co-operate."

Notice the clear threat here to take matters into his own hands, binding the Johannesburg confederates to the letter of their appeal to him. It is a curious irony that Mr. Hammond, whom Jameson picks out as one who could be relied on to fall in with this expedient for "rushing" the weaker brethren, is, of all the leaders, the one who has most bitterly resented the improper, he would almost say the perfidious, use made of the letter. It is to Hammond, too, that he appeals to give the

[1] See above, S. Jameson's telegram.

signal in his wire of the same date to his brother at Johannesburg :—

"Dr. Wolff will understand. Distant cutting British Bechuanaland Police have already gone forward. Guarantee already given.[1] Therefore let J. H. Hammond telegraph instantly all right."

Meaning, presumably, as in the telegram to Harris, that the police entrusted with cutting the Pretoria wire were beyond recall. But what J. H. Hammond in reply did telegraph, under the name of "Hays," was this :—

"Wire just received. Experts' reports decidedly adverse. I absolutely condemn further developments at present."

Even more explicit was Mr. Phillips' simultaneous wire to Mr. Beit :—

"It is absolutely necessary to delay floating. If foreign subscribers insist on floating without delay, anticipate complete failure."

This wet blanket Dr. Harris duly forwarded to Jameson on Saturday.

Upon receipt of Hammond's message, Jameson gives up Johannesburg as a bad job, roundly accuses it of "funking," and tries one last desperate "bluff" on Cape Town. The following was sent first thing Saturday morning :—

"There will be no flotation if left to themselves. First delay was races, which did not exist ; second, policies—already arranged. All mean fear. You had better go as quickly as possible and report fully, or tell C. J. Rhodes to allow me. I stand to lose fifty good B.S.A. Company's Police —time expires next week, and so on, as can tell them nothing."

But Cape Town was not to be bluffed. The mad folly of a move into the Transvaal without so much as the pretext of a disturbance within its borders was one possible to Jameson's fevered brain, as he chafed upon the frontier, but unthinkable in the cooler distance of Cape Town. Holden was pressing

---

[1] See above, S. Jameson's telegram.

AN AFRICAN CRISIS

across country to Pitsani on horseback, laden with the Johannesburg arguments to show that action at the moment was hopeless. Heany was coming round by rail to the same goal. The only thing was to—

"Stop Zahlbar till Heany sees him."

As Colonel Rhodes put it in a telegram. So Harris ordered a special train for Heany from Kimberley to Mafeking (for to go round by rail from the Rand to Mafeking you must dip down into the Colony and then northward again along the Transvaal border), and telegraphed meanwhile to Heany himself :—

"Lose no time, or you will be late."

And to Jameson :—

"It is all right if you will only wait. Captain Maurice Heany comes to you from Colonel F. W. Rhodes by special train to-day."

And again, a few hours later, with a final bowing to the inevitable :—

"Goold Adams arrives Mafeking Monday, and Heany, I think, arrives tonight; after seeing him you and we must judge regarding flotation, but all our foreign friends are now dead against it, and say public will not subscribe one penny towards it, even with you as a director. Ichabod!"

It may be well to remind those who do not know their Bible as well as the conspirators apparently did, and who, therefore, have taken "Ichabod" for a dark and sinister code word, that it is, being interpreted, "the glory has departed."

That the sender of the telegram, in spite of Jameson's bluff, never doubted that he would now await the Rand messengers and abide by their message, is shown by the telegram, "Cactus" to "Toad," which was sent at noon on Saturday :—

"Have arranged for Heany. Dr. Jameson awaiting Heany's arrival Keep market firm."

Meanwhile, on Saturday morning, the train from Johannesburg had come in, and Messrs. Leonard and Hamilton (the

Chairman of the National Union, and the Editor of the *Star*, the Uitlander organ), had laid bare the utter disunion and chaos reigning at Johannesburg, the suspicions aroused upon the "Flag Question," upon which more anon, and the consequent insistence by a section that the whole question of the Government of the future should be settled before taking a step further against the Government of the present. Their account was such as to make Harris echo Jameson's theory that "all means fear." He telegraphs to Jameson at two o'clock :—

"You are quite right with regard to cause of delay of flotation, but Charles Leonard, Hamilton of *Star*, inform us movements not popular in Johannesburg; when you have seen Captain Heany, let us know by wire what he says; we cannot have fiasco."

And at the same time to Colonel Rhodes :—

"Charles Leonard says flotation not popular, and England's bunting will be resisted by public. Is it true? Consult all our friends and let me know, as Dr. Jameson is quite ready to move, and is only waiting for Captain Maurice Heany's arrival."

* * * * *

The net result of the interview which Messrs. Leonard and Hamilton had at Groote Schuur was to convince Mr. Rhodes that the whole affair was over.

Here on the very date originally fixed for the revolution, were the border supports adjourned *sine die*, and the Johannesburg revolutionaries at sixes and sevens.

Perhaps Mr. Rhodes was secretly relieved. Some time before, in the presence of another confederate, he had had a talk with Jameson in which he had wavered as to the whole design.

"I think, after all, we will give it up," he had said.

"No. I'm d——d if we do now," was the Doctor's curt reply; and the man of schemes yielded to the man of action.

It is not suggested here that the moment's vacillation was due to a moral scruple; but merely that, to adopt the words of the Cape Committee, "there is no evidence that Mr. Rhodes

AN AFRICAN CRISIS

ever contemplated that the force at Pitsani should at any time invade the Transvaal uninvited. It appears rather to have been intended to support a movement from within."

That movement from within Mr. Rhodes regarded as now in abeyance; and as the result of the conference one of the two Johannesburg deputies went from Groote Schuur to the Telegraph Office that Saturday afternoon and sent off a reassured and reassuring telegram, which has, so far, escaped the various fishing inquiries, and is here made known for the first time.

He reported Mr. Rhodes' satisfactory assurances, said that it was all right about Jameson, and told the Johannesburg leaders to "go on quietly" with their movement—a "new programme" had been "agreed upon."

As for Mr. Rhodes, he drily told Government House, which was anxiously watching the apparent signs of rising storm at Johannesburg, that the Johannesburg Reform Movement had "fizzled out like a damp squib."

Such then was the situation on Saturday evening. It was on that date that Jameson had originally arranged with Johannesburg to move. He had now been stopped. Heany and Holden were due at Jameson's camp. For them he was waiting, and Cape Town now knew how absolute a veto they were carrying. Evidently nothing was further from the minds of Mr. Rhodes and those with him than the idea of Jameson accepting that veto for the date fixed only to "take the bit in his teeth" and dash in on the morrow.

The Chartered Company's office was closed as usual on a Saturday afternoon, and the confederates in Cape Town went to bed that night to sleep. Let us hope they slept well. It was some time before some of them got a night's sleep again.

Chapter VII

A HITCH, AND A FALSE START

WHAT had caused the sudden hitch which had thus brought the Johannesburg Revolt to a standstill? The "Flag Question." And what was the "Flag Question"? Much has been conjectured about it, and in many quarters the theory is accepted that the rock on which the Johannesburg Revolt finally struck was the discovery of the Johannesburg leaders that while they were only working for reform, Mr. Rhodes was planning to "jump the Transvaal"—to re-annex the Republic to England, or, as it is absurdly put by some, to the Chartered Company. It is this suspicion which more than anything else seems likely to damage Mr. Rhodes' career in Cape Colony.

The facts seem to be these.

The "Flag Question" had never bulked large in the previous history of the movement. Johannesburg is a cosmopolitan place, and to raise the question of the ultimate future of the country would be to court disunion. The platform of the National Union had always been that of simply reforming the existing Government. That was the only programme which could be avowed by a constitutional agitation, and the only one which could command the sympathies of enlightened Afrikanders in the Cape and the Free State. The most loyal Afrikander in Dutch Cape Colony, however satisfied with the British flag for himself, would be up in arms the moment anybody proposed to force it on his cousins in the Transvaal by arms or by a *coup d'état*. The memories of the last "War of Independence" were too fresh.

Nevertheless, as time went on and the Transvaal contemptuously repudiated the advances of the National Union Uitlanders to cast in their lot with the Republic, the aggressively English section in the Union began to grow in strength, and the old formula, "We want nothing to do with Downing Street," became less and less confident. The writer remembers well, returning to Johannesburg in the middle of 1895, when some years had elapsed since a former visit, and talking over this very question with two of the foremost National Union leaders. I had learnt to regard the Afrikander formula, should a Johannesburg Revolution ever come, as the *mot d'ordre*. What was my surprise to find these leaders beginning to ask each other whether their movement was not losing more strength within, than it gained without, by adopting this platform.

"What!" I said, "You think of waving the Union Jack? I thought it was an axiom that 'flag-wagging' in Johannesburg would ruin everything?"

"With the Progressive Boers, yes. But where *are* the Progressive Boers? One could wait if there were signs of progress, however slow. But look at the reactionary legislation! We go from bad to worse."

"But," I asked again, "even if you regard your friends among the Boers as no good, what about the Afrikander section of your own followers? Surely they will be choked off at the first word of re-annexation?"

"We are not so sure. It *was* so; it would be so now if the Government had met our advances towards citizenship halfway. But as it is—you do not know how bitter feeling has become. There is a small section, but it is the keenest of all, which talks in this way:—'We aren't allowed to have a Transvaal patriotism: very well, let's fall back on our English patriotism. We are nothing to this Government. If we have got to make a revolution, let's make it under the grand old Union Jack.' And the Republican platform does not 'enthuse' these men a bit."

I do not mean that this was the last word of the conversation, or that the leaders I refer to had actually made up their minds in this sense; but the conversation showed the current of thought, and it must be remembered that it preceded the genesis of the actual plot by months.

But in the actual plot all these questions were left over. The first thing was to make the *coup*, to dispossess the present Government on a clear issue of its own misgovernment, and having done so, to submit the question of what should replace it to a plebiscite of all the inhabitants.

The actual government of the Reformed Transvaal would be a part of the great settlement which must follow the downfall of the Unreformed Transvaal, and which would be guided by many factors not calculable beforehand: such as the temper of the Uitlanders, and the completeness of their *coup*; the temper of the Boers, of South Africa at large, of British colonists, of Great Britain and the Colonial Office.

If Mr. Rhodes had any cut-and-dried plan for forcing all these factors into acceptance of the British flag, it is the belief of the present writer that not a soul was in possession of that plan. But it is incredible that he would have risked so much but for the hope that this result would be arrived at, and arrived at without civil war, either immediately or as a proximate result of the upheaval. It was an old saying of his about the Boers: "I know what I feel about my flag—so I do not expect them to give up theirs." He would have worked with the Transvaal if the Transvaal would have worked with him towards a scheme of South African co-operation such as all really Progressive Afrikanders have been willing at some time to accept: a scheme allowing the Republics to keep their own flags and a very complete measure of State autonomy, while at the same time accepting the hegemony in South Africa of the Power which guards the coasts and owns the greatest area of territory.

But his sympathy with the Boer determination to preserve Republican forms was less a moral and sentimental one than it was the recognition by a practical man of practical factors in a situation. For the same Republican formula on the lips of Johannesburg cosmopolites, who dreamed of swaggering themselves in the foretop of a brand new Separatist Industrial Republic, he had no sympathy at all. Had the contest between old and new come to the point at which he, with that finger in the pie which he had been so careful to secure, could have the controlling word in the settlement, nobody who knows Mr. Rhodes can doubt what that word would have been. But in that case, the Boers, led by Paul Kruger and his Hollanders, having themselves to blame for the overturn of their polity, not even Mr. Rhodes' Afrikander supporters could have reproached him for taking advantage of the fact to solve at one blow the intricacies of South African union caused by clashing sovereignties.

After all, to submit the question to the vote of the entire white population of the Transvaal, Boer and Uitlander, was to entrust it to those who alone had a right to settle it. Supposing for a moment that the majority settled it in the English Colonial sense, and could make the minority abide by the vote (a thing most improbable), then the South African problem would be solved at one stroke. With the Cape, Natal, and the Transvaal all British Colonies, surrounded by British territory, the little Free State in the centre of South Africa would have been like a nut between the crackers. It may be that this tempting prospect lured Mr. Rhodes away for once from the saner and, as it happened, fairer-minded and more straightforward opportunism which had always hitherto guided him on this question. But it is the conviction of the present writer that whatever was in his heart Mr. Rhodes was waiting upon events, and that his only settled plan was to secure a hand in the settlement and use it for getting the Transvaal into the best relations with the British Colonies and the British Empire which might then prove feasible short of civil war.

To sum up, the *status quo* was assumed as to flag both at Groote Schuur and in Johannesburg; and oddly enough the people who first brought the matter into prominence on the

Rand were some well-meaning British Jingoes who had lately rushed back to Johannesburg determined to be in at any revolution which might be going. One of these men—and a capital fellow he is, full of pluck and pugnacity, and immovably solid in his convictions—went about the streets in the latter days of December with a little toy Union Jack, which may have come off a Christmas tree, tucked away in his waistcoat pocket as some people will wear a temperance ribbon. He would engage in conversation with anybody supposed to move in the outer revolutionary circles, and sound them on their loyalty to the flag, producing the Christmas tree emblem at an appropriate moment from his pocket to lend emphasis to his remark, "That is the only flag I'll fight under."

This sort of talk brought the matter into discussion. It gave a handle to three classes in the revolutionary councils.

A certain number of Afrikanders, old National Union men, had joined the movement, and induced friends to join, at a time when the anti-Downing Street formula was a more genuine affair than it had since become.

Then there were the Americans, who were inflamed at that moment with the anti-English sentiment raised by Mr. Cleveland's bellicose message about Venezuela. It is an odd illustration of the ramifications of our world-wide interests, this vital link between the swamps of Guiana and the Rand conglomerate; but so it was. Our American cousins were at that moment full of the sentiment of championing pseudo-Republics menaced by grasping John Bull, and Republicanism in the Transvaal was at least not more unreal and corrupt than in Venezuela. It is out of this atmosphere that Mr. Hammond, as an American citizen, eventually came to emerge as a doughty champion of the Transvaal "vier kleur." Excited compatriots accentuated his position at the time of the crisis, and made great capital of it on his behalf later when he was a captive of the Government.

A third section which caught at the handle afforded by this question, was the inevitable party of delay, which, as we have seen, had seized several pretexts for re-opening large questions already.

In the latter days of December, one after another questioner brought the "Flag Question" to the notice of the leaders; and on Christmas Day there took place in the house of Colonel Rhodes a secret meeting, a strange Christmas meeting enough, not of the Reform Committee (which did not then exist), but of the revolutionary junto which formed the nucleus of that Committee.

At this meeting the Colonel was asked point-blank whether there was a private plan between himself and his brother and Dr. Jameson to hoist the Union Jack?

Colonel Rhodes had never heard of such a thing, and said so. Nothing could have been more explicit or more emphatic than his disclaimer. And whatever other deficiencies he may be charged with in the difficult part which he had to play at Johannesburg, he had one singular advantage, especially enviable in that community, and that was that not one of his associates for a moment doubted his honour and his word at any point.

However, the result of the discussion was a triumph for those who wished to delay. One or two of the leaders insisted on a distinct pledge from Mr. Cecil Rhodes. Now, it was argued, the case for adjourning everything is unanswerable; we can do nothing till this question of principle is settled. It was necessary to send agents by train to confer with Mr. Rhodes personally, and they could not be back under four or five days.

So it came about that on the 26th, the day advertised by the National Union for a great public meeting, the manifesto which was issued by its President was accompanied by a notice of adjournment of the meeting to the 6th January. So, too, it fell that the President of the National Union and the Editor of the *Star* left Johannesburg on the eve of the time originally appointed for action and came to Cape Town. Their mission succeeded, as we have seen. Mr. Rhodes gave "satisfactory assurances," while Jameson's impatient brushing aside of what he regarded as a merely factious dissension, is on record in the cipher telegrams.

Nevertheless, the raising of the discussion at this precise moment proved fatal.

It was an interesting question no doubt—with what particular sauce the Transvaal should eventually be served up at the banquet of nations. But, as Mrs. Glass began her immortal recipe, "*first catch your hare.*"

* * * * *

We must now pass from Johannesburg and from Cape Town to Pitsani. We saw in the last chapter how on Saturday, the 28th of December, the confederates at Cape Town went to bed with easy minds under the impression that they had secured a breathing space.

At five o'clock that Saturday afternoon Jameson walked into the office at Pitsani and sent off this remarkable message:

"Received your telegram Ichabod *re* Capt. Maurice Heany. Have no further news. I require to know. Unless I hear definitely to the contrary, shall leave to-morrow evening and carry into effect my second telegram of yesterday to you, and it will be all right."

The pretext for this new departure seemed to Jameson an excellent one. He had that day received a Reuter's telegram representing the situation at Johannesburg as acute, and renewed remarks reached the camp of the kind reflected in one of the cipher telegrams about "Boer shareholders holding rival meeting on Limpopo." This time rumour said that the Boers in the Zeerust and Lichtenburg districts were being assembled in view of the proposed public meeting which was to have taken place that evening at Johannesburg, and that it was intended to surround the town. Jameson did believe in hostile movements of Boers in the Zeerust district sufficiently to send a spy, one Bates, to reconnoitre. Jameson had long ago discussed the possibility of movements of this kind suddenly threatening to cut him off from his friends, and had said to one or other of them in an off-hand way that of course it was understood in that case that he would act at once, without waiting for any signal. The writers of the letter of appeal deny that there was ever any such agreement, but to this day Jameson maintains that some kind of understanding to that effect there was.

Be that as it may, in his then mood the dubious "final arrangement" struck him as a capital piece of bluff for Cape Town, for it is evident that he had now decided in his own mind that the time had come for applying his rule of "shoving things through."

He knew that Heany could not reach him till Sunday, and he can hardly have overlooked the facts that the Chartered Company's Offices, to which the above telegram would be delivered like a bolt from the blue, would probably be shut on Saturday afternoon; while the Mafeking telegraph connection would be shut off on the Sunday.

On Sunday morning (having, of course, received no answer to a telegram which at that moment had not yet been delivered) Jameson proceeded to his next stage of action: from "I will go unless I hear," to "I must go whether I hear or not." At nine o'clock that morning he handed in a message to Cape Town and another to Johannesburg. The first was addressed to Dr. Harris, and says simply:—

"Shall leave to-night for the Transvaal. My reason is, the final arrangements with writer of letter was that, without further reference to them, in case I should hear at some future time that suspicions have been aroused as to their intentions amongst the Transvaal authorities I was to start immediately to prevent loss of lives as letters state. Reuter [telegrams] only just received, even without my own information of meeting in the Transvaal, compel immediate move to fulfil promise made. We are simply going to protect everybody while they change the present dishonest Government, and take vote from the whole country as to form of government required by the whole."

The Johannesburg message was addressed to Dr. Wolff:—

"Meet me, as arranged before you left, on Tuesday night; which will enable us to decide which is the best destination. Make J. W. Leonard speak. Make cutting to-night without fail. Have great faith in J. H. Hammond, A. L. Lawley, and miners with Lee-Metford rifles."

The references in the telegram to Cape Town have been explained in advance. The telegram to Dr. Wolff may be translated : " Come out to meet the column on Tuesday night, and decide whether it should march to Pretoria or Johannesburg. Start the revolution with an harangue from Advocate Leonard, Q.C. Serve out the arms, and the miners will fight, ready or no, when I set the example."

When Heany and Holden arrived, they could no more shake a determination like this than a pair of butterflies could stop a traction engine. He brushed them aside, swearing that with his lads he could kick the persons of the burghers " all round the Transvaal." We have seen what Jameson's training and experience had been, and what formula for success he had derived from it. Unluckily, the Kimberley doctor knew little of the Boer, living aloof and speaking an unknown tongue; and he had something yet to learn.

From this point forward to Doornkop, Jameson moves not like a human thing accessible to human expostulation or authority, but rather like some blind instrument in the hand of Fate.

Chapter VIII

THE GREAT FIASCO

ON Sunday evening the Resident Magistrate at Mafeking (lately Imperial, now Colonial) was surprised at supper by a noise like cheering from the direction of the Police barracks (the Police, lately Imperial, now Company). About the same time Inspector Fuller of the Cape Police saw that the men were being paraded in full kit, marching order; saw Colonel Grey rallying some troopers who at first declined to fall in; and proceeded to investigate. He reports:—

"I followed the column on foot and found that they were taking the main road to the Protectorate, but seeing a cart and six mules belonging to the Company move off in the direction of the Buurman's Drift Road to the Transvaal, I took a short cut on to this road. When I got about half-way between these two roads, I heard the command given to form to the right, and then some one, I was too far off to recognise the voice, or distinguish the words, made what I thought was a short speech, after which a cheer was given, and column of route was again formed. The head of the column then wheeled to the right, left the Protectorate road just past the township, and came into the Transvaal road where I was standing. I estimated the number as they passed me in the moonlight to be about 160 men with four guns. As Major White passed me he bade me good-bye. I returned the greeting, and told him at the same time that I was reporting the whole affair. He said, 'It's all right, old chap, you can do what you like; the wires are cut.'"

The after-history of the men who set forth so light-heartedly, lies buried under the successive accretions of two legends. The first is the Raider legend, which first obtained currency, and was embodied in a certain ballad by a Poet Laureate, a catch now fallen upon evil days of derision. But now there has grown up a great Boer legend only less fearful and wonderful. This chapter is the result of a patient (if almost despairing) effort to confront, collate, and reduce the two to the ascertainable maximum.

Mafeking and the Pitsani camp are about twenty-seven miles apart. About 160 to 170 of the men had been collected at Mafeking, including two troops which were still Bechuanaland Border Police, the rest being now Company's men. At Pitsani were 373 to 380. At each place, on Sunday afternoon at Pitsani, on Sunday evening at Mafeking, there was a parade called, at which the secret was let out and some sort of speech or appeal made. At Pitsani Dr. Jameson made the speech, Colonel White and Sir John Willoughby adding a few words. At Mafeking Major Coventry and Colonel Grey did the speaking. "We cannot keep it from you any longer," said Major Coventry. "It is all bosh about fighting Linchwe." [It had been put about, to account for the drilling, that there was to be a police visit to an insubordinate petty chief in the neighbourhood.] "We are going straight to Johannesburg. We want you all to come. It will be a short trip, everything has been arranged for." The troop addressed seems to have contained a good many hangers-back. There were murmurs and questions. Several of the men wanted to know whether they were going under Queen's or Company's orders. "I cannot say that you are going under the Queen's orders," said Colonel Grey frankly, "but you are going to fight for the supremacy of the British Flag in South Africa."

At Pitsani the men seem to have been better prepared by the prevailing gossip about trouble in the Transvaal. But even there Jameson himself could not quite repress the same kind of questionings. He read the letter of appeal from the five Johannesburgers, or a snatch from it, laying special stress, of course, on the women and children in danger, and said that he was sure not a man would hang back from the rescue. Of course there were cheers, but there were also questions. Where were they going? To Johannesburg. Would there be fighting? Probably not a shot, as everything had been carefully arranged for a surprise; but if need arose they need have no fear of being left to fight it out alone. There were two thousand armed men in Johannesburg; the Cape Mounted Rifles would rush to the rescue; to say nothing of the Imperial forces in Natal, and the Rhodesia Horse in the north. There would be a bonus for the special service, and, in short, if any one's heart was not in it let him fall out and stay behind. Jameson wanted no flinchers.

Then there were more cheers, and doubters and grumblers fell into the background. How could a lot of English lads, careless fellows with rifles and a belt full of ammunition, refuse a madcap adventure proposed by a man in authority,—and such a man as " Dr. Jim "?

And so they started, and trotted in the moonlight over the level veld, across the invisible line which separated a camp of exercise from an incredible violation of international comity.

Before the start (says the Dutch legend) the canteen was thrown open and the troopers were made free of it, to imbibe what it is a special irony under the circumstances to call "Dutch courage." The effects of which (continues the same authority) were grotesquely visible at the start. Some of the riders fell off their horses, and rifles, saddles, and bandoliers were picked up along the first few miles of the route next day. This last statement is well witnessed. Perhaps some few men deserted during that first night. When the columns met next morning, no trooper was *minus* any of his accoutrements. And the free drinks are mere legend. The canteen was open in the usual course for the men to buy.

Here is something else, however, which is credibly attested. An essential part of the plan was the cutting of the telegraph wire—" Secure Telegraph Office silence," as one of the cipher telegrams puts it. And one wire was cut, sure enough. The southward wire to the Colony was cut south of Pitsani, and again south of Mafeking. But the really important wire, running to Pretoria by way of Zeerust and Rustenburg, was not cut, by reason of the trooper who was sent to cut it being, in plain words, drunk. He started on his errand carrying with him the most elaborate and detailed instructions. He was to cut the wire in two places, so many yards apart, take it so far into the veldt, and bury it so deep. He did cut certain wire, and he did make an effort, at least, to bury it in the veld. But the wire which he cut was that of the peaceful railing by which a farmer kept his cows in. Then with a good conscience he reeled back. In the whole tragi-comedy there is no grotesquer touch than this, which the writer had from a resident on the spot.

The two columns effected their junction at the village of Malmani, 39 miles from Pitsani, less from Mafeking. It was five o'clock on a Monday morning, and great was the surprise of the few folks who were stirring. The united force numbered some 512 men, all mounted, with about 30 pack horses and a posse of Kafirs leading them, with eight Scotch carts and three Cape carts drawn by horses or mules and loaded with ammunition and with a small amount of provisions, with eight M.H. Maxims, one 12½-pounder and two 7-pounders.[1]

Besides Dr. Jameson, the officers apparently in command were as follows (the local rank is put first, that in the Service given in brackets): Lieut.-Col. Sir John Willoughby, Bart. (Major), Royal Horse Guards (in general military command); Major Hon'ble Robert White (Captain), Royal Welsh Fusiliers; Lieut.-Col. the Hon. Henry F. White (Major), Grenadier Guards, in charge of M.M.P.; Lieut. Col. Raleigh Grey (Captain), 6th Dragoons, in charge of B.B.P.; The Hon. C. J. Coventry, a Militia Officer, added another title, and several Guardsmen were attached to the Staff. One invalid officer who happened to be staying at

---

[1] The force was under 600, counting the seventy odd native drivers, leaders, etc. Men and natives carried 50,000 rounds of ammunition, and there was the like amount in the carts. There were also some 45,000 rounds for the Maxims, and for the other guns about 120 each.

Mafeking for his health, went along in his own cart in civilian clothes " to see the fun."

Sir John Willoughby was in some ways the most seasoned of these warriors. He had acted in the vague capacity of adviser to Jameson at the time of the Matabele War, and had a hunting reputation and a Derby win to his credit. But taking the officers as a whole it cannot be said that Jameson had surrounded himself for his enterprise with the fighting flower of the British Army. Rather the Company had got a jovial lot of titled young Guardsmen " seconded," dwelling upon that fringe of civilization which parts Society from Bohemia. One of Cromwell's psalm-singing Ironsides would have loved, especially in view of the sequel of the combat, to draw an edifying contrast between these cavaliers, with their rackety troop of young ne'er-do-weels, and the pious fathers of gross families speaking the nasal speech of modern Roundheads, who were to give them their Dunbar.

A certain number of the troopers, no doubt, perhaps a half, were fairly seasoned South African irregulars. They were spoken of at the time as " the lads who smashed Lobengula"; but this was not correct. Most of those who fought in the first Matabele War were settlers, or became settlers. The " Rhodesia Horse," up at Bulawayo, had more title to such a description. The backbone of the column was the B.B.P., or strictly, the ex-B.B.P. Of the M.M.P., the Company's force proper, a surprising proportion were very young, from 18 to 25; and of these many were recent arrivals in South Africa, some of them, indeed, quite green, but for such drilling as they had got in camp during the last few weeks. There was a sprinkling of Afrikanders, a few of them with the typical Franco-Dutch names.

The route from Malmani to Krugersdorp may be followed in the map prepared beforehand by Major " Bobby" White, who had gone over part of the ground in October, besides visiting Pretoria and making elaborate sketches of the environs with military topographical annotations; all which maps and plans, needless to say, were duly carried along and found among his papers.

The distance to be covered must not be thought of as a stretch of trackless veld. From Malmani a plain road ran straight before them and they followed it as far as Krugersdorp. A road—that is to say, a South African cart-track of the usual kind, a strip of ruts and horse-tracks, with a little something done to make the bad places passable, pick out the drifts, etc.

On this road there is a canteen of some sort every two hours on horseback; and the Boer legend has it that the column stopped and drank at every store. Were that true the march would have been a wonderful performance indeed. Of the stores specially built for the column, as we have seen, four were passed on the journey. Here and there appear the homesteads belonging to the farms along the line of country An ordinary South African traveller on horseback, decently mounted and in the habit of riding journeys, not one of a troop, would cover the distance from Mafeking to Krugersdorp (somewhere between 120 and 140 miles at most) in two days to two and a half days, sleeping most of the night.

The column went along with scouts, advance guard, and flanking columns, the artillery and Scotch carts in the middle. The order of the march was as clearly laid out beforehand as the route. Elaborate instructions for Quartermaster, for Transport Officer, and so forth were also among the papers, signed "J. Willoughby, Colonel, O.C. Column." Here is a memorandum marked—

Orders for Intelligence in charge of Scouts (special party).

1. A party of 12 picked men will be detailed for advanced patrol.
2. Captain Lindsell will be in charge, 6 men will be employed and accompany him unless more are detailed.
3. Captain Lindsell's party will always start $\frac{1}{2}$ hour by day and $\frac{1}{4}$ of an hour by night before the column moves.
4. He will report himself to O.C. Column before moving off.
5. This party marches independent of the main body, and will regulate its pace to about 5 miles per hour.

6. The party will halt at places named by O.C. Column.

7. One man of the party will march about 100 yards ahead of the remainder and one man 100 yards in rear.

8. A guide will accompany the party.

9. The officer in charge will endeavour to obtain all the information he can of the road ahead, and will warn all stores of the approach of the column, so that forage and food may be prepared ready for issue on the arrival of the column. He will inform all persons he may meet, that if they keep quiet they will not be molested in any way, and that the column has no hostile intentions against the inhabitants of the country. In case of any hostile demonstration, he is to fall back, sending back a message with the fullest information as to nature of such; and any important information, as to any movements of armed bodies, should also be sent back at once to O.C. Column, stating whether the information be hearsay or otherwise and from whom obtained.

The message should state exact time, place of its despatch, if possible, in writing.

This party is not to scout to the flanks, as this will be done by the advanced guard, but caution must be exercised in approaching a village, defile, or any awkward piece of country.

Ascertain about water, how far and how many horses can be watered at same time. See that water is boiled for coffee, etc.

Everything, however, was not done quite so much "according to Cocker" as all this. In particular, the halts made at the stores were not long enough to allow the men to eat the bully beef and biscuits provided. It was a case of off-saddling, standing about, sitting, or lying to rest for a while without sleeping, and off again. Two hours was about the longest halt, save once in the dark when the road was lost.

So the column jogged along, walking, cantering, and trotting by turns. From Malmani the column pushed on in order to pass a defile, noted as dangerous by the topographical "Bobby," at the Lead Mines. This was achieved at a scamper, soon after five p.m. Otherwise, the only incident of Monday was the first official challenge. A quaintly formal communication came to hand from the Commandant of the Marico district[1] to the Head Officer of the expedition of armed

[1] Under the old South African Burgher Law, each district has a Commandant, a permanent official, who "Commandeers" in any emergency a

troops at Malmani Eye, warning him to retire with his force over the frontier and not conflict with the law of the land, with the Convention, and with international laws. A characteristic Jamesonian composition was the reply: "Sir,—I am in receipt of your protest of above date, and have to inform you that I intend proceeding with my original plans, which have no hostile intentions against people of Transvaal, but we are here in reply to an invitation from the principal residents of the Rand to assist them in their demands for justice and the ordinary rights of every citizen of a civilized State.—(Signed) JAMESON."

On Tuesday morning the column reached the farm of Mr. Malan, a Volksraad member and near connection of General Joubert, where the remount horses were in readiness, as before described, and the worthy raadslid himself came out to express his astonishment and anger at the apparition. He did so quaintly enough. Approaching Jameson, he exclaimed in an aggrieved tone, "Jameson! what do you come bothering me like this for?" He might well resent the service which, all unwittingly, he had been made to render the column; but, as it turned out, it was no service at all. The horses, as we have seen, were a job lot bought up from a coaching company. Many of them were probably quite unused to the saddle; and either because they proved intractable, or because they could not be caught, or because it was not thought worth while to stop long enough for the exchange, little advantage was taken of their presence, and the column rode on mostly with the same horses.

That morning the column was caught up by a mounted messenger, one of the troopers who had declined to join, riding post haste with the first word from the High Commissioner, telegraphed up to Mafeking on Monday to the Resident Commissioner. He had ridden after them for eighty miles, all night, and would have caught them some hours sooner, but

certain proportion of men from his district, sending round from farm to farm.

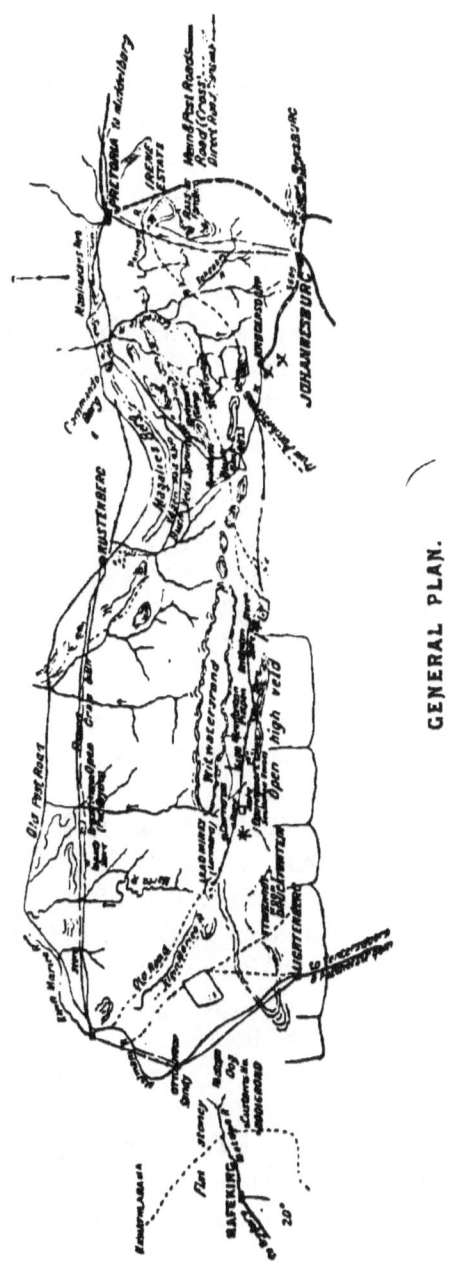

GENERAL PLAN.

that he himself was caught by a party of Boers on the border
—a party which at first meant to follow Jameson, but received
orders from Pretoria by telegraph to await some imaginary
supports which were expected to pour into the country in
Jameson's wake. A Landdrost had opened his despatches
and read them, with the natural result that he was forthwith
allowed to proceed.

The column was halted when the messenger came up with
it. He carried a separate despatch for each officer, as well as
one for Dr. Jameson. In these Mr. Newton, the Resident
Commissioner at Mafeking, simply repeated the High Commissioner's brief message, directing Dr. Jameson to return
immediately, saying that the violation of the territory of a
friendly State was repudiated by Her Majesty's Government,
and adding, for the benefit of each several officer, that they
were rendering themselves liable to severe penalties. There
was no eagerness to peruse these billets. The messenger found
his way to one of the officers, who said, "Take them to Sir
John Willoughby." Willoughby said, "Take them to Dr.
Jameson." Dr. Jameson said, "Take them back to Sir John
Willoughby; he is in military command." After half an hour
the messenger got his answer that "The despatches would be
attended to"—and the column moved off.

A more picturesque meeting was that about three o'clock on
Tuesday afternoon with a grandson of President Kruger, a
lieutenant (*Anglice*, inspector) of police at Krugersdorp. This
young man, formerly a Government clerk, has military ambitions, and once went spying to Mafeking with absurd results.
He is a favourable specimen of the young Transvaaler of the
new generation, and was quite lionised by the interviewers
lately in England. Hearing a rumour of the advancing force,
young Eloff rode out burning to distinguish himself, coolly
went up to the column when at Mrs. Boon's farm, and was
passed through to the officers, whom he asked by what right
were they entering the Transvaal with an armed force. The
question was somewhat difficult to answer, and it was evaded

by putting the young gentleman under arrest and taking away his arms, with the remark that they would be returned to him at Johannesburg. Eventually he was treated with all due courtesy, his arms were returned to him, and he was left behind on parole to remain rooted to the spot for an hour after the column left. His next appearance was after Jameson had fought and lost, when he led a detachment of burghers into the streets of Johannesburg, where they let off their feelings and a quantity of blank cartridges.

New Year is a great visiting-time for the Boers, who make up parties and go round to friendly homesteads. One or two parties of this kind were descried, and at first taken for a hostile force. Only at midnight on Tuesday (New Year's Eve) came the first sign of hostility from the Boers who were hanging about the column. A few score men were keeping it in view and retiring before it as it advanced. As the column reached a place where the road mounts some rising ground, a few Boers shot in among them from over the brow. It was a brief and dropping fire, and only one man was wounded. The reply in the midnight darkness was rather a matter of form, though the guns were got into play in one minute.

Early on Wednesday morning the column received despatches both from the British Agent at Pretoria and from the leaders at Johannesburg. A messenger with a safe conduct brought from Sir Jacobus de Wet a more peremptory veto telegraphed up by the High Commissioner:—

"Her Majesty's Government entirely disapprove your conduct in invading Transvaal with armed force; your action has been repudiated. You are ordered to retire at once from country, and will be held personally responsible for the consequences of your unauthorized and most improper proceeding."

This time Jameson wrote his reply, and a very characteristic one it was:—

"DEAR SIR,—I am in receipt of the message you sent from His Excellency the High Commissioner, and beg to reply, for His Excellency's information, that I should, of course, desire to obey his instructions, but, as I have a very large force of both men and horses to feed, and having finished all my supplies in the rear, must perforce proceed to Krugersdorp or Johannesburg this morning for this purpose. At the same time I must acknowledge I am anxious to fulfil my promise on the petition of the principal residents on the Rand to come to the aid of my fellow-men in their extremity. I have molested no one, and have explained to all Dutchmen met that the above is my sole object, and that I shall desire at once to return to the Protectorate.—I am, etc., JAMESON."

The Johannesburg despatches were brought in soon after by a couple of cyclists, who met the column about ten o'clock with a scribbled note from Colonel Rhodes, and a scribbled postscript by Mr. Phillips, which will appear in another chapter.

This scrap of paper told Jameson, reading between the lines, that he was taking the Johannesburg leaders by surprise, that they had not yet made any overt move against the Government, but that they had armed a number of men, and were prepared to applaud his audacity, and to suggest explanations of his action. The note ended by asking whether they should send him out men to show him a suitable place to pitch his camp at the outskirts of Johannesburg, where he was expected to arrive that evening. He was not offered any military help; evidently there was not the barest idea of his requiring any.

In reply to this note Jameson at first said in an off-hand way, "No. It didn't matter."

Then, after consulting with Willoughby or one of the others, he added, as a kind of after-thought, "Tell Colonel Rhodes we are all right. The only thing is, it might be as well, perhaps, to send out an escort, say a couple of hundred men, to conduct me in, just to show that I am not coming as a pirate."

On their way back with this message the cyclists were captured in the Boer lines, then closing upon the column, and the message was not received at Johannesburg till four days afterwards.

To return to the column.

The exact tenour of the cyclists' despatches was not communicated, but it went round that Johannesburg had sent welcoming messages, and there was some cheering.

About midday the column came in sight of Krugersdorp, the western terminus of a railway line which runs along the "reef" through Johannesburg, Johannesburg itself being fifteen to twenty miles away.

The gold reefs on which Johannesburg is built are generally described as running along for fifty miles from east to west. The village of Krugersdorp (about 1,500 to 2,000 souls) is a kind of western outpost of that line of reef. As the column sighted Krugersdorp it would also sight in the neighbourhood the signs of mining: headgear, heaps of tailings, etc., and would feel as if it were now really at the beginning of Johannesburg.

But if Krugersdorp had rousing associations for the raiders, so it had for the Boers, who were now cantering up from district after district on their sturdy little ponies to this appointed meeting-place. For, by a dramatic coincidence, which must have inspired the farmers with patriotic memories, within gun-shot of the Krugersdorp market-square rises the stone obelisk of Paardekraal, commemorating the struggle and triumph of their "War of Independence" against British troops in 1881.

The cyclists had warned the column that some few hundred Boers were waiting for it at Krugersdorp, and as small parties were also seen hanging upon its skirts, and as the formation was hampered at this point by a quantity of wire railing, the approach to the little town was made warily. Four or five miles off was the last store that the column was destined to touch at—Hind's store; and here it enjoyed, for an hour and a half, its last quiet rest. For some reasons, however, the arrangements for feeding men and horses were a failure here. Neither got much to eat.

Close to the store the column surprised a party of Boers watering horses. These were not fired on with rifles or Maxims, and had made off long before the field guns, now pushed forward, reached the advance guard. A few rounds were fired after the retreating party. The column learnt at the store that the Boers before them were now nearer 800 than 300.

The country here rolls in low downs or ridges across the route. At the entrance to the town from the west the road, mounting one of these ridges, forks; the north fork (to the column's left front) leading between the houses; the south fork (to the right front) leading round among mining properties. All along the ridge was seen from a mile away to be occupied by Boers. After reconnoitring the north fork, the column took the south one. A little to the north (left) of this, on the top of the occupied ridge, conspicuous to the column on the sky line, stood a disused "battery-house" of the Queen Mining Company: that is to say, an iron-roofed shed which had contained ore-stamping machinery. Surrounded by heaps of "tailings"—the mud-heaps left by ore crushing and washing—this formed a natural fort with earthworks ready made; and the trained eye of old Cronje, the Commandant of Potchefstroom, had hit upon this as the place to hold. Moreover, the road to it was flanked at longish range by a farmhouse and plantation to the north, and by some old prospectors' cuttings—ready-made rifle-pits—to the south. These on the rising slope: in the depression midway between this ridge and that on which the column now faced the Boer lines lay a "vlei," or stretch of standing water, crossed by the road at a narrow drift.

Before a shot had been fired, Sir John Willoughby sent a messenger under a flag of truce carrying this quaint message:—

"1st January, 1895.—To Commandant-in-Chief, Krugersdorp, from O.C. of the friendly force *en route* to Johannesburg.

"SIR,—I have the honour to inform you that in the event of my meeting with any hostile opposition in my advance through Krugersdorp, I shall be bound to shell the position and the town, and hereby give you due warning so that peaceable inhabitants and women and children may leave before 4 p.m. to-day.

"I have the honour to be, sir, yours,
"JOHN WILLOUGHBY, Lt. C.C."

The Commandant—Malan of Rustenburg—returned no answer. When the time had elapsed, the guns were brought to bear, and presently a hole was neatly knocked right through the gable of the battery-house, which the few Boers who were in it hastily vacated. None of them were hurt. The artillery fire was next turned along the ridge where puffs of smoke told of a line of invisible sharp-shooters, and a large quantity of shrapnel shells were blazed away, the artillerymen, under Captain Gosling and Captain Kincaid Smith, making good practice in bursting the shells just over where the puffs of smoke were. The Boers, who had no artillery up as yet save an old 7-pounder, replied with rifle fire; and desultory firing went on at long rifle range from both sides, till presently Col. White (in charge of the advance guard of about 100 men) ordered it to advance and charge the Queen battery-house position.

We say "Colonel White ordered." The responsibility is not quite clear. The officer commanding the column was, as we have seen, Sir John Willoughby; but a difference as to seniority in command had arisen between him and Major White, and as the operations proceeded it became more acute (if troopers' gossip is accepted). In fact, according to the descriptions given by some troopers, it was never quite clear throughout the whole march who was in command. Sometimes Dr. Jameson would give an order, sometimes Sir John Willoughby, sometimes one or other of the Whites, and sometimes Major Grey.

Whoever ordered the charge, it is dubious what the troopers were intended to do upon reaching the ridge. They had no swords, and could only have fallen upon the Boers with the butt ends of their rifles. The idea seems to have been that they had only to gallop forward and rush the position and the Boers would jump up and run away, exposing themselves to the fire of the troopers and making way for the column. However, the question what they should do when they reached the Boers was not destined to arise. The Boers, lying prone along the ridge, protected by stones and the lie of the ground, had no intention of getting up and exposing themselves. Most of them were protected by a line of rock "outcrop": a natural rampart which, in the geological formation of the Transvaal, creates endless positions of defensive strength. Then, at the battery-house, there were the "tailings," and southward there were the prospectors' trenches already mentioned : which, by the way, served in the sequel for burying some of the dead.

MR. JOHN HAYS HAMMOND.
From a Photograph by DUFFUS BROS., *Johannesburg.*

While the artillery fire was rattling on to the ridge, the Boers lay low, cautiously refraining from any attempt to put up their heads and take aim. They stayed quite still where they were, having found that the shrapnel, though sending up dust and splinters of stones, burst harmlessly over them as they lay. The Boers say, as a matter of fact, not a single Boer was wounded here except one man who had the skin taken off his thumb and went on firing. This is simply explained. Shrapnel does not burst upwards and downwards, but opens out in a horizontal plane, fan-like. If the Boers had been obliging enough to stand up it would have cut them to pieces, but a very few inches of ground mixed with stones sufficed to break the projectiles when fired low, and when fired higher they simply passed over the Boers' heads. So tightly, however, did the shrewd farmers hug the ground that a galloper, after surveying the prostrate and motionless Boers at one end of their positions, reported to the column "so many killed"; and the apparent silencing of the ridge as a whole led to the illusion that a charge would get through without difficulty. Between two and three o'clock, accordingly, the Boers on the ridge saw a sudden movement of the troops nearest them. A manœuvre was executed which much impressed them for the moment. A narrow clump of men galloping towards them suddenly opened out at the word of command, to right and left, and came on in a single long straight line in open order. The Boer does not drill and has no manœuvres, and he—for a moment—admired accordingly. On the charge came, about a hundred strong, with a ringing cheer; till from 1,000 yards the range diminished to 500, 300, 200. At this point the riders splashed into the "vlei," and as they did so right along the ridge and from the flanking positions the Boers opened fire, emptying saddle after saddle. A score of men tumbled off. The frightened horses plunged and scattered. The men not killed or wounded stopped, jumped down and replied to the hail of bullets, firing over the backs of their horses or from the ground.

The charge was checked.

A moment more and the cross-fire in the "vlei" was too hot to be withstood.

The survivors turned round and galloped back, or crawled away into a clump of reeds at the side of the "vlei" for cover, where they were shortly afterwards taken prisoners as they lay among the reeds. Some thirty prisoners were so taken, and during the night which followed, the Boers carried away another thirty killed and wounded; the wounded to Krugersdorp hospital.

As the stragglers from the charge got back to the column the officers took council together. The utter failure of the manœuvre dashed the spirits of the troopers. It seemed that less than half of those that went had returned, and it takes very seasoned troops to treat a sacrifice of sixty per cent. with indifference. At five o'clock the Boers noticed the column in two parts turning off the road and making a move southwards, evidently to turn the position. In this direction lie the farms Randfontein and Vlakfontein; which were the scene of the rest of the fighting.

As it grew dusk, some undecided movements were made and unmade, which the Boers could not understand, and which shall be given in the words (slightly shortened) of one able to speak with authority for the other side :—

"Two guides were obtained, the column formed in the prescribed night order of march, and we started off along a road leading direct to Johannesburg, hoping to slip through in the darkness.

"At this moment heavy rifle and Maxim fire was suddenly heard from the direction of Krugersdorp, which lay one and a half miles to the left rear.

"We at once concluded that this meant the arrival of reinforcements, for we knew that Johannesburg had Maxims, and that the Staats-Artillerie were not expected to arrive until the following morning.

"To leave our supposed friends in the lurch was out of the question. It was determined at once to move to their support.

"Leaving the carts, escorted by one troop, on the road, we advanced rapidly across the plateau towards Krugersdorp in the direction of the firing.

"After advancing thus for nearly a mile the firing ceased, and we perceived the Boers moving in great force to meet the column. The flankers on the right reported another force threatening that flank.

"It was feared that an attempt would be made to cut us off from the ammunition carts, and a retreat on them was ordered.

"It was now clear that the firing, whatever might have been the cause thereof, was not occasioned by the arrival of any force from Johannesburg.

"Precious moments had been lost in the attempt to effect a junction with our supposed friends. It was now very nearly dark. In the dusk the Boers could be seen closing in on three sides, viz.: north, east and south. The road to Johannesburg appeared completely barred, and the last opportunity of slipping through, which had presented itself an hour ago when the renewed firing was heard, was gone, not to return.

"Nothing remained but to bivouac in the best position available.

"But for the unfortunate circumstance of the firing, which we afterwards heard was due to the exultation of the Boers at the arrival of large reinforcements from Potchefstroom, the column would have been by this time (7 p.m.) at least four or five miles further on the road to Johannesburg, with an excellent chance of reaching that town without further opposition."

On the slope slanting down to a "pan" or "vlei," then, to which a few men with pannikins found their way for much-needed water, the column camped at nightfall, some two miles south of their first fighting position. Lying in a depression, they were to some slight extent covered, and all lights were put out except one in the ambulance wagons, where there lay about thirty wounded, or otherwise disabled and knocked up. Using this light for a mark the Boers went on firing into the camp all night, sometimes from only a few hundred yards away, killing some horses, stampeding others, and harassing the tired men. They also killed here two troopers, who were hastily dug into the ground, for a friend of the writer's who went over the scene next day was shocked to see the feet of one of these poor fellows sticking out from the heap of earth which his comrades had shovelled over him.

As the night, thus wearily spent, wore on, things began to look black to the Doctor. He had staked everything on the idea that he could force his way through at the first onset. He had failed, and knew that the Boers must be massing all round him. Indeed, forces had been seen and heard from at very long range behind, before, to right and to left. Only the Maxims had kept them at a respectful distance while the column moved, the artillerymen sitting astride and sweeping the rear ground while the mules dragged the guns along.

The High Commissioner's messages had practically made an outlaw of him, and twenty miles away, at Johannesburg, his confederates, evidently undreaming of his bitter need, were comfortably waiting to see him march in in triumph. Sombre thoughts must have passed through Jameson's mind as he sullenly waited for dawn down there by the "pan" surrounded by the troop of raw young fellows whom on his sole responsibility he had led into this position.

At four o'clock in the grey dawn, Jameson despatched a second message for Johannesburg, a verbal one for one of his men to carry through the Boer lines. But even then he was not going to make it a cry of despair. "I am all right," was the effect of the message, "but I should like a force sent out to us." It was only a little change from the earlier request for a patrol, "just to prevent me from looking like a pirate," but the little change meant much.

The trooper to whom it was entrusted duly got through the Boer lines in the darkness. What came of the message at the other end we shall see later. To get through was not difficult for individuals. It was a straggling camp, to which the Boers gave a fairly wide berth, and, as a matter of fact, with whatever object or pretext, some thirty or forty young fellows out of that column, few of them over nineteen years of age, did get separated from the camp and straggled through into Johannesburg during that night, almost all eventually reporting themselves to Colonel Rhodes at his private house, some turning up disguised in the clothes of miners.

As the light came, the column moved on across the railway embankment of the Potchefstroom railway. A number of Boers had taken up their position behind this, and as the mules struggled up the embankment, tugging the Maxims behind them, severe execution might have been done (so a Boer critic remarks) by turning these guns on to the surprised Boers, who skeltered across the embankment and took up their position on the other side as the column passed it.

At about seven o'clock, as the column was moving along

under fire, among mine properties, a new despatch arrived by messenger from the British Agent, completing the former discouragements by supplying a copy of the proclamation in which, among other things, all British subjects in the Transvaal were called on to "abstain from giving the said Dr. Jameson any countenance or assistance." To drive one last nail in the coffin of any hopes which the Doctor had entertained that at the last moment Johannesburg might find out the truth and rally to his assistance, the bearer of the proclamation was accompanied by a member of the Reform Committee, Mr. Lace, who explained that he had come by arrangement between the Committee and the Government to assure Jameson of the fact that the Committee had made an armistice, and could therefore do nothing.

On all sides, therefore, Jameson was now cast off, a fair quarry for his enemies. It was an hour or more before he told Sir John Willoughby the heavy news. Better sullenly play out the losing game.

The long running fight now enters on a phase when the column, having crossed the railway embankment, zigzagged through depressed ground rather broken by "vleis," seeking for an unexposed passage across the next rise eastward; while the Boers, similarly impeded by broken ground, but able to wait their time, made large circuits at longish range from the column, till it finally walked into a sort of trap, when they closed in upon it.

The Boers say that the body which finally headed the column off would hardly have kept up but for a drift across one of the "vleis," pointed out to them, as it happened, by a Cape Colonist. Had they failed to get in front of the column among this broken ground, it would probably have got through to Johannesburg; for in a straight line as the crow flies there was hardly anybody there at that time to oppose it, though thousands were massing in the neighbourhood.

Generalizing from the accounts of both sides it would seem that as long as the column continued its detour southwards

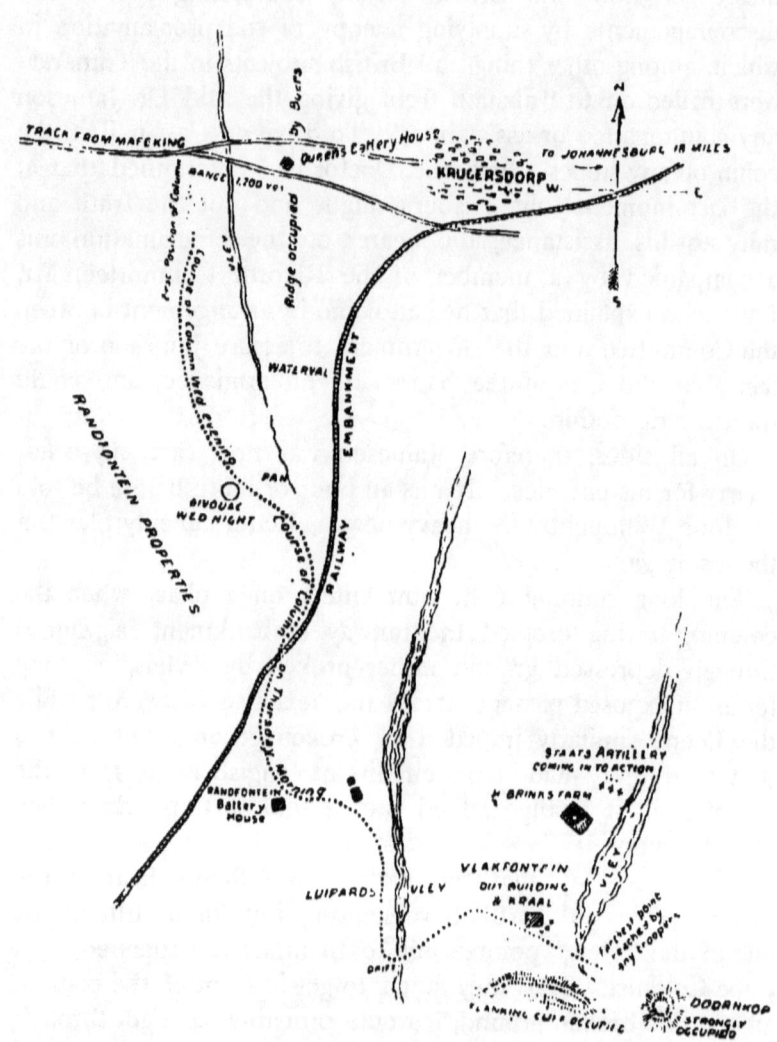

PLAN OF BATTLEGROUND.
(Scale about 1½ in to a mile.)

keeping up a fire before and behind (for bodies of Boers were now visible in both directions), there was no great opposition; but the moment it attempted to force any likely position for continuing its march eastwards, that position was held. Very determined attempts were made twice at least before the end. A Boer narrator speaks of a charge attempted by an officer and half a dozen men, in which the officer and three of the men were killed. Chief Inspector Bodle cleared a little ridge with two troops of M.M.P. Colonel Grey, with the hardy B.B.P., was shot in the foot, but went on as if nothing had happened. Sub-Inspector Cazalet went on with a wound, to be shot again in the chest in the last scene.

On the Randfontein farm some Scotch carts were abandoned, and the column continued the detour by a drift through Luipaard's Vlei to Vlakfontein farm, where, at Farmer Brink's outhouse (five or six miles south and slightly south-east of Krugersdorp), they were to make their final stand.

Here there was an outbuilding, and a disused cattle kraal with stone walls the height of a man, which offered cover till flanked, and was at once occupied by one troop. As the morning grew into day this outbuilding became the Hougoumont round which the fusillade of battle roared heaviest. The Boers on their side took advantage of a wall, and venturing to nearer quarters made their rifle fire less inefficient than it had been for the most part as regards the actual number of killed and wounded. Men and horses dropped on all sides. In the column the feeling grew that unless it could burst through the Boer lines at this point it was done for. The Maxims were fired till they grew too hot, and, water failing for the cool jacket, five of them jammed and went out of action. The 7-pounder was fired till only half an hour's ammunition was left to fire with. One last rush was made and failed; and then the Staats Artillery came up on the left flank, and the game was up.

The fact is that by mischance, or misled by the volunteer guides who were now found to have slipped away, the column was at the mouth of a *cul de sac*. It must either stop or throw itself at a rising ground with cover flanked by other rising ground with cover. Doornkop, which has christened the battle, is an isolated kopje, or stony hill, conspicuous for a mile or two round; but it was not actually reached. It is a thousand yards further on in the direction the column was going. It was strongly held, and warm indeed would have been the reception of the luckless little force if it had come to rounding that hill. But what did the actual mischief was a flanking ridge on the right (southern) flank, an abrupt low cliff as seen by the column, placed roughly as shown in the accompanying plan; which also exhibits the direction in which the Staats Artillery on the left (northern) flank came into play as the decisive factor.

Of actual combatants at this time the Boers say they had only 700 or 800. Indeed, the Boer legend swears that those closely engaged, apart from supports, were but fifty well-placed men; while those who stopped the last charge were exactly seven! The Boer legend adds that General Joubert found on inquiry at the hospital that all Jameson's wounded save one bore the spoor of a new pattern of rifle of which there were but fifty all told in the hands of burghers. Here, however, the records of the St. John Ambulance Brigade, which went up from Cape Town and evolved order from chaos at Krugersdorp, are available to explode the myth. They show that practically all the raiders' wounds were Martini-Henry. It was these seven champions, the Boers add, rather than the other fifty or the 700 or 800 engaged all along the line, who commanded the little gap attempted by the last charge, and saving their fire till the troopers were close, killed six of them and the last hope of the rest together. The other troopers sought shelter again on the farm, and shortly afterwards, while the Staats Artillery from the other side was finding range, between eight and nine o'clock on Thursday the 2nd of January, 1896, a white flag was seen waving over Farmer Brink's outhouse. The so-called battle of Doornkop was at an end.

And here must be recorded one more grotesque fact. Not even in its surrender was this raid fated to be romantic. The white flag used on this occasion was not, as a matter of fact, a torn shirt plucked from a weary trooper, but was the white apron of an old Hottentot " tanta " who was standing somewhere at hand on the farm when it was borrowed from her to be waved as an emblem of peace.

Those who first noticed the white flag were the seven Boers at the drift already mentioned, and very glad they were, for they had just come to the end of their ammunition. They walked forward as the firing ceased, and went in the direction of the Maxims, their idea being, as one of them afterwards explained, that they didn't know exactly what was up, but thought that if the parley proved unsatisfactory in other respects, they might at least run away with a Maxim or two. It was to one of these that Willoughby entrusted the following note :

"To the Commandant of Transvaal Forces.—We surrender, provided that you guarantee a safe conduct out of the country for every member of the force.

"(Signed) JOHN WILLOUGHBY."

The answer came back in a quarter of an hour, of which the following is a translation :

"Officer.—Please take notice that I shall immediately let our officers come together to decide upon your communication.

"COMMANDANT."

The " Commandant " who signed this note was Potgieter, of Krugersdorp.

In about half an hour came this further answer (translation) :

"John C. Willoughby.—I acknowledge your letter. The answer is that if you will undertake to pay the expenses which you have caused the South African Republic, and that you will lay down your arms, then I shall spare the lives of you and yours. Please send me the reply to this within thirty minutes.

" P. A. KRONJE,

" Commandant, Potchefstroom."

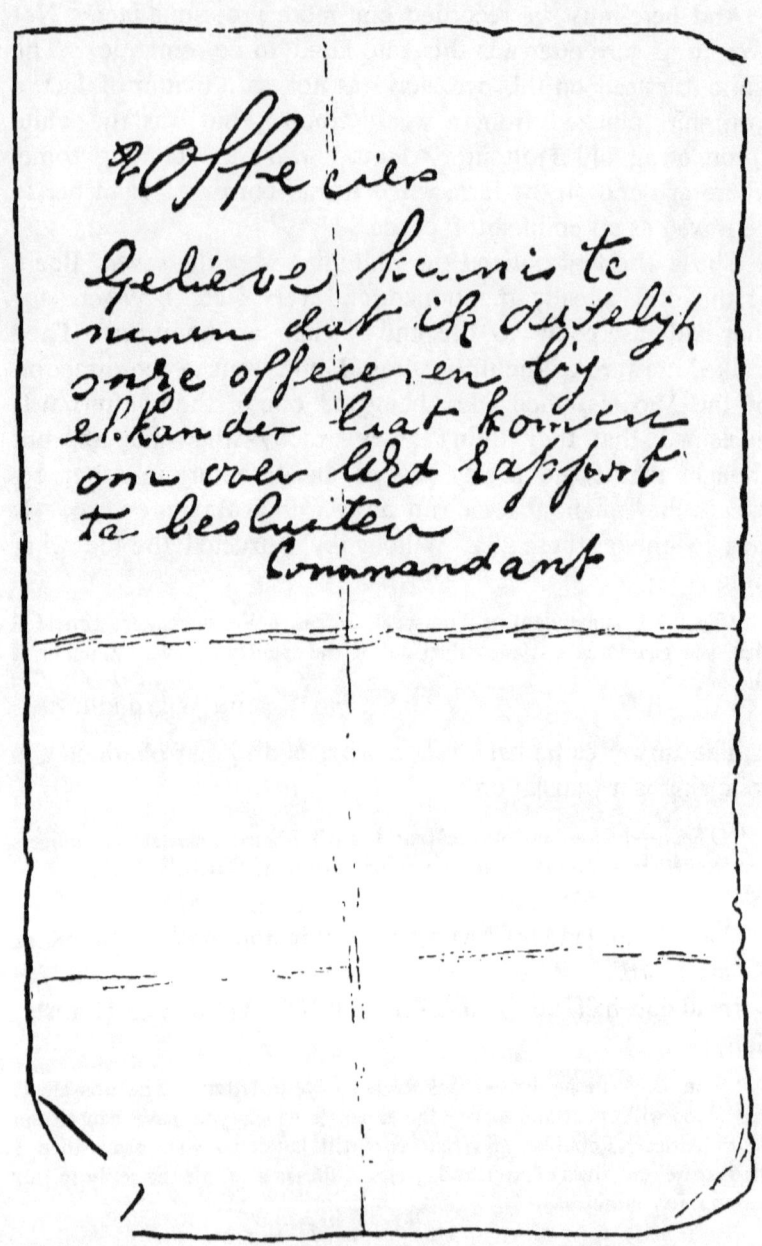

FACSIMILE OF POTGIETER'S REPLY TO WILLOUGHBY.

FACSIMILE OF CRONJE'S LETTER OF CONDITIONS.

The inference was that the terms thus proposed came from the senior Commandant, which, indeed, Cronje might fairly be called, and that they were the result of the consultation announced by the anonymous Commandant in the previous message. The Force had been guaranteed expenses in the letter of invitation, and Sir John may well have been glad to get off so easily. Cronje, on the other hand, had no reason to refuse conditions so far as his previous instructions from Pretoria had gone; for the word passed round to the Commandants at an earlier stage of Jameson's progress through the country, and before any fighting had taken place, that is to say when the Pretoria Government was not quite sure how things would go at Johannesburg, was to allow Jameson's Force to return scot-free across the border provided they disarmed. So, at least, Sir Jacobus de Wet had telegraphed to the High Commissioner on December 31st. Be this as it may, Sir John Willoughby jumped at the terms offered, and within a quarter of an hour sent back a note of which neither side, as it happens, kept a copy, but of which Sir John's memory, which has not been disputed, is as follows:

"SIR,—I (or we) accept your terms, on the guarantee that the lives of the whole force are to be spared. I now await your instructions as to how and where we are to lay down our arms. At the same time I would ask you to remember that my men have been without food for the last twenty-four hours.—I have, etc., your obedient servant,

"JOHN WILLOUGHBY."

The column was quickly surrounded by about five hundred Boers, who galloped up from various directions, and the troopers began to stack their arms and soon all were given up. At this point, and not sooner, according to Cronje's own affidavit, arrived Commandant Trichardt of the Staats Artillery with orders from Commandant-General Joubert, which were explicit enough, viz.: That the troops should be given five minutes to lay down their arms unconditionally, and if they did not comply within that time firing should be resumed. Meanwhile, Commandants Malan and Potgieter, having joined Cronje in conversation with Jameson and Willoughby, had put in their word, Malan having had to ride all the way from the Queen's Battery, where he was still stationed, and Malan scolded Cronje for going beyond his powers. Turning to Jameson, he said:

"*Your* life and your officers' lives we do not promise to spare. We shall hand you over to the Government at Pretoria, and they will decide what is to be done with you."

Jameson merely bowed. He was in no mood for bargaining, and seemed to have relapsed into a kind of sullen stoicism, though one Boer narrator avers that the hand holding the switch—his only weapon throughout the fighting—trembled at this ominous speech of Malan's. The same Boer narrator even goes so far as to add that Jameson said, as if to himself, but aloud, "My last hour is come," and that a Boer standing by told him with rough kindliness to keep quiet and cheer up, as nothing very bad would be done to him. But these embroideries are such as always grow up round an incident of this kind. The officers were taken off to the Court House at Krugersdorp, fed, and driven to Pretoria, a distance of fifty miles, in carts. The men were conducted thither under a strong escort on horseback, and a sorry spectacle they made, weary and dispirited as they were. A few tried to raise their spirits by singing snatches of "After the ball was over." Officers and men alike were well treated by their captors who, mindful of Sir John Willoughby's remark about the fasting condition of his men, provided them with a good meal before starting them for Pretoria, besides sharing their own biltong and biscuits with some of the more exhausted ones before moving off the field of battle.

And so the raiders were marched off to prison, where their communication with the outer world was stringently conditioned, and from that time till their arrival in England weeks afterwards not a single official, friend, or newspaper in South Africa dreamed that their surrender had been anything but unconditional. Had it been known that their lives, though not their liberties, were secure under the promise upon which they disarmed, several events might have fallen out, for good or ill, otherwise than they did, as we shall presently see. Here all that need be added is to record the final decision on a technical military point which eventually afforded weeks of heated controversy. When all the facts had been thrashed out, Mr. Chamberlain received from the War Office, a quarter, by the way, by no means inclined to be lenient to the raiders, the following report:

"In reply, the Marquis of Lansdowne, having consulted with his military adviser, desires me to observe that, whatever position Mr. Cronje may hold in the Transvaal Army, he decidedly, on the occasion in question, acted as an officer in authority, and guaranteed the lives of Dr. Jameson and all his men if they at once laid down their arms.

"The terms prescribed were accepted by Dr. Jameson's force, and they surrendered and laid down their arms, and no subsequent discussion amongst the Transvaal officers could retract the terms of this surrender.

"I am, therefore, to acquaint you, for the information of the Secretary of State for the Colonies, that the Secretary of State for War concurs with Mr. Chamberlain in considering that the surrender was completed on Sir John Willoughby's acceptance of Commandant Cronje's terms, and was subject to these terms and conditions."

The Government of any large European Power, of the United States, or of a British Colony, would have been extremely sensitive if it found itself in the position into which the Transvaal Government was unwittingly betrayed by the Commandant's insufficient reports. The Transvaal Government has never shown a moment's qualm. Military operations are conducted in a rough and ready manner by Boers. They treated their prisoners decently, and handed them over to the Queen to punish. What did it matter that being misinformed by their own agents they, in turn, misinformed the High Commissioner, and traded on their apparent generosity in sparing lives which they were really under an obligation to spare? That is their way of looking at it. This same Cronje was found guilty of obtaining the surrender of the British garrison in Potchefstroom at the close of the war in 1881 by what was

either a barbaric ruse or an unaccountable failure to remember
the terms of an armistice. The wrong in that case was proved,
admitted, and redress made. In this case Cronje did not
really "practice to deceive." A mixture of kindheartedness
and eagerness to settle the matter off his own bat probably led
him to make more favourable terms than he had any right to,
and afterwards a certain characteristic looseness over small
obligations and willingness to let awkward things slide, led
him to let his arrangements be brushed aside by the other
Commandants and say nothing about it in his report. He is
a very religious man. When the shelling was going on he was
squatting on the ground in a position which struck one of his
companions as being exposed. "Come over here; this is
better," said the companion, but old Cronje remained squatting and replied: "God has called me here to do a certain
work. If God means me to be taken I shall be shot wherever
I sit, and if He does not I am as safe here as anywhere else."
It was he, too, who at one point gave an order to fire at the
horses, as it would stop the column just as well. His own son
was wounded during the battle. A tough, shrewd old Boer,
whose kindliness, fatalistic religion, and crookedness about nice
points of honour are all thoroughly typical.

Excluding the two legends already spoken of, there are a
few personal incidents of the fighting picturesque enough to be
added here. A young Boer named Jacobsz was moving forward to give a drink to one of the wounded troopers after the
first charge, when another wounded man, mistaking his intention, shot him with a revolver, and was at once riddled with
bullets himself. It was in the vengeful volley fired among the
disabled in connection with this incident that Major Coventry
received his very severe wound near the spine. It has been
mentioned that during the running fight on Wednesday evening the column picked up a couple of volunteer guides, presumably Transvaalers, and some of the raiders attribute to
these guides the final misdirection into a *cul de sac*. The Boer
story is different. They say that at a point of the fighting

where the range was short some of the Boers recognised one whom they knew acting as guide to the column. They fired at him till at last he fell, when one of them seized the occasion to run forward, turn him over, and make sure of the traitor's identity. He came back and said with a groan: "Yes. It is ——."

On the story that has now been told certain questions arise.

Was the surrender inevitable? Did the column show heroism or the reverse? What is the truth about food, water, and ammunition? What were the odds in numbers and position? Why were so few Boers killed? Was the march itself an achievement? Were the causes of failure accidental or inherent?

Partly these questions have been answered by the narrative.

There seems to be no doubt that if the troops had not surrendered when they did they could not possibly have escaped from their position, and they would have been shot down like sheep. 2,000 Boers were close to the field of battle at the time of the surrender, and by that evening there were nearer 8,000 men, on the average neither better nor worse than the average of Jameson's few hundred troopers. The odds, counting only those who were actually firing at the moment of surrender, were odds of position rather than of numbers, but consider the supports in the background! It might have been gratifying to their countrymen if the little force which everybody disavowed and cold-shouldered, when things became hopeless, had chosen to die singing as Wilson's patrol did, as Englishmen have died again and again and again in Africa as elsewhere. But men who die like that generally know what they are fighting for. Even Leonidas might have surrendered when the Persians found the path round the mountain, if he had just heard that official Sparta regarded him as a foolish filibuster. When they gave in they were minus some twenty per cent. of combatants. There were seventy-six casualities. There were thirty men hurt or sick in the wagons. There were twenty-seven killed on the spot or mortally wounded. They had been engaged continuously for twenty-one hours. Some of the officers had literally had no lie-down sleep since they started, for they were busy overseeing arrangements during the brief rests at the stores, while the men, as we have seen, had not done very much better. Longer rests while they were about it, with time to eat comfortably, and a more even pace in between, without breaks of walking, would have cost both men and horses far less fatigue. Forty miles riding a day is no hardship to a South African who is "hard" when he starts. Unfortunately, some of the troop were by no means "hard"; in fact, were not riders at all, for the Boers, when they got to Krugersdorp, were astonished to find the breeches of some of them sticking to the saddle with blood. That the commissariat had gone all wrong, in spite of the stores and a small amount of provisions carried on the Scotch carts, is beyond doubt. The Boers testify that many of the men fell ravenously on the rude fare which their captors made haste to share with them at the surrender. It is not true that they had fired away all their ammunition. There were plenty of cartridges left for rifles and Maxims, though the $12\frac{1}{2}$-pounder had only ammunition left for half an hour more. The lack of water in the final position is shown by the jamming and disablement of more than half the Maxims. As to the so-called record march, the rush for the Rand, etc., here again one extreme has been followed by another. It was undoubtedly a good piece of work for a troop of the size and equipment of the column. Many of the Boers, singly or in small parties, had made infinitely better riding, as might be expected, between the distant districts where the alarm ran from farm to farm, and the rendezvous at Krugersdorp. Some, indeed, arrived with dead-beat ponies, carrying their biltong and their biscuits, but no rifle, and had to be supplied from a small arsenal run out to Krugersdorp by train from Pretoria under the nose of Johannesburg. For the military conduct of the raid nobody has ever said a good word; but as to the general conduct of the men, the odd thing about the too heroic legend which first went forth to the world is that the first to spread it were the Boers themselves. An early interview with a Boer official eye-witness, published in Johannesburg, speaks of "the brave fellows seeming not to value their lives at all," etc., etc. After discussing the point with critics, eye-witnesses, and partisans of each side endlessly, the writer's conclusion is that there were some in the column who behaved extremely well, some who behaved badly, and a large mass of "food for powder," which went through the business without calling for special comment either way. Perhaps, in the last analysis of most fighting, brilliant episodes excepted, the truth is something similar. Some of the officers showed a good deal of *sang froid* of the kind which Boers would regard as foolish, and some of the attempts to rush a position here and there by small bodies, if not quite in the reckless style of Fuzzy Wuzzy, were very determined, and roused the admiration of the Boers as they quietly lay there and potted off the rash youths; but the fighting as a whole was not impressive on either side. The mystery of the Boer killed and wounded is one of the strangest. No one doubts that their loss was insignificant; but apart altogether from the raider legend, which dreamed of wagon-loads of weltering Boers and awful carnage wrought by shrapnel and Maxim, there is a curious persistence and sincerity about the doubts with which men qualified to judge still receive the official Boer total of two killed by the enemy (one being poor Jacobsz shot by mischance), and two shot by accident by their own side. That reduces the butcher's bill for twenty-one hours' almost continuous fighting, by men, some of them good shots, armed with the very latest make of rifle, and assisted by field guns, to one man really shot by design. To give one single instance of the contrary evidence, one of Jameson's officers, cool, observing, and of the rigidly matter-of-fact English type, saw a cart containing at least three or four dead bodies in unmistakable Boer clothing.

"But are you sure they were all dead? We know there were

five wounded in Krugersdorp Hospital, one of whom died afterwards."

"You cannot mistake the way a dead man lies. I saw their hands wagging, so——, as the cart moved," with a gruesome realistic gesture.

"But why should they conceal? How do you explain the discrepancy?"

"I don't explain. I am simply telling you what I saw. I don't trouble my head about it."

The only motive suggested to counterbalance the natural wish of the aggrieved Republic to pile up its case for blood-money is the policy of cultivating the idea that God fights for the Boers. The extraordinary disproportion in killed which has marked all fights between Boers and English in the Transvaal, has made some of the more ignorant and superstitious farmers firmly believe that the Lord of Hosts would be constant to the side of the small battalions were their country invaded by the French and German armies together. Two, say the sceptics, is a favourite official number of Boers killed. It was two at Majuba. The ineradicable doubt had to be recorded here; but the writer, on a balance of probabilities, fully accepts the official version, and thanks Heaven the kill was not larger. The cover, and the defensive tactics, explain a great deal. The only use of Jameson's Maxims, but a very substantial use, was in keeping up such a clatter and sputter at the edge of the Boer positions as to spoil their shooting, hence the comparatively small death-roll of the column. The Maxim, in fact, was a weapon rather of defence than of offence.

The net result on the mind of a plain man from discussing with experts why Jameson's invasion of the Transvaal was a dead failure, is that it failed simply because it was an invasion. Completer surprise might have saved it, but when once a few Boers had time to choose a position and mass, the odds were tremendous, even had the column been twice as big. In a battle of sharp-shooters, with the geological formation of the Transvaal, the man who can sit still is equal to ten men who have to move. Had it been the Boers who must expose themselves and get past at all costs, and Willoughby who had only to play the waiting game, the result would have been exactly the opposite, whatever the numbers. Perhaps, with modern arms of precision, the battle tends to be more and more with the defence force in any country, unless that force is reduced through its belly. Which is, perhaps, just as well for the cause of peace.

Chapter IX

JOHANNESBURG TAKES ITS COAT OFF

[THE thread will now be taken up by turns by the Special Correspondent of the *Cape Times* despatched to Johannesburg in December when everything seemed to be threatening an outbreak. On the 20th Mr. Lionel Phillips made his speech at the opening of the new Chamber of Mines, fearing that unless the Government came to terms with the industry, " it would end in that most horrible of all possible endings—bloodshed." A more rattling speech made by Mr. Fitzpatrick at the Old Barbertonians' dinner about the same time helped to show that there was something more than the usual grumble in the air. Looking back now, we connect Mr. Phillips's speech with Jameson's visit at the same date to Johannesburg. But at that time nobody dreamed of any link between Jameson and Johannesburg further than that both began with a J. What all South Africa did conclude at once was that the capitalists had at last thrown in their lot with the National Union, and that some unusual demonstration was being prepared for. The *Cape Times*, taken somewhat by surprise, hailed the conversion of Capital to Reform, and described the Kruger-Hollander *régime* as the "Sick Man of South Africa," declaring that, as with the Sick Man of Europe, the one anxiety of neighbours now was to get the break-up decently and peacefully over. Both Sick Men have somewhat taken up their beds and walked since then—thanks to the disunion of their heirs presumptive. But at the close of December, 1895, it seemed the enterprising journalistic thing to send a Special Correspondent to the Rand, in time for the obsequies; and the Assistant-Editor of the *Cape Times* went up accordingly. He came in for a stirring experience. The " I " of any personal reminiscences is, therefore, in the Johannesburg chapters, not the Editor's, but his.]

I REACHED Johannesburg at sunrise on Christmas Day. A great meeting of the National Union had been advertised for two days later.

Trouble looming, the people of the great mining town seemed to draw nearer to Church. Many a non-attendant became a church-goer at Johannesburg on Christmas morning. A "cab round" convinced one that all the churches were crowded. At the English churches there was an inspiriting heartiness about the services; one could not but be struck by the emphasis with which the prayer for the Queen's Majesty was intoned, and at the vigour of the congregational response. Devotions over, the people of Johannesburg spent the Christian festival in quite the orthodox way—in home gatherings and veld outings, winding up with a sacred concert at the Wanderers' Club, and the usual singing of "God Save the Queen" at the close.

Next day a special National Union Manifesto, signed by the President, Mr. Chas. Leonard, was put into people's hands just as they were streaming out to the racecourse at high noon. The manifesto set forth the Uitlander grievances in plain terms, and pointed out the duty of the Government in equally emphatic language; but postponed the mass meeting to January 6th. Generally, the tenour of the manifesto may be summed up in the following concluding paragraph :—

"We have now only two questions to consider: (*a*) What do we want? (*b*) How shall we get it? I have stated plainly what our grievances are, and I shall answer with equal directness the question, 'What do we want?' We want: (1) the establishment of this Republic as a true Republic; (2) a Grondwet or Constitution which shall be framed by competent persons selected by representatives of the whole people and framed on lines laid down by them—a constitution which shall be safeguarded against hasty alteration; (3) an equitable franchise law, and fair representation; (4) equality of the Dutch and English languages; (5) responsibility to the Legislature of the heads of the great departments; (6) removal of religious disabilities; (7) independence of the Courts of Justice, with adequate and secured remuneration of the judges; (8) liberal and comprehensive education; (9) efficient Civil Service, with adequate provision for pay and pension; (10) free trade in South African products. This is what we want. There now remains the question which is to be put before you at the meeting of the 6th January, viz.: How shall we get it? To this question I shall expect from you an answer in plain terms according to your deliberate judgment."

The effect was electrical. In a twinkling the scales fell from the eyes of the townspeople as they found themselves face to face with the possible consequences of the manifesto. Feeling, which had been growing in intensity day by day with the publication of reports of meetings held at the mines along the Reef, now reached a most acute stage, and the manner of the receipt of the manifesto by the Pretoria authorities was awaited with much concern.

Miners and artisans employed at the scores of mines east and west of the town, addressed nightly by one or other of the prominent leaders in the Reform movement, had been hurriedly indoctrinated into the principles of National Union faith, and, as events showed, the majority displayed a ready willingness to subscribe to the creed, and to stand up for it. There were notable exceptions. Jameson had spoken of his reliance on "miners with Lee-Metfords": but a Lee-Metford is a fearsome tool in the hands of a miner who has never handled even an ordinary gun. Some of the men, late comers who cared nothing for the quarrel as compared with daily wages equal to a week's pay in England, were slow to move. And, oddly enough, those odd Celts the Cornishmen, whom some thought likeliest to prove ugly customers when cornered, were the first to escape cornering by taking to their heels from the scene of danger. Such men, if taxed with desertion, repeated the stock phrases of the Krugerite and renegade Press about "capitalists' trick," "it'll all come off our wages," etc., etc. But this later.

Everywhere excitement reigned. People had no thought

for aught but the manifesto. The distractions of the race-course and the totalisator were powerless against the all-absorbing theme of conversation. Faith that can remove a Grand Stand has indeed done wonders at Johannesburg.

But the people were not unanimous. So much was clear from the very commencement. There were at first two camps. There was the Anglo-Saxon camp, comprising Englishmen, Welshmen, Irishmen, Scotchmen, Canadians, Australians, Americans, and Colonists from the Cape and Natal. These elements were solidly ranged on the side of the Union and the manifesto. Then there was the Continental camp, comprising Germans, Frenchmen, and the Scandinavians (including Swedes, Norwegians, Danes, and Finlanders). These had no liking for the manifesto. They admitted the gospel truth of every line of it, but they would not listen to a word about guns, and turned their faces in eager expectation towards Pretoria.

Chief amongst these was Mr. Langerman, Mr. J. B. Robinson's representative at Johannesburg (not the Max Langermann who joined the Reform Committee). Mr. Langerman's protest was taken to indicate that Mr. Robinson remained a staunch Krugerite.

Of all the Rand millionaires, Mr. J. B. Robinson is reputed the richest, and he is the one who has most obstinately clung to the policy of looking to Pretoria for favours rather than to the united effort of the Uitlanders for freedom. It is, or rather it was before the present crisis forced every man to choose between two sides, difficult to say why Mr. Robinson should be so much disliked throughout South Africa. It was then, of course it is still more now, impossible to discover any one who would say a good word for him. The ill-natured stories told about the foundations of his fortune in the early days of the Rand, and about his present entertainments lavished upon Society in Park Lane, are in both cases much the same sort of stories as are told about many other rich men; and if it was contemptible to find a mining magnate standing aloof from the cause of the mining city, it was, after all, not so very long since other capitalists, now staunch reformers, gave up the habit of making their account with the back stairs of Pretoria. Perhaps what made people dislike this attitude particularly in Mr. J. B. Robinson was the obvious connection of it with the strange vendetta against Mr. Rhodes which has possessed Mr. Robinson's soul for many years past. Nobody quite understands this vendetta, which appears to be carried on solely from one side. It is said to date from some obscure squabble in early Kimberley days. Purely to gratify this Mr. Robinson had lately started a most expensive anti-Rhodes daily paper in Cape Town, since defunct, power of attorney over which he vested in Mr. Rhodes' most malignant local political opponent, and to which he himself cabled from Park Lane during the most disastrous period of the crisis hundreds and thousands of pounds' worth of messages demonstrating, day after day, that Mr. Rhodes was fallen, must be fallen, ought to be fallen, irretrievably and for ever.

But this is anticipating. Mr. Robinson's paper at Cape Town was the first to inflame the Dutch vote against him by raising the cry of "treason" when the crisis came. His papers at Pretoria and Johannesburg, one of them openly subsidized as a Government organ, were simply busy in their habitual work of fostering disunion and discouragement in the Uitlander ranks. It is a singular illustration of the remissness of the Johannesburg capitalists in the educative part of the Reform movement that the entire morning daily Press of the town was so far left in the hands of papers owned and conducted in the Government interest, the dynamite monopoly interest, the canteen interest, the Robinson interest, anything but the Reform interest, which was confided solely to the afternoon *Star*. The other morning paper was more mischievous even, because more read, than Mr. Robinson's. This, the *Standard and Diggers' News*, openly boasts itself the Government Gazette, and had been preaching for years the doctrine that the Pretoria Codlin, not the Johannesburg Short, was the true friend to the working-man; that the miners on the Rand should distrust their natural leaders and look to the Government. The steady drip of this teaching may probably be credited with much of the disunion between men and masters, which was to sap and destroy the supreme effort of the community to throw off its bondage.

All day and all night the situation remained uppermost in men's minds. The insinuation that the leaders of the movement were flagomaniacs (local phrase for Jingoes) was denounced indignantly.

Meantime, what of the Government at Pretoria? Before the manifesto was twenty-four hours old it became patent that the Government had awakened to the seriousness of the aspect of affairs. Compromise was in the air early on the following day, Friday, December 27th. Means had been taken to let Mr. Kruger know that Johannesburg was well armed, and that a crisis of a grave character was nigh at hand. Two leading citizens from the Rand interviewed the President and wired satisfactory news. There was division in the councils of Pretoria. The Executive trenched upon what General Joubert considered his province, as Commandant-General, in despatching quick-firing guns to the Rand, an order which the General, who was not yet forced by events to recant his confessed leaning towards the Reform movement, countermanded. But among the Uitlanders, too, the "split" became wider with every hour, though the defection from the manifesto was not yet bold enough to detract much from its force and pressure on the Government. The bellicose bearing of Reform adherents began to create much concern amongst the trading section of the community; especially was this manifest in the ranks of what was known as the Mercantile Association, a body somewhat similar in character to the Chamber of Commerce, though not possessed of the Chamber's power and commercial influence. The members of the Association were mostly of foreign extraction, a good sprinkling being of Semitic origin and of that Continental type of Semitism in which the

AN AFRICAN CRISIS

fiercely patriotic blood of the Maccabees does not run strong. The Association watchword was that to talk of war or revolt was criminal, while to murmur "Lee-Metford" was blasphemy to the God of the Till. How unattractive at some times and places becomes the attitude which at other times and places we applaud as "a sober sense of law and order"!

All this time no very clear notion was held concerning the controlling power of the agitation. As seen in a previous chapter, Mr. Chas. Leonard, who signed the manifesto on Christmas Day, left for Cape Town the same night, twelve hours before the document became public property. He was wrongly supposed to have fled from instant arrest.

In their dilemma men instinctively turned towards the magnificent red brick building at the corner of Simmonds Street and Fox Street, within a stone's throw of the Exchange. This building was the headquarters of the Consolidated Goldfields of South Africa Company, popularly known as the "Goldfields." People turned towards this building because Colonel Rhodes, as the chief representative of the Company on the Rand, had his headquarters there, and because the leaders of the Reform movement frequented the building. It was, moreover, observed to be the rendezvous of various military-looking men—some of them retired or half-pay British officers, and some old Mashonaland officers. Gradually the "Goldfields" became the focus of interest in the town, and for once in a way the holy ground "between the chains" at Eckstein's Corner, the Throgmorton Street of Johannesburg, became of secondary importance.

Friday was a day of painful uncertainty, and people discussed with much speculation what President Kruger really meant when he said that a tortoise has to put its head out of its shell before one could chop it off—a saturnine response offered to certain burghers who pestered "Oom Paul" about the rising turmoil at Johannesburg. (He was on tour at the time, and the scene of the speech was Bronkhorst Spruit, an '81 battle site.)

The answer came with the rising sun. Saturday, December 28th, deserves to rank amongst the days most big with fate in the annals of the Rand. President Kruger sent his message swift and severe. "Obey the law," he said to Mr. J. B. Robinson's representative who had journeyed to Pretoria to ascertain how the land lay around the Presidential stoep. "Trust in autocratic clemency!" Thus Johannesburg read the message, and, thereupon, Johannesburg took the step that launched the town into the throes of revolution. It openly raised a citizen army. The indecision and irresoluteness that had characterized the day before—this had vanished, and in its place there showed a determination to await with confidence the next development of events. Even Mr. J. B. Robinson's representative declared for the manifesto. Carried with the flowing tide, confident in the strength, if not the policy, of the Reform leaders, Mr. Langerman came back to the Rand and reported that he told the President to his beard that "there can be no retreat from the manifesto. Johannesburg is one and indivisable." "Then I shall know how to deal with Johannesburg," rejoined Mr. Kruger. The shot was a random one, no doubt, but it was strangely prophetic. Twelve days later—but this is anticipating. . . . And Oom Paul, too, was to have his hour of panic before then.

An advertisement appeared in the papers, headed, "Enrol! Enrol!" the object being the protection of life and property from the rabble—or from——? Well, from anybody who might attack.

The credit for the formatiom of the first force available for this or any other service belongs to the Australians. Led by Mr. Walter D. Davies (called Karri Davies from importing karri-wood), who at the time of writing still languishes in Pretoria gaol for the crime of refusing to sign a petition, the Australians assembled ostensibly for the purpose of forming a Red Cross Australian Brigade. It was, however, impossible to completely banish the political element, and thus we find these Red Cross advocates declaring that, "if we do fight, let it be on the side of right and justice." That spoke plainly. The Americans met, too, for the purpose of forming a deputation to engage in a straight talk with Mr. Kruger. The Americans professed themselves desirous of maintaining the integrity of the Republic; but the deputation was to explain that, if the Pretoria Government utterly ignored just demands, and by its action precipitated war, the Americans would array themselves on the side of the Uitlanders.

The effect of this tumult and excitement was shown in the growing activity of the Cape Government Railway Offices on Market Square. From early morning the offices were besieged by panic-stricken people, anxious to escape from what they regarded as a doomed city. They cared not whither they went, provided only they crossed the Vaal in safety. Those who had friends in the Cape Colony booked through; others betook themselves to Kroonstad, Bloemfontein, and other places in the Free State. By three o'clock in the afternoon, eight hours before the time of departure, people boarded the train as it stood in the station yard at Braamfontein, preferring the discomforts of a stuffy compartment on a sweltering summer's day, to the risk of losing their seats when the rush set in at night. Anticipation was realized. When the train drew up at ten p.m. at the Braamfontein Station, where the trains are "made up," a mile or so from town, a crowd of more than a thousand persons seized it, and scrambled into such compartments as had not been already taken. But the most maddening scene of all was that which took place at the town (or park) station. Four or five thousand people greeted its approach, and then there was such a fight for seats as never before was witnessed. People who had booked first-class, and had anticipated a clean and comfortable bed for the night, found themselves glad enough to sit in second-class compartments four and five in a row. Wealthy gold-bugs disguised themselves and hid under the seats and behind the petticoats of their womenkind from the jeers of the men who stood on the platform. The women and children were cheered and wished God-speed on their journey. At midnight the train of carriages, twenty-two in number, steamed away towards border — and safety. And thus the Great Exodus commenced.

Sunday brought little relief from the excitement of the times. Those concerned in matters of defence, or defiance, as the case may be, proceeded with their precautions and preparations. The clergy had their say to-day. Nearly every church was crowded, and at nearly every church the theme was the same. To do the English ministers credit, they put a bold face on matters, advising the sterner members of their congregations to quit themselves like men. To show the unanimity of the pulpit, let us take extracts from sermons delivered on this day by the Rev. J. S. Darragh, Rector of St. Mary's (English) Church, and the Rev. P. G. J. Meiring, pastor of the Dutch Reformed Church :—

ENGLISH CHURCH.

"A man can only preserve his own self-respect by showing respect to the feelings and sentiments of others. Abstain, therefore, from bluster and equally from 'funk'— a vulgar word for a very vulgar thing—which some, of whom one expected better, have been displaying to a painful extent. Only by calmness, union and moderation will the conviction be brought home to those in authority that the constitutional agitation for our just rights is in earnest and means to be heard. It is preposterous to imagine that the majority can be ruled for an indefinite period by a minority, which is not their superiors in intelligence, honesty or capacity for government ; yet the peaceful vindication of rights cannot fail to be

DUTCH CHURCH.

"The end of the year has come, and should be a most serious time for our Government that is reaping, in the unrest which pervades the community, the fruit of the indifference and contempt with which the new population has been treated by the Volksraad. As a congregation belonging to the Church of the people of the country, we feel at one with the people, and are resolved to share their weal and woe ; accordingly we cannot but pray in this serious time, when the most threatening rumours are whispered abroad, that the people, through their Government and Volksraad, may recognise the mistakes of the past, and with the opening of the new year engage in such measures by which every reasonable cause of hampered by declamation on the one hand, or cowardly truckling on the other. May he (the President) learn to rule an unfortunate tongue and temper, and talk no more of chopping off tortoises' heads. Even tortoises have the indefeasible natural right to protrude the head on occasion. It is an insult to the President's intelligence to imagine him capable of turning a deaf ear to the reasonable rights of the people reasonably urged, as they have been recently in a lucid and temperate document."

discontent may be removed. If any of us possess any influence with the Government, let us consider it our solemn duty to use that influence in moving the Government at the proper time to give solemn assurances that just concessions will be made in relation to the new population, and right and justice done. Remember that we shall never be able to justify before God and the bar of posterity the shedding of blood and the rending asunder of the two great elements of the white population in South Africa because of comparatively insignificant grievances, if such shedding of blood is not prevented by any activity on our side."

It was sentiments such as these that parsons sent the people away to ponder over. The Reform leaders redoubled their exertions to-day, being in session at Saratoga House, Doornfontein, the residence of Colonel Rhodes.

Monday, December 30th.

Monday might be called the day of the great Reform rally. The cruel suspense that had dominated the early days of the crisis had entirely disappeared; so far as could be gathered from spoken utterance the several factions had settled their differences; all now stepped into line with the object of presenting a united front towards Pretoria—all save the Germans and Frenchmen, who at a conference between Sunday night and Morning morning, decided to await the pleasure of their consuls at Pretoria. Even the mercenary Mercantile Association had been won over. The leaders of the movement assured the leading spirits of the Association that nothing had been forgotten; that organization had done all that human experience and prevision could effect, and that they could only injure and hamper the supreme effort by allowing their own immediate and personal interests to remain uppermost in their minds. Realizing that they were not alone in the dangers that might overtake the community in the throes of the national change sought for, the members of the Association confessed their confidence in the leaders, albeit they took the precaution to form themselves into a separate Committee of Defence.

Public confidence in the movement was further enhanced by an authoritative announcement that Mr. J. B. Robinson's representative and the Barnato Bros. saw no escape from choice between the two alternatives. "He who is not for the National Union is against it." The view taken was that Johannesburg had gone too far to recede. "Let the Charter of our liberties be effectually conceded—or Heaven protect the right." Thus, the mouthpiece of the National Union, which vigorously preached revolution hour by hour.

Early this morning the rumours of the past few days concerning the possession of firearms became a demonstrated fact. Rifles had been served out at certain mines the day before. Men began to appear in kharki suits, with bandoliers and smasher hats. Still, nobody seemed to know how matters were to be brought to a head. The impression was that the leading mining companies would precipitate events by closing down the mines on the morrow, the last day of the Old Year, and thus throw thousands of white men, and tens of thousands of blacks on to the Pretoria Road—an expedient which made sober heads frown. It was given out that there was no lack of firearms and ammunition, and that at the Simmer and Jack there was a stand of one thousand arms and a Maxim. On the whole, the impression prevailed that the subscribers to the manifesto were fully prepared for emergencies.

The effect of all this war talk and war preparation upon the trade of the town may well be imagined. There was an immediate and general advance of 100 per cent. in the price of the most essential articles of food; bakers doubled the price of bread—from 6*d.* to 1*s.* per 1 lb. loaf; all credit was suspended, and orders for supplies coming forward from the ports were countermanded. Hour by hour the commercial panic raged, and in the afternoon flour reached 100*s.* per bag; forage, 100*s.* per 100 lb.; and so on.

The news from Pretoria was more hopeful. Government was disposed to be conciliatory. President Kruger even went so far as to inquire of a Rand American deputation what he should do to avert a revolution. "Make the best possible terms with the National Union," sententiously replied the deputation, and forthwith returned to the scene of tumult. The homogeneity of opinion on the Rand, and the well-circulated report that the leaders could back their words by blows had great moral force at Pretoria. President Kruger received Rand deputations freely, and was by no means niggardly in his promises. The news came that the Executive Council at the morning meeting had decided to remove the special duties on foodstuffs forthwith. Johannesburg accepted the removal of the duty as one instalment of reform demanded by the manifesto. Pretoria vacillated—Johannesburg "bluffed."

The panic amongst the less confident spirits grew proportionately in intensity, and the exodus assumed the look of flight from a plague or a siege. Women and children left by the thousand; Cornish miners from the East Rand took to their heels, not stopping for their pay, to be presented with derisive white feathers; thousands of natives, mine and house boys cleared, and racehorses were sent far from the reach of the field-cornet on commandeering purposes bent. The determination with which the movement was being pursued at the mines along the Reef was shown in the arrival in town about noon of wagon-loads of women and children and household goods. Shelter for the fugitives was quickly provided. The Wanderers' Club gave up their magnificent hall, the East Rand Proprietary Mines gave up their building and offices for conversion into bedrooms, and the Turf Club vacated Tattersall's with the same humane object. All was enthusiasm; the unanimity was wonderful. Recruiting for town protection and for district duty went on all day, and good care was taken that

Pretoria was kept well informed of it. Miners and artisans thronged the town, and everywhere there was excitement and ferment. There was, of course, much opposition to extreme measures, especially on the part of property-owners and tradesmen; but the events of the day had greatly popularized the National Union Manifesto; people regarded the Union as the winning side, and flocked to it accordingly.

All was going merrily, when at five o'clock in the afternoon, the leaders of the movement received the news of Dr. Jameson's entry into the Republic.

The Reform Committee, as a body, did not yet exist.

Although there had been much anxiety in the inner circle about Jameson's impatience, they had been so reassured by their Cape Town confederates so fully and so lately that the news that Jameson had broken his tether came with a shock.

On the previous morning—the very morning of the day when Jameson started—the reassuring messages reported in an earlier chapter had culminated in the receipt of a cipher message, never hitherto published, addressed to Mr. Percy Fitzpatrick by one of the two emissaries in Cape Town sent down to get the flag difficulty settled and Jameson checked. This important unpublished cipher was to the following effect:—

We have received the necessary assurances from Rhodes. Evidently the misunderstanding is in another quarter. [The reference here was to one of those loose impressions current at the time, as fully explained in a former chapter, about the supposed attitude of the British Government towards the conspirators or towards any outbreak in the Transvaal.] *Go on quietly with preparations without any haste. New programme agreed on.*

It is a curious and significant fact that the first actual news of Jameson's movement reached the Reform leaders neither from him nor from their own Intelligence Department, but from a Government official at Pretoria, who conveyed the news wishing to sound the leaders as to their attitude.

Later, Mr. A. Bailey received a wire from Cape Town—yet another of the few cipher telegrams that have never yet seen the light either in newspaper, Blue-book, or Green-book. I obtained a copy of the message the day after. It ran thus:—

The Veterinary Surgeon has left for Johannesburg with some good horseflesh, and backs himself for seven hundred. [= with 700 men.]

In these bizarre terms was conveyed news of a proceeding that was to set armies and fleets in operation, and to disturb the relationship of two of the great world-powers, to say nothing of the peace of South Africa.

The only other intimation of the move sent to Johannesburg from Pitsani or Mafeking was the telegram recorded in a previous chapter, which said that "Dr. Wolff will understand that distant cutting." (This active go-between was now in Johannesburg.) Dr. Wolff, unfortunately, denied that he understood anything of the kind.

Feeling that Jameson had "put them in the cart," the ringleaders hastened to in-span other people. Let the representative breadth of their own Johannesburg movement be put on record at once! The "Reform Committee" was formed. And here let one telling fact be mentioned to show that Jameson's audacity did inspire, if it also amazed and alienated. Threats and persuasions were needed to get some Committee men's names down, till the Jameson news leaked out; and then they "came tumbling over one another to join," says an eye-witness. By Tuesday the Committee numbered sixty-four of the leading men of Johannesburg.

The position of the leaders was one of painful perplexity. Some explanation they must give about the Jameson news to the crowd of leading residents who kept pressing for priority of position on the "Reform Committee" roll. Men of various races and creeds were banded together, and while some were swept off their feet by the proof that *somebody* at least was in deadly earnest, others were certain not to welcome the new development. The American section of the Committee, for instance, hot from the Venezuela excitement, would scarcely relish any seeming association with the Imperial factor. The Committee, in short, were at sixes and sevens on this point.

For some hours after its receipt the news was kept within the Reform Committee circle, and preparations calculated to strike the eye and to reassure were feverishly pressed forward.

When, late at night, the news was published throughout Johannesburg, the dominant note was rather anti-Jameson than pro-Jameson. There was a revulsion against outside interference, which by many was construed as from an Imperial quarter. Johannesburg, as the news spread, was dumbfounded by the audacity of the thing. There was a babel of dubious comment. "Who told Jameson to come in?" "Whose quarrel is this: ours or the Charter's?" These questions were bound to be asked.

Feelings were further damped by the news of a terrible tragedy which had marked the panic-stricken exodus by rail. A packed train which left Johannesburg for Natal the previous evening had run off the rails near Glencoe, injuring thirty-one and killing twenty-one of the fugitives, men, women, and children. Distraught relatives were naturally inclined to hold the Reform leaders vaguely responsible, though the accident was more directly traceable to the deficiencies of the Netherlands' cars on the train—and therefore to a characteristic feature of the Unreformed Transvaal.

The worst thing was the leaders' utter military unreadiness. When the news came the conspirators had but 1,500 rifles in their possession, of which only 500 were unpacked. The balance of the guns, and the majority of the Maxims did not reach the Simmer and Jack Mine until the following day—at the moment when Jameson dashed across the border the Maxims were *en route* to the Rand concealed in consignments destined for the Simmer Mine.

There was wild unpacking that Monday night, leading Reformers pulling grease-covered rifles out of secret places till their arms ached.

AN AFRICAN CRISIS

The Hon. "Charlie" White, and Captain Heyman, two of Jameson's officers whom the surprise move found still at Johannesburg, swore that nothing would stop Jameson in his march to the Rand—not even 10,000 men. This assurance was contagious; the Committee took heart, and awaited developments.

In the meantime wagon-loads of rifles and tons of ammunition were brought into town from the Simmer and Jack Mine, and stored in the "Goldfields" building. Three Maxims were brought in and located at the Rand Club for general exhibition. No attempt was now made to conceal the real state of affairs, so far as the intentions of the Committee were concerned. The rumour that the town had plenty of guns acted as a great public stimulus. More mass meetings were held, and more corps formed—of course, all for "the protection of life and property," and the defence of the town. Defence, not defiance, was still the watchword. The Scottish Brigade was formed on this eventful day, a brigade which before many days were over numbered 1,100 men, none of whom ever shouldered a gun. The cyclists of the town, a large athletic body, likewise formed a Women and Children Protection Brigade, and further decided to stand up for their rights.

The Anglo-Saxon section of the Uitlanders remained loyal towards the Cause, and towards one another. The "Moderates" hedged once again. This section, largely composed of German members of the Stock Exchange and merchants, held another meeting, and decided to approach the Government and beg it to appoint a Commission, to be presided over by Chief Justice Kotzé, to report to the Volksraad at the special session opening on the 9th January, then ensuing, upon the following matters: (*a*) the amendment of the Grondwet; (*b*) the alteration of the law with regard to the franchise; and (*c*) the granting of further privileges in connection with education. The most prominent people concerned in this movement were Mr. Langerman (Mr. J. B.

Robinson's representative), Mr. S. B. Joel, and Mr. Harold Strange.

What attitude the Government assumed was indicated in the following proclamation issued in a "Gazette Extraordinary," and published by the Government War Commission at Johannesburg late on Monday evening :—

"Whereas it has appeared to the Government of the South African Republic that there are reports in circulation to the effect that earnest endeavours are being set on foot to bring into danger the good order at Johannesburg ; and

"Whereas the Government is convinced that should such reports be of a truthful nature, endeavours of such a kind can only emanate from a small portion of the population, and that the greater portion of the Johannesburg population is desirous of maintaining order, and is prepared to support the Government in its endeavours to exercise law and order :

"So it is that I, Stephanus Johannes Paulus Kruger, State President of the South African Republic, with the advice and consent of the Executive Council, according to Art. 913 of the Minutes thereof, 30th December, 1859, hereby earnestly warn those evily disposed and command them to remain within the bounds of the law, the alternative being that those who do not hearken to this caution must answer to it on their own risk ; and

" I further make known that life and property shall be protected, where attacks thereupon may be attempted, and that every inhabitant of Johannesburg who is desirous of maintaining order, to whatever nationality he may belong, is hereby called upon to support and assist me, and the officials are ordered to do the same.

" And, further, I make known that the Government is at all times prepared to duly consider all grievances which are laid before it in a proper manner, and to lay the same for treatment before the Legislature of the country without delay.

"GOD SAVE COUNTRY AND PEOPLE."

The leaders of the movement met late in the evening at the "Goldfields" to discuss the situation as it appeared in the light of the Jameson development ; but nothing definite was decided. The only game that the hesitating Committee could play was the waiting one. As to their own status and

AN AFRICAN CRISIS

position, however, the Committee spoke with no uncertain voice. They formally declared themselves the Reform (sometimes called the "Defence") Committee of Johannesburg, and thus constituted, they awaited the arrival of the morning's news from Pretoria.

The gradual formation of the Committee and its programme as first adopted, are shown by the following message and the names appended to it; it was despatched to the High Commissioner on Monday night :—

"JOHANNESBURG, SOUTH AFRICAN REPUBLIC,
"*December* 30, 1895.

"Whereas certain deputations which proceeded to-day to Pretoria have returned with unsatisfactory answers and promises of inconsiderable concessions, this meeting resolves to abide by the manifesto issued by the Chairman of the National Union and to send a deputation of representatives to-morrow to request from the Government to give a definite answer within twenty-four hours, failing which this meeting decides to approach the Government of Her Majesty to secure its intervention for the purpose of establishing rights and averting internal strife.

"(Signed)
Francis Rhodes,   Lionel Phillips,
A. P. Hillier,   W. F. Gilfillan,
V. M. Cement,   Gordon Sandilands,
Abe Bailey,   H. A. Wolff,
S. W. Jameson,   H. A. Leith,
F. R. Lingham,   Max Langermann,
A. L. Lawley,   J. J. Lace,
W. St. John Carr,   George Farrar,
J. Percy Fitzpatrick, Walter E. Hudson,
John Hays Hammond,   John G. Auret,
E. P. Solomon,   J. W. Leonard."

Thus, on Monday, 30th December, did Johannesburg take off its coat to begin.

Chapter X

THE IRENE MYSTERY AND THE NACHTMAAL SURPRISE

BUT what, the mindful reader will ask, what has become all this time of the surprise attack on the Pretoria arsenal, which, according to Chapter II., was to have been almost the first move in the revolution?

It will be remembered that it was Johannesburg which was to have the controlling hand in its own challenge to the Government. Jameson's part, so far as it was ever clearly arranged at all, was to be merely a diversion, and a diversion which could be carried off under the pretext of an emergency police incident for the protection of life and property.

When the existing Government was paralysed, and its police withdrawn (as did actually occur); when a Provisional Government was declared at Johannesburg; when the improvised forces of this Provisional Government were occupied at Pretoria or on the Pretoria Road; a case would be created, plausible enough, for the Johannesburg leaders accepting the services of certain police, lately the Chartered Company's, who would then come in to police Johannesburg.

It is one thing to start a revolution in a community like Johannesburg. It is another thing to direct it. When the Government withdrew its police, if anything like an Alexandria riot had supervened the case for throwing troops in from outside would have been so cogent that, failing Jameson's police, Imperial forces would probably have had to be moved up. The emergency once provided for by Sir Henry Loch, in fact, would have arisen.

It is only by remembering this point about the original plot that many things in what actually happened become intelligible : such as the uncertainty of Jameson's destination, when he moved of his own accord, whether Johannesburg or Pretoria ; the entire absence of any arrangement for effecting a junction with Jameson, or for Johannesburg forces going out on that side at all ; the construction of defensive works and posting of forces upon a design evidently framed with an eye towards Pretoria, not towards Krugersdorp ; and last, the Mystery of the Irene Estate, which greatly puzzled and alarmed the Pretoria Government at the time, and the story of which is here told for the first time.

"Why was no step in the Pretoria part of the plot ever taken?" One step was taken. Johannesburg, in fact, threw out its outposts as far as the Irene Estate, almost within gun-shot of the church steeples of Pretoria. Almost immediately after the issue of the manifesto, steps were taken to store rifles and ammunition at this convenient spot. The Irene Estate, formerly the property of the late Mr. Nellmapius, was now in hands sympathetic to the Reform movement (though it does not follow that the owner was necessarily more cognisant of the way in which his property was to serve the revolution than worthy Volksraad member Malan in the matter of Jameson's remount horses). The estate was a very handy depôt. The expedition to it was placed in charge of the son of a well-known ex-commandant of Colonial forces, who, however, like nearly everybody else in the affair, was not taken fully into the confidence of the conspirators. At the time of starting, he was told that he was to go in charge of a trading expedition, and to take with him a couple of men of the farming class who could speak the taal and give the time of day to any Boer they might encounter in their travels.

The expedition consisted of a couple of well-laden "buck-wagons" drawn by oxen. These left Johannesburg on the day following the issue of the manifesto. The first halting-place was to be the Irene Estate, and the expedition was to await at that spot further instructions.

Arriving at the farm, the expedition received orders to off-load, and store their goods in buildings on the estate. They did so, and during the work the men first learned the nature of the expedition in which they were engaged. They rose to the situation, did their work with speed and with a will, and soon had everything in apple-pie order. Then they awaited developments.

Strange to say, on the Tuesday following, orders came that the goods were to be loaded up again and returned to Johannesburg with all possible despatch.

Again the men worked like Trojans, and had their wagons full and their teams inspanned in double-quick time. But how to reach Johannesburg unseen by the Boers! For the country was now all astir from the news of Jameson, and the splendid rally of the Boers to cut him off. The Pretoria road was likely to be much frequented, and by just the sort of parties that the pretended traders did not want to meet.

The happy thought struck the young Englishman, or rather Welshman, in charge of the expedition, to avoid the President's highway, and striking across the veld hit an ordinary farmer's road leading to the Rand.

Thanks to this idea, and good luck, and hard work, he managed to reach Johannesburg without encountering any too inquisitive party.

The wagons passed the toll gate on Hospital Hill late at night, and proceeded to the "Goldsfields" building, where the "goods" were again off-loaded—and were supposed by the crowd to be part of the warlike stores brought nocturnally from the Simmer and Jack Mine.

The men in charge had a narrow escape of capture. Whatever the source from which Pretoria drew its cognisance of the revolutionary plans, that cognisance was specially and anxiously alive to the menace to the seat of Government. The information even covered the fact that there was cause for search at "Irene." And on the Tuesday morning a small force under Mr. Malan, son-in-law of General Joubert, was sent out to investigate. When the party reached Irene, the birds had flown. The high road was scoured—but, as we have seen, the birds had flown otherwise.

And that is the Irene Mystery, which there is now no harm in telling.

But the nerves of Pretoria were still fluttered, and it was not till Thursday morning that President Kruger would let the artillery go out of the capital, even to meet Jameson. General Joubert, who has been accused of treason for not responding to the urgent messages from the front, had actually given orders to the artillery to start, when the President interposed to stop it. He could not have the capital exposed to assaults from Johannesburg

* * * * *

Now, why was the assault from Johannesburg never attempted? Why were arms ordered out to Irene, only to be ordered back again, like the men of the "gallant Duke of York"?

The reason is simple; even to absurdity. The Johannesburg leaders had just discovered that the Boers keep Nachtmaal!

Christmas and New Year are great times to take communion. At the end of December and beginning of January, Church Square at Pretoria is white with the tents of outspanned wagons. Bearded farmers, and fat frows, and families, by scores of wagons, drawn from the Pretoria district up to several days' journey distant, have come to town to partake of Nachtmaal; and in each wagon, along with the Bible, comes the rifle—in case of game on the way, or thieves, or other need. At any rate, those who had no rifle with them could soon be supplied. It was a ready-made garrison!

So when Jameson suddenly precipitated matters, and Johannesburg sent to spy out the land at Pretoria, lo! the Church Square was thick with Boers.

The Pretoria surprise was a wild and hazardous idea in any case. But with Pretoria full of Boers, it dissolved into thin air. To this day there are many, eager revolutionaries at the time, who do not know that it was ever dreamed of.

As it was, the preparedness of the Government shows that the scheme was confided to one too many. But had it been confided to two or three more, surely some one or other would have known his South Africa well enough to remember the institution of Nachtmaal!

As it was, the geese of the Capitol were not more useful to Rome than the Boers in the Church Square were to Pretoria. "Once again," the Boer historian of the future will remark, " we were saved by our religion!"

Chapter XI

A PREMIER'S "APPLE-CART"

THE news of the raid ushered in a drama at Cape Town scarcely less moving than that enacted at Johannesburg, save that at Cape Town the action was mostly behind the scenes. At nine o'clock on Sunday morning, the 29th of December, the telegraph office opened, and, to quote the words of the Cape Committee of Inquiry, "it is in evidence that the telegram from Dr. Jameson of the evening of the 29th, as well as that of the morning of the 29th, were both handed to an official of the Chartered Company some time between ten and eleven a.m. on that morning."

Imagine the feelings of Mr. Stevens when he decoded, one on the top of the other, the message, "I shall go unless I hear," and the message, "I shall go in any case this evening!" He took a cab and dashed off to Three Anchor Bay, where Dr. Harris lived. He found Dr. Harris breakfasting. The Secretary of the British South Africa Company took Mr. Stevens' cab and posted out to Groote Schuur, while Mr. Stevens was despatched to the telegraph office to "keep Mafeking open."

But the operators could not ring Mafeking.

At Groote Schuur Mr. Rhodes, closeted with the two Johannesburg emissaries, to whom was shown Jameson's startling messages as soon as he could escape from a maddening tablefull of guests at luncheon, walked up and down with his hair roughed up, repeating mechanically from time to time: "Now just be cool. Let's think this thing out. Now just be cool," and so on.

It seems clear that Jameson's two messages threw Mr

Rhodes into a kind of fatalistic vacillation. An impulse of irritation with his old friend for breaking away was followed by a rush of confidence that the man who was neither to hold nor to bind had flung himself into a great enterprise, and would somehow carry it through.

Between three and four o'clock Dr. Harris returned from Groote Schuur to Cape Town with a message signed "Unbegangen," a private code name for Mr. Rhodes, as follows:—

> "Heartily reciprocate your wishes with regard to Protectorate, but the Colonial Office machinery moves slowly, as you know. We are, however, doing our utmost to get immediate transference of what we are justly entitled to. Things in Johannesburg I yet hope to see amicably settled, and a little patience and common sense is only necessary. On no account whatever must you move. I most strongly object to such a course."

The reader's first thought will be, how oddly worded the beginning of the message is as a reply to Jameson's breathless telegrams, with no part of which it seems to connect. The Cape Committee of Inquiry were fairly puzzled by this Protectorate reference. It might even be suspected that the intention of the first part was to detract from the emphatic veto of the second part and turn the whole telegram, on some pre-arranged plan of interpretation, into a blind. But apart from any other reason against this, the telegram was never made use of as a blind, nor shown to any one in justification during the difficult days which followed. Long afterwards, it came to light without Mr. Rhodes' approval by a sort of accident.[1] More plausible, perhaps, is the theory that the veto was genuine, and that the calm and philosophic beginning of it was deliberately calculated as a cold douche for the ardent recipient. If Jameson was "bluffing," the best way was to dismiss his threat of going in as nonsense. If he was not bluffing, but really meant what he said, then any veto at this point was a mere matter of form.

[1] Mr. Stevens gratified the curiosity of the Select Committee by producing the draft, and his superiors seem to have disapproved the disclosure as prejudicing Jameson, whose trial was then imminent.

Whatever the intention of the telegram, it was never sent. When Mr. Stevens took it to the office on Sunday, the line to Mafeking was still closed. He tried and tried again, until late that evening. Early next morning he again took the telegram to the office, and ascertained that the wire had been cut. In the end he did not leave the telegram at all at the office—another evidence, by the way, that it was not a sham veto intended merely to be put on record. By the time that communication with Mafeking was restored matters had passed into a new phase, Mr. Rhodes having folded his hands and left everything to Fate and the High Commissioner; and Mr. Stevens seems not to have sought or received any further instructions.

At eleven o'clock that Sunday night the Imperial Secretary, who had gone to bed, for South African hours are early, was roused by an urgent message from Mr. Rhodes. He hurried to Groote Schuur. Mr. Rhodes at once told him of Jameson's telegrams received that morning. He mentioned in a general way that he had tried to stop Jameson, but could not communicate, said that there was a chance that the messengers from Johannesburg, who would have reached the Doctor after the despatch of his morning telegram, might have changed his mind, but did not conceal the fact that he fancied Jameson would now stop for nobody.

At that season of the year the Governor abandons Government House for a country villa at the suburb of Newlands. From his midnight interview at Groote Schuur the Imperial Secretary went home to spend a few sleepless hours before going to Newlands House to rouse Sir Hercules Robinson untimely from his slumbers. A phrase in the following note has become historical :—

"NEWLANDS HOUSE,
"*Monday, December 30th*, 1895, 5 a.m.

"MY DEAR SIR HERCULES,—

"I hope you will come to town early. There is, I fear, bad news from Jameson. He seems to have disobeyed Rhodes, and to have taken the bit between his teeth.

"Yours, etc., GRAHAM BOWER."

Sir Hercules Robinson *did* "come into town early" that Monday morning, and confronted with admirable coolness the perplexed situation. The first thing was to find if Jameson had actually started. He telegraphed to the Resident Commissioner, Mafeking, mentioning Jameson's violation of the border as a rumour, asking if it were true, and directing Mr. Newton, if so, to send a special messenger on a fast horse ordering him to return immediately, and carrying appropriate warnings, peremptory in tone, also to Jameson's officers. It was the first message to go through on the restored wire.

Thanks to the success of the troopers sent to cut the southward wire, and the drunken failure of those who should have cut the wire to Pretoria, Cape Town, like Johannesburg, had its first authentic news of the raid from President Kruger's capital. Earlier on Monday morning the British Agent at Pretoria, Sir Jacobus de Wet, had sent a telegram which puts on record what a tension public feeling had reached already before Jameson's move was heard of:—

"Great excitement prevails here, and a feeling of disturbance and insecurity is very strong on both sides. Rumours of fully armed strong force of burghers freely circulated. Disturbance may happen at any moment; it is a critical state of affairs. Should I call on President South African Republic, and ask him what provisions have been made for protection of law-abiding British subjects?"

This Sir Jacobus followed up by another telegram, recounting that the President had just sent for him, when General Joubert had read a telegram from the Landdrost of Zeerust, giving the news. Sir Jacobus de Wet had assured the President that he could not believe the force consisted of English troops. General Joubert said they might be Mashonaland or Bechuanaland Police, but whoever they were, he would take immediate steps to stop them. The President wanted to know what the High Commissioner had to say to it, and the British Agent, poor man, turned upon by the Executive Council in its dismay, was driven almost wild by a block on the wires, which prevented him from receiving the answers from Government House, clearly defining the High Commissioner's attitude towards Jameson, till he had sent a number of more and more agitated messages, one of which concluded : "The Government has already sent for me twice. Possibly blood has already been shed."

Meantime, Sir Hercules Robinson had to deal with Mr. Rhodes, an old political co-worker, to whom he found himself in a tryingly new relation. Mr. Rhodes must be made to range himself either as an ally of the High Commissioner against Jameson, or as an abettor of Jameson against the orders of Her Majesty's representative. Sir Hercules was prompt to present the alternative, but in view of the ascendency which Mr. Rhodes had come to wield alike in the Colony and in Downing Street, he must have been glad to receive, as he did on Monday morning, the remarkable cablegram which Mr. Chamberlain had despatched on the previous day, showing that Sir Hercules would have Her Majesty's Government behind him in sternly asserting the Queen's treaty obligations :

"(Strictly confidential.)

"It has been suggested, although I do not think it probable, that an endeavour might be made to force matters at Johannesburg to a head by some one in the service of the Company advancing from Bechuanaland Protectorate with police.

"Were this to be done, I should have to take action under Articles 22 and 8 of the Charter. Therefore, if necessary, but not otherwise, remind Rhodes of these Articles, and intimate to him that, in your opinion, he would not have my support, and point out the consequences which would follow."

This message, dated from London, 5.30 p.m., the 29th of December, and therefore despatched just between the time of the parade at Pitsani and the parade at Mafeking preliminary to starting, is an odd coincidence, and sounds like a case for the Psychical Research Society. A Minister of the Colony (Sir James Sivewright) has even had the indiscretion to refer to it once in debate as matter for inquiry. But, as Mr. Chamberlain afterwards explained in the House of Commons with great simplicity, it was really due to the fact that Mr. Secretary Fairfield, who has South Africa under his special wing at the Colonial Office, had been led by the publication of the Leonard Manifesto in the *Times* of the previous day, and by the growing confidence of certain club and private rumours, as described in a previous chapter, to convey an urgent representation to his Chief, which made the latter feel that he must at once put the High Commissioner on his guard.

The High Commissioner then took steps to corner Mr. Rhodes at once, but Mr. Rhodes was not to be found. Instead of sitting in the Premier's Office in Grave Street, besieged by long queues of callers waiting to see him in one or other of his multifarious capacities, he discreetly remained all day in the umbrageous seclusion of Groote Schuur.

Some years ago, when Mr. Rhodes decided to leave off living *en garçon* at the club, and to take unto himself a house, he bought an old Dutch grange, with rococo gables and a pillared stoep in the ancient colonial style, built on the Rondebosch slopes of the Devil's Peak. This he restored, lined it with teak, filled it with the old Dutch furniture now becoming rare, and bought up the best piece of Table Mountain to create a free menagerie for all Cape Town to wander in by stocking the labyrinthine glades and woods with antelopes, rare birds, and all the fast disappearing fauna of South Africa. It is his habit to get up at five or six in the morning and go for a gallop along some of the immensely various mountain paths of this great pleasance.

On Monday, the 30th of December, 1895, those who sought Mr. Rhodes at Cape Town learnt that he was at Groote Schuur, and those who sought him at Groote Schuur learnt that he was riding the slopes of Table Mountain.

The Blue Book contains two stiff and formal letters from the Imperial Secretary to the Right Honourable C. Rhodes, Rondebosch, of which this sentence strikes the key:—

"I have called several times at your office this morning for the purpose of conveying to you His Excellency's instructions for the immediate recall of Dr. Jameson, but you have not, so far as is known, been at any of the public offices, or at the British South Africa Company's offices. I therefore send this note by special messenger to your private residence."

Which two letters evoked the following undated, laconic, and characteristically informal reply:—

"MY DEAR BOWER,—

"Jameson has gone in without my authority. I hope our messages may have stopped him. I am sorry to have missed you.

"Yours,
"C. J. RHODES."

Meanwhile, the persistence and reality of the apprehensions roused at the Colonial Office that Sunday and Monday were again shown by the receipt at Government House of a telegram following up the warning about Jameson's possible intentions. Sir Hercules had crossed the first warning by a message remarking (on the strength of Mr. Rhodes' "damp squib" expression) that the movement at Johannesburg seemed to have collapsed through internal divisions, and that leaders of the National Union would probably now make the best terms they could with President Kruger. To this (Saturday) telegram Mr. Chamberlain now replied: "Are you sure Jameson has not moved in consequence of collapse? See my telegram of yesterday." It was not till very late on Monday or early on Tuesday morning that Sir Hercules got Mr. Chamberlain's reply to his definite news of the crossing of the border: "Your action," said Mr. Chamberlain, "is cordially approved. I presume that Mr. Rhodes will co-operate with you in recalling Administrator of Matabeleland. Keep me informed fully of political situation in all its aspects. It is not understood here. Leave no stone unturned to prevent mischief."

Mr. Rhodes was not destined wholly to escape being cornered on this first day of the crisis.

The first intelligence of the raid to the Cape Government,

Mr. Rhodes' colleagues in the Cape Ministry, came not from him, but in due official course from Mr. Boyes, Resident Magistrate at Mafeking. He wired on Monday to his chief, the Attorney-General, nominally 8 a.m. (received in Cape Town when the wire was restored at 1 o'clock), reporting the departure of the Mafeking part of the column, 150 strong, and stating their intention of joining another column from Pitsani, under Jameson, as a rumour "currently reported." Mr. Schreiner had this about two o'clock, and so utterly scouted the "currently reported" story that he sent back a stiff "snub" —so the magistrate afterwards complained—beginning "your agitated telegram received." But on the heels of Mr. Boyes' telegram came a more detailed one from Inspector Fuller of the Cape Police, and at last, instead of snubs, semi-apologetic instructions had to be sent north. The local officials were advised of the correct attitude of the Colony towards an "unauthorized mad proceeding," and told to keep quiet watch along the border, and telegraph any news.

Mr. Schreiner could not believe his eyes, nor could Mr. Faure, the Minister for Agriculture, the first of his colleagues whom he happened to meet, but the reports were too circumstantial.

None of Mr. Rhodes' colleagues, and few of his friends, have been closer to him than his late Attorney-General. Of German parentage, but born and educated in the Colony till he went to Cambridge and London, the Honourable W. P. Schreiner, Q.C., is perhaps the sincerest, as he is quite the most intellectual, specimen of the young Afrikander patriot in Cape Colony, where those who call themselves by this name are apt to be of no great parts and of still less straightforwardness. All the Schreiners are clever, are in earnest, are headstrong, fine minded, and a little incalculable. Some of the genius which Olive Schreiner put into the "Story of an African Farm" this brother has turned into the dry channel of Roman-Dutch law. Another brother and another sister are extraordinarily earnest Temperance reformers. A profound and subtle legal scholar, sharing with Mr. Rose-Innes the leadership of the Cape Bar, Mr. Schreiner was carried into politics at the chariot wheels of Mr. Rhodes. He was likely to go far, because his rather paradoxical mind has sincerely arrived by some strange speculative course at nearly all the identical fossilized beliefs which make up the mental equipment of the most ignorant member of the Afrikander Bond. Mr. Rhodes found in him a young lieutenant who would defend all the Afrikander side of his policy with both brains and conviction, while Mr. Schreiner fell in love with Mr. Rhodes' personality; which, with all its crudities, casts a strange spell on many men of different temperaments. No man in all South Africa was more truly cut to the heart by the Jameson Raid than Mr. Schreiner, but he has risked his ambitions and lost ground with many of those whose leadership he was almost winning away from Mr. Hofmeyr, now out of Parliament, because since the raid, he will insist on speaking of Mr. Rhodes always with sorrow rather than with anger.

The critical meeting between the two colleagues was thus one for a psychological novelist.

On the fateful Sunday evening Mr. Schreiner had seen Mr. Rhodes for a few minutes and asked: "Have you seen Charlie Leonard?" "Yes," said Mr. Rhodes indifferently, "I have seen him." "For goodness' sake," said Mr. Schreiner, "keep yourself clear from that entanglement at Johannesburg. If there is any disturbance they are sure to try and mix you up with it."

Mr. Rhodes, as Mr. Schreiner observed to the Select Committee, is not a man of many words. He shrugged his shoulders and said, "Oh! that is all right."

On Monday evening Mr. Schreiner hurried out to Groote Schuur with the amazing telegrams from Bechuanaland. Mr. Rhodes was still on the mountain side. Mr. Schreiner left an urgent message asking to see him, and after supper, Mr. Rhodes' confidential man went across and asked him to come over at once. Mr. Schreiner hurried through the wood in the dark—he lives on the edge of Mr. Rhodes' grounds—Mr Rhodes' man lighting him with a lantern.

For three hours the two colleagues were closeted in Mr. Rhodes' library. It was a significant, and in a sense a memorable interview, because it typified the great struggle between Afrikander sympathies with the Transvaal and Afrikander devotion to Mr. Rhodes over which so many friends and supporters have agonized since.

The library at Groote Schuur is a cosy, teak-lined room, furnished in keeping with the old-fashioned Dutch style of the house. The principal feature of the book shelves is a unique collection of "cribs" of almost the whole of classical literature,—cribs carefully made and typewritten to Mr. Rhodes' order, and sumptuously bound. On one wall hangs a tattered Union Jack from some scene of battle, also a flag taken from the Portuguese by Mr. Rhodes' pioneers at the time of the "Manica Incident," when that funny little scuffle took place at Massikessi which ended so differently from the scuffle at Krugersdorp.

Nothing could be more dramatic, nor, to those who know Mr. Rhodes' manner, more expressively accurate, than Mr. Schreiner's own account of their talk :—

"I went into his study with the telegrams in my hand.

"The moment I saw him I saw a man I had never seen before. His appearance was utterly dejected and different.

"Before I could say a word, he said : 'Yes, yes, it is true. Old Jameson has upset my apple-cart. It is all true.'

"I said I had some telegrams.

"He said : 'Never mind. It is all true. Old Jameson has upset my apple-cart,' reiterating in the way he does when he is moved.

"I was staggered. I said : 'What do you mean, what can you mean?'

"He said : 'Yes, it is quite true, he has ridden in. Go and write out your resignation. Go, I know you will.'

"And so I said : 'It is not a question of my going to write out my resignation'; but I elicited from him a good many facts in relation to this matter, and I told him that it was his duty to convene a Cabinet meeting at once.

"During this entire interview Mr. Rhodes was really broken down. He was broken down. He was not the man who could be playing that part. Whatever the reason may have been, when I spoke to him he was broken down. If it were unfair I would not say it, but it is true. He could not have acted that part; if he did he is the best actor I have ever seen. He was absolutely broken down in spirit; ruined.

"I said: 'Why do you not stop him? Although he has ridden in, you can still stop him.'

"He said: 'Poor old Jameson. Twenty years we have been friends, and now he goes in and ruins me. I cannot hinder him. I cannot go and destroy him.'

"That was how he put it. That was the attitude he assumed to me. Much took place between us. I do not want to go into that. I left in very great distress. It was impossible to do anything on that night, and I left with the understanding that the first thing in the morning he would convene the Cabinet.

"We did meet. It was never after uncertain, from the moment that we met Mr. Rhodes there, that Mr. Rhodes must resign."

It should be added that though Mr. Schreiner frankly told the Select Committee that he was not certain in his own mind that part of Mr. Rhodes' agitation may not have been due to the threatening cablegram which had been communicated to him from Mr. Chamberlain that afternoon, yet that he personally had no doubt, after all the subsequent disclosures, that Mr. Rhodes did strongly disapprove of Jameson going in at that time. He added :—

"You would ask me for my theory why Mr. Rhodes did not use more energy and vigour in stopping Dr. Jameson. I have given you all that I could gather from him when he, in a heart-broken way, said, 'Poor old Jameson, poor old Jameson, we have been friends twenty years, he is ruining me now, but I cannot go and pull him back.'"

In short, from Mr. Schreiner's point of view,—

"His honour rooted in dishonour stood,
And faith unfaithful kept him falsely true."

When Mr. Rhodes did meet his Cabinet he set himself desperately to hold it together long enough to give Jameson time to get to Johannesburg, and in the sequel, through a conjunction of causes, the resignation which he hastened to place in the Governor's hands, and which neither the Governor nor Mr. Chamberlain would accept as long as there was hope or pretence of Mr. Rhodes co-operating with them against Jameson, was only accepted by telegram when the Governor was on his way up to Pretoria. An emergency Ministry was then gathered together by Sir Gordon Sprigg, lately Mr. Rhodes' Treasurer-General, but a person with whom the formation of Cape Ministries is almost a habit, and that Ministry, having survived the emergency, seems now fairly rooted to its bench.

With Mr. Hofmeyr soon afterwards Mr. Rhodes was scarcely less frank than with Mr. Schreiner. His two interviews with the Bond Leader, the last they are likely to have for many a long day, may fitly conclude this chapter, the contents of which are mainly personal. The relation between these two men, each so strong and shrewd, and sure of what he himself wanted, has been one of the curiosities of Cape politics, of which for half a dozen years they had been the great twin brethren. The writer well remembers a little birthday feast at Mr. Hofmeyr's house, when a presentation was made to him by Members of Parliament in connection with his retirement from the Chamber where he had so often made and unmade the Ministries he would never enter. It was Mr. Rhodes who proposed his friend's health. He recalled how, when he himself first entered Cape Politics, in the first bitterness after the Transvaal struggle, he was an arrant rooinek Britisher; how, in Mr. Hofmeyr, the leader of the opposite party in the Colony, he had found the fairest of opponents, yet the staunchest of allies; how they had gradually come to find that their points of view were not so dissimilar, and at last to work gradually together. "People have disputed whether I led Mr. Hofmeyr or Mr. Hofmeyr led me," said Mr. Rhodes in his blunt way. "I say that our minds worked in the same direction," and then came a curious passage—it struck one hearer, at least, as curious at the time—"Every man," Mr. Rhodes said in a hesitating way, "works for personal ends. Mr. Hofmeyr's personal end was, nothing for himself, but it was to get the best position he could for his own people in this country." The speaker paused, and one half expected him to add that *his* personal end was to do the like for *his* countrymen, but he broke off, concluding lamely—" and therefore I ask you to drink to Mr. Hofmeyr, as a true patriot," and buried his remarks in his glass of champagne.

Mr. Rhodes did not conceal from Mr. Hofmeyr that he knew more than appeared on the surface about all that had led up to Jameson's move, and Mr. Hofmeyr did not, at that first interview, waste time on reproaches, or moralities, or ejaculations about being hoodwinked by his friend up to the very moment of the crisis. With that practical mind of his he set himself to induce Mr. Rhodes to come out with a strong public repudiation of Jameson, but Mr. Hofmeyr and the High Commissioner and Mr. Chamberlain together could not wring that out of the Cape Premier. Had they known all, they would not have tried. That Jameson had gone in without his consent; that the sudden move was a surprise to him; that he had tried to stop Jameson too late; so much Mr. Rhodes would say, but not a word more, nor would he conceal that so far from a spirit of denunciation, he cherished a wild hope that Jameson might somehow win and tumble Paul Kruger down.

"You will not pretend to me," said Mr. Hofmeyr, for indeed there had never been any pretences in their relations, "that you have mixed yourself up with this outrage from an overwhelming democratic sympathy with the poor, down-trodden, working-men who are now drawing big wages on the Rand?"

"No," said Mr. Rhodes coldly, "I shall not pretend," and they parted, each knowing well that this was the parting of the ways of their two careers.

Days afterwards, when the worst was over, friends who could not face the rending in twain of the joint-party which had looked to the two as leaders, contrived to bring them together for another interview. In the meantime Mr. Hofmeyr, already denounced by the zealots of the neighbouring Republics as one of the Rhodolaters who had brought this trouble on South Africa, had been compelled to make public various bitter expressions. He now justified himself. He spoke with emotion. He declared it was difficult not to use the word perfidy. "I could explain better," he said, "if you had ever been a married man. You were never married. I have not yet forgotten the relation of perfect trust and intimacy which a man has with his wife. We have often disagreed, you and I, but I would no more have thought of distrusting you than a man and his wife think of distrusting each other in any joint undertaking. So it was till now; and now you have let me go on being apparently intimate while you knew that this was preparing, and said nothing." Perhaps Mr. Rhodes felt that the reproach was just. Perhaps he felt that it was over-charged and that Mr. Hofmeyr was pretending to take the popular and conventional view of a position, the tangled casuistry of which he at least might have done justice to. At any rate he was not able or willing to pour forth the exculpation which seemed to be expected of him, and sullenly or stoically he let pass the storm, and with it the opportunity for patching up any kind of peace.[1] Mr. Hofmeyr was left free to take whatever steps against Mr. Rhodes might be demanded by just indignation or by political exigencies. He has taken few public steps. But he does not come of a forgiving stock.

Such was the upsetting of a Premier's apple-cart at Cape Town. We must now go back to the powder-cart at Johannesburg.

---

[1] It seems that Mr. Hofmeyr had used the same matrimonial illustration to other less intimate persons, one of whom had repeated it to Mr. Rhodes just before the meeting with Mr. Hofmeyr. Thus the effect was somewhat staled.

Chapter XII

A BOOM IN REVOLUTIONS

TUESDAY, December 31st.—The last day of the old year dawned upon a position of unparalleled complexity. Here was a town entirely, as events proved, unprepared for the serious work of war, with Jameson marching to its relief on the one hand, and Pretoria preparing for attack on the other. Public opinion was bitterly hostile towards Pretoria, yet shrank from joining forces with Jameson. This was in the early hours of Tuesday morning, December 31st. The Reform Committee then made up their minds to accept the situation as just described, and formally repudiated Jameson. Through their organ,[1] they disavowed "any knowledge of, or sympathy with, the entry into the Republic of an armed force from the Bechuanaland side," and denied having been "in any way privy to the lamentable step." At an early hour of the morning the Committee published the following solemn declaration :—

"SIR,—I am directed to state for the information of the public that it is reported a large force has crossed the Border into Transvaal territory, and to say that this has taken place without the knowledge of the Committee. A deputation consisting of Messrs. Lionel Phillips, J. G. Auret, W. E. Hudson, D. Lingham, and Max Langermann is leaving this evening to meet Government in reference to the situation.

"By order,
"A. KELSEY,
"Secretary Reform Committee."

[1] The *Star* was not *officially* the Reform Committee's mouthpiece; but practically it became so, and a very vigorous and eloquent one.

Unhappily, nobody could yet make up his mind to provide Johannesburg as Pretoria was presently provided, with the simple clue to the mystery, viz., that Jameson had been first invited and then stopped or adjourned.

The air thus cleared by simple repudiation of Jameson, the Committee were free to consider again the question "Under which flag," which the new development made again insistent. Was it to be the Union Jack, the Stars and Stripes, or the "Vierkleur"? The matter was a weighty one, and on it the unanimity of the Committee, and, therefore, as it then seemed, the success of the Cause depended. The matter was earnestly debated in the Council Chamber of the "Goldfields" building. Only the day before Captain Mein of the Robinson, as typical a Yankee as ever chewed tobacco, declared that Americans did not want the British flag, but if it came to a matter of choice between the English flag and the Pretoria Government they would fight for the former. But the Jameson news changed this attitude, and Mr. J. H. Hammond, pressed by excited compatriots, insisted that the Committee should now publicly register the previous formal decision of the smaller junto to abide by the flag of the *status quo*.

But where was the flag to hoist? Mr. Hammond first tried to borrow a *vierkleur* from a Government official, who, however, could not be persuaded that the purpose was not one of insult. Eventually, the necessary bunting was secured from a linen-draper. He brought this into the room where the Committee was now sitting in perpetual session, and somebody set the example of signifying allegiance to the flag of the Republic with uplifted hand.

At half-past eleven a figure was observed by the crowd outside the "Goldfield" offices to emerge upon the balcony, and point up at an unfurled *vierkleur*, with its red, white, green, and blue stripes; one or two other figures came out and also pointed up. Such was the formal public act of dedication.

Thousands of people who loitered in the vicinity looked on with silent amazement, not knowing what it all meant. The

"Flag Question" wrangling had never extended to the people at large.

Subsequently the flag was hoisted to the roof of the building, and from that position it fluttered unmolested in the breeze until the downfall of the Uitlander cause, when bunting of this particular make became more in request at Pretoria.

The "Flag Question" settled, the Committee now turned their attention to a matter of more cogent importance. It was known that the burgher forces had been instructed to repel the invasion, and, although Johannesburg had formerly and officially repudiated Jameson, it was deemed politic to put the city into a state of defence against a possible surprise. Compromise was now once again in the air, and the bearing of the Reform Committee might be gauged from the following official notice posted on the "Goldfields" doors shortly after high noon :—

"Notice is hereby given that this Reform Committee adheres to the National Union Manifesto and reiterates its desire to maintain the independence of the Republic. The fact that rumours are in course of circulation to the effect that a force has crossed the Bechuanaland border, renders it necessary to take active steps for the defence of Johannesburg and preservation of order. The Committee earnestly desire that the inhabitants should refrain from taking any action which can be construed as an overt act of hostility against the Government.

"By order of the Committee,

"J. PERCY FITZPATRICK,

"*Secretary.*"

The military preparations were very much *en evidence* now. Throughout the night arms and ammunition had been served out at the "Goldfields" office and at the Simmer and Jack Mine. At an early hour of the morning the townspeople were afforded other signs of the thorough preparedness, as it then appeared, of the Reform Committee. Some strings of horses, between fourteen and fifteen hands, were brought into town, some from the Robinson Mine, others from the Simmer and Jack, the Langlaagte Estate, and other places. The ponies were taken to Reform Committee stables, where they were saddled and accoutred, and generally made ready for service in the field. There was a business-like air about the whole proceeding. Colonel R. Bettington, an old Colonial hand, was in charge, and the forces that were being mounted now became known as Bettington's Horse. There were two troops each sixty strong, of as serviceable a body of men as could well be imagined. Their uniform was kharki suits, with leggings, smasher hats with red bands.

As fast as companies of twenty or thirty were mounted and accoutred, they departed, and great commotion was occasioned by a body of them riding out in the direction of Viljoen's Drift on the Vaal River—the popular surmise being that they had gone to guard the Vaal River bridge.

Recruiting was continued at a brisk pace throughout the day. Nearly a dozen different agencies were employed. Several mines had shut down the previous night, and the men thus liberated flocked into town to enrol in the Reform Committee's forces, to receive arms, and to undergo drill. As the men were enrolled they were formed into companies under commanders, who for the most part had had some experience of Kafir warfare, and were at once marched to one or other of the several squares, and put through their first drill.

Offers of outside assistance, from the Colony and Natal, poured in upon the Reform Committee, and the publication of this fact stirred a lively spirit in town. "South Africa is with us!"

The commonplaces about avoiding bloodshed flickered out. The glitter and trappings of war caught the popular imagination, and the changing humour of the town responded to the morning's preparations. By the luncheon hour, war-talk held the streets. Men now began to doubt whether, after all, the Reform Committee had done well and wisely in repudiating Jameson. Rumour came in that Jameson had engaged a large number of Boers in the course of his march, and had beaten them off; that he was pressing on victorious towards the

Golden City. "He'll be here on Thursday," was the cry that went up, and the manner of his reception was already being discussed.

The ferment increased hour by hour. Tradesmen commenced barricading their shop windows and doors, and armed their employees for the protection of their premises, while jewellers removed their valuables to safe keeping in the vaults of the Johannesburg Safe Deposit Company. Great excitement was occasioned early in the afternoon by the receipt of a wire from Pretoria to the effect that a well-known townsman had met the Executive Council and represented the perfect organization and equipment behind the Uitlander movement.

"The President was amazed," so ran the wire, "at the large number of Maxim guns which are at our command, and was especially staggered at the Nordenfeldt guns in the possession of the Reform Committee." He might well be. They had no such thing as a Nordenfeldt among them.

The panic of the cautious and the mercantile had its natural sequel in a run on the Banks. All day long the banking halls were thronged by people madly anxious to withdraw money. Nothing but gold would suffice. People who were leaving drew their all. People who had money about them in the shape of paper converted it into sovereigns, and the notes of the National Bank of the Transvaal, so far as street exchange was concerned, were at a discount. The biggest run of all was upon the National Bank, from which, on behalf of the Government, the Post Office Savings Bank was supplied. Numbers of customers of this institution withdrew their deposits to the last penny. Some at once transferred the gold to the Standard Bank, whilst others took the hoard home and secreted it about their farms. One farmer took three thousand British sovereigns, which he said he would bury in his land. The National Bank kept open after hours to meet the demand; but all requirements were satisfied, the Bank receiving a special consignment of gold from the State Mint.

Another development of the situation was the formation of

a field ambulance corps, and a hospital corps. The doctors of the town and district to the number of seventy, met at the Rand Club, and appointed an Executive consisting of the leading medicos. The St. John Ambulance Association undertook to provide nurses, orders were placed for all necessary requirements, and the Wanderers' Pavilion, the Rand Club, and the Freemasons' Hall were placed at the disposal of the Committee for hospital purposes. In this connection the following advertisements were published :—

AMBULANCE NURSES REQUIRED.

ALL QUALIFIED NURSES OR LADIES willing to assist in case of need, please apply, personally, so soon as possible for instructions to

Dr. HUNT PHILLIPS,
70, Jeppe Street, or
Dr. F. H. SIMMONDS,
87, Jeppe St., Von Brandis Sq.

By order,
ST. JOHN AMBULANCE SOCIETY.

AMBULANCE CORPS.

VOLUNTEER STRETCHER BEARERS
required for the
AMBULANCE CORPS.

Apply to Johannesburg Ambulance Committee,
Masonic Hall,
Jeppe Street.

To the eternal fame of such ladies as still remained in Johannesburg, there was no lack of offers in reply to the first-mentioned advertisement. Ladies came willingly forward to discharge their part in the national movement; their names were duly enrolled, and as far as time and circumstances would permit, they were instructed in the principles of First Aid. Another humane feature of the crisis was the formation of a Relief Fund in aid of such as might suffer in consequence of the movement. The first subscribers comprise the following : [1]

	£
H. Eckstein & Co.	10,000
Lionel Phillips	5,000
Consolidated Goldfields	15,000
George Farrar	10,000
Lace & Thompson	5,000
Lingham Timber Syndicate, Ltd.	1,000
Abe Bailey	5,000
S. Neumann & Co.	10,000
Barnato Bros.	10,000
Fehr & Du Bois	1,000
H. B. Marshall	2,000
W. D. ("Karri") Davies	1,000
W. H. Adler	1,000
Victor Wolff	250
Johannesburg Hebrew Congregation	100

The disposal of this princely fund was entrusted to the Rev. Mr. Kelly, who discharged his duty to the general satisfaction.

With the growing tension of feeling in the streets as the day wore on, a crowd of men, estimated at ten thousand, assembled in the neighbourhood of the "Goldfields," and anxiously awaited some sign from the Committee. A new fear was in the air. The distribution of arms had been suspended, and rumour got abroad that the Reform Committee was not so well prepared after all. The thought was maddening, and there were loud and persistent calls for some one or other of the leaders to come out and explain.

"Make J. W. Leonard speak," Jameson had remarked in one of the cipher telegrams; and the eloquent Q.C., brother

[1] As this list is published it should be added that Messrs. Barnato, Bailey, and Lace eventually, on some pretexts about the application of the fund, refused to contribute the second instalment of their donations, and should therefore be credited with only half of the amounts stated.

of the National Union Chairman, now stepped into the breach. Addressing the multitude from horseback, Mr. Leonard declared that every precaution that prudence combined with capital military knowledge and political sagacity could take had been taken to ensure the safety of the town. There were, he declared, sufficient organized, armed, and equipped men ready to cope with any force the Boers might send against them. There would be a satisfactory settlement of the difficulty before long. There was a Reform Committee, which was practically a Provisional Government, consisting of the best and strongest men that could be found in the place, who were taking charge of affairs. The constitution of such a committee was inevitable. It was, however, only provisional, and there was no intention to go back on the feelings of the people of this place or to impose upon them anything of which they might not ultimately approve. Needless to say, these sentiments were cheered to the echo. There was now a Provisional Government, and the first shadow of its authority appeared almost immediately in the shape of a small detachment of mounted riflemen who rode up and stationed themselves in front of the "Goldfields" building.

This informal declaration of a Provisional Government stimulated activity amongst Government officials. A meeting was hastily summoned, and at its close the Commandant of Police came outside the Government Buildings and addressed a gathering of some hundreds, chiefly of the Boer class. Amongst other things, he said that they wanted to maintain the independence of the State. If necessary, they were prepared to resort to force of arms, though they sincerely trusted that no such ultimatum would be necessary. He counselled them all to keep their mouths shut and not create any disturbance. The Government relied upon the townspeople coming forward in case of need, and arms would be served out if necessary. *There were several thousand Boers outside the town in case of emergency*, but they trusted they would get over the difficulty without their aid.

This emphatic statement concerning the army of Boers which thus early in the crisis were massed near Johannesburg sounded as if the Government was well prepared beforehand for *something*, if not exactly for the raid.

The next official tribute to the seriousness of the situation was even more striking. The Commandant of Police agreed with the Reform Committee that to "avoid possible collisions,"

MR. CHARLES LEONARD.

he should entirely withdraw the Government police from the town. The Committee undertook to police Johnnnesburg. The first function of a Government was thus deliberately transferred to the rebels. At eight o'clock that evening the S.A.R. police, commonly known as "Zarps," mounted and foot, about one hundred strong, fully armed, were marched from the police station in the town to the police barracks on Hospital

Hill, a position of great strategic importance, which, in the event of hostilities beginning, must have been assaulted by the town forces as a first necessity. The revolutionary plan for such an emergency was a night attack.

Here the Zarps joined forces with a number of burghers who were camped in the depressions a little further along the veld.

It should be added here that the Committee performed the task which thus devolved upon it, of policing Johannesburg, to admiration. This aggregation of cosmopolites, so often described as containing some of the scum of the earth, was never governed so orderly, before or since, as during the brief reign of Uitlander authority. The Uitlander Government was prohibitionist and martinet. Canteens were closed by absolute fiat. The contents of some were bought up regardless of expense and destroyed. For a few days the chronic scandal of undetected thefts and murders in broad daylight utterly ceased. An informal court of first instance was set up under Trimble, the head of the Government Detective Department, lately extruded as not being a burgher—an absurdity which had cost the Government the resignation of the last Afrikander State Attorney. This court was summary. One man, caught red-handed breaking half-drunk into a store, was flogged; and that he did not dispute the justice of his punishment may be assumed from the fact that when brought up later to testify against the Committee's usurpation of magistracy he declined blankly to remember either why he was flogged or by whom, or anything about it except that he was uncommonly sore next day.

As the afternoon closed in, with the Government and the revolution thus openly in the lists, Mr. J. W. Leonard's oratorical gifts were again called into requisition to give the right bent to the rising fever of excitement. He addressed the "Afrikander Brigade." Some 7,000 or 8,000 persons assembled "between the chains," and Mr. Leonard spoke from the balcony of Eckstein's building. They had, he declared, borne with tyranny long enough, and the people were going to tell the tyrants once for all that they were face to face with the issue. Let them not fear men born and bred on the same soil as themselves. Other speakers followed in similar if less eloquent strain, and the assembly eventually dispersed to the strains of "Rule Britannia."

During the afternoon two remarkable messages reached the Provisional Government of Johannesburg. Mr. Eugene Marais wired an appeal from Pretoria asking the Committee to meet an unofficial deputation representative of the enlightened and educated burghers, to discuss the situation in the endeavour to effect a compromise. The request was at once complied with, and thereupon an intimation was received from the Executive Council at Pretoria stating that the deputation would have official status. President Kruger further wired requesting a palaver, to extend over twenty-four hours, "with the intention of coming to terms if possible."

This looked well. The Provisional Government willingly consented to twenty-four hours' palaver. The deputation came over from Pretoria in the evening, Mr. Marais being accompanied by Mr. Malan, son-in-law of General Joubert. The Conference took place at the "Goldfields," and it was then that Government representatives were first made acquainted with the character of the forces which were behind the Uitlander movement and of the military character of the organization. The members of the deputation were passed into the "Goldfields" building through an armed guard, and each was furnished with the password for the day. Here it may not be inappropriate to indicate the means that were taken to guard the headquarters of the revolutionary party. The building, three storeys high, has its entrance, a fine large doorway set in a framework of ornamental terra-cotta work, on the Simmonds Street side. There is another entrance from the Fox Street side, but this is by means of a narrow doorway, through a tortuous yard and a narrow passage. The main door was closed and barricaded, and so too were the ground floor and first floor windows of the whole building. Access was, therefore, possible only through the narrow back doorway in Fox Street. But it would probably have been easier for the proverbial camel to go through the eye of a needle than for a Reform Committee foe to enter openly the headquarters of the agitation. The place was converted into a citadel, impregnable save against the assaults of cannon. It was held day and night by the employees of the Goldfields Company, all armed, and supplied with sufficient ammunition and provisions to stand a siege. The corps in charge, officially enrolled as the Devil's Own, consisted of a grand body of men, not humble quill-drivers, but athletes and men who for the most part had had military training and experience. Amongst them were the "eleven fine diamonds" which were despatched from De Beers a few days before the upheaval set in. No better guard system could have been devised. The visitor had first of all to be provided with the password, which was changed every twelve hours, sometimes, especially during the summit of the crisis, more frequently The password was known only to members of the Provisional Government, and their trusty men. I was fortunate enough to have enjoyed the confidence of the revolutionary leaders, and was notified as a special favour of every change in the shibboleth for the day. So many of the secrets of the "Goldfields" have been made public since those eventful days, that no harm can now possibly be done by disclosing the character of the words which passed one from the vulgar crowd in the street into the innermost recesses of the Reformers' citadel. "Quebec" was one of the first, a curious choice; "Maxim" was another; "Citadel," a third; "Ricochet," a fourth; "Fortification," a fifth; and oh! the grim humour of it, "Doornkop" was one of the last. There were a dozen others, but they were for a few hours' duration only, and were upon disuse chased from the memory by more pressing considerations. The password had first of all to be whispered to a double guard on either side of the doorway, and repeated every few paces upon the silent demand of one or other of the armed men who lined either side of the passages and staircase from the street to the rooms where the Executive was to be found.

It was under circumstances such as these that the Government deputation were admitted to the headquarters of the Provisional Government of Johannesburg. The password for the night was, if memory serves, "Maxim." Having passed the passage and staircase and reached as far as the inquiry office, the deputation were brought to a standstill, whilst their guide announced their presence to a body of men occupying the board room. After a pause of a couple of minutes the word was passed for the deputation to enter. Messrs. Marais and Malan passed in, and there beheld the conclave, fifty of the leading men of Johannesburg, all the members of the Reform Committee in town, seated round the table.

Entering with his shirt-sleeves rolled up, black with grease to the elbow, Mr. George Farrar artlessly begged the deputation to excuse him, "as he had been unpacking rifles for some hours."

The deputation gave an account of its mission, which led one of the Committee to sum up, "In short, the Government holds out the olive branch?" and the deputation accepted that description, though Mr. Marais remarked that Jameson would undoubtedly be stopped with the full force of the Republic. If the Committee would send a deputation to Pretoria, things would be amicably settled, and they would get practically what they asked in the manifesto. The Government offered the two persons of its deputation to Johannesburg as hostages for the safety of the proposed deputation from the Reform Committee; but the Reformers politely waived that.

Messrs. Marais and Malan made it quite clear that they had been commissioned to come by the Executive, and cited as a token of the Government's pacific intentions the fact that it had that evening withdrawn the police from the town.

The meeting accepted the invitation, and Messrs. Marais and Malan returned to Pretoria by the special train which had been kept waiting. On the way to the station a call was made at the Rand Club, and there the deputation, in an incidental sort of way, were shown a Maxim.

The question in the crowded streets that night was, "Where was Jameson? Had he beaten off the Boers? Would he get through?" That was uppermost in men's minds, as they saw the Old Year out. The current of public opinion had changed marvellously during the day. In the morning the Reform Committee had repudiated Jameson, and the excited populace had upheld the repudiation. But that was twelve hours ago, and a great deal had happened since then. The Government were afraid! The Government wanted to palaver! The Government had made the first overtures! Why repudiate Jameson any longer? Why not join forces with him, and bring Oom Paul finally to his knees? These were the sentiments one heard expressed amongst the war party in the street.

Inside the "Goldfields" building the same sentiments began to take shape. On this night news came that the High Commissioner was repudiating and recalling Jameson, Mr. Chamberlain approving the High Commissioner's action. This news at first created consternation; then indignation. The very men who had found it necessary to repudiate Jameson in the morning—they, a revolutionary camarilla with no international obligations—were now furious with Her Majesty's representative for doing the like. Downing Street, like the absent, is always in the wrong.

What made things worse in the inner circle was the rooted impression already referred to, that the Colonial Office, at the last moment, had "come in." It had gone round diligently just before this that Chamberlain was behind Jameson. Chamberlain must be behind Jameson! Yet here was Chamberlain disavowing Jameson, and spiking his guns. Curses sounded loud and deep.

I chanced to be present in the "Goldfields" building at midnight at this fateful time, and discussed the situation as it now existed, with one of the Executive of the Reform Committee;

and there could be no mistaking this attitude towards the pro-, clamation.

Mr. Chamberlain's ears must have tingled for the things said in the "Goldfields" building during the moments while the Old Year passed away, and 1896 was born.

Wednesday, New Year's Day.—The Reform Committee loyally observed the compact that had been made overnight with the official deputation from Pretoria. Ere the last wassail-note was sung for a "happy New Year," Messrs. Lionel Phillips, G. Auret, Abe Bailey, and Max Langermann, a representative rather than a personally powerful deputation, left for Pretoria. Here they were not admitted to the holy of holies. Sir Theophilus Shepstone used to say that you could trust Paul Kruger's word, but you must be extraordinarily careful to tie him down exactly as to what that word was. To facilitate the elasticity on this point, which the Transvaal Government always provides for where possible, the Government appointed a Commission as a buffer between itself and the Johannesburg deputation that it had invited.

The Commission consisted of Chief Justice Kotzé, Judge Ameshoff, and Mr. Kock, a member of the Executive Council. There were mutual explanations. Friendly discussion of grievances and remedies ensued at length, and one momentous admission was made.

Mr. Phillips frankly and boldly avowed that the Reform Committee were aware of Dr. Jameson being on the border with an armed force, and had an arrangement with him "in writing" to come to their help if called on, but declared that he had crossed the border without their knowledge or consent.

Mr. Kock was staggered.

"If you have arms in your hands, and have invited Jameson, then you are rebels!" exclaimed the Councillor.

"You may call us what you like; we only ask for justice, and we shall stand by Jameson," rejoined Mr. Phillips.

Then the conversation turned on the question of stopping Jameson without bloodshed. The deputation said they had no means of stopping the Doctor; but as proof of good faith they offered their own persons as hostages that Dr. Jameson would leave Johannesburg peacefully and retire across the border, if he were allowed to come in unmolested.

"Who are the Reform Committee?" queried one of the Government Commission, and then this guileless deputation, to show, as they said, their *bonâ fides*, telegraphed to Johannesburg for a complete list of the Committee. The list was sent, and proved very useful indeed when arrests had to be made in the following week.

Having elicited all possible information, the Chief Justice declared that he and his colleagues were not authorized to make a settlement. They had simply to report to the Executive Council what had passed. The two deputations separated only to meet again in the afternoon. Then the Chief Justice produced a written statement embodying the decision of the Executive. This document was referred to at the trial of the Reform Committee, and ran as follows:—

"Sir Hercules Robinson has offered his services with a view to a peaceful settlement. The Government of the South African Republic has accepted his offer. Pending his arrival no steps will be taken against Johannesburg providing Johannesburg takes no hostile action against the Government. In terms of the proclamation recently issued by the President the grievances will be earnestly considered."

The Rand deputation believed that their cause was won. The promise just recorded was vague maybe on the larger political question, though clear on the immediate military one. But the Government Commission had done its work so as to convey the maximum of assurance with the minimum in black and white, and at the Pretoria Club a crowd of sympathetic Pretorians was assured, by Mr. Abe Bailey and the others, "We have got *all* we wanted!"

Many bumpers of champagne were drunk in honour of the event.

In these terms, with these hopes, and to these libations,

was concluded that armistice between the Reform Committee and the Government which has one simple justification.

The leaders knew that the town was not really ready to fight, for *it had not ammunition to last an hour!* As the plot was first arranged, Johannesburg was to have got in 5,000 rifles, and one million rounds, and Jameson was to have come in with a larger force and a spare rifle to every man in it. Alas! 1,000,000 cartridges means thirty tons, and all had to come in concealed in machinery! Nobody had thought of that difficulty. So when Jameson rushed, the Johannesburg leaders doubted, not for a moment his getting through, but their own plight when he did so. The armistice gave them time to turn round they thought.

Very early on Wednesday morning a couple of cyclists were despatched from the Johannesburg headquarters to communicate with the column. Colonel Rhodes scribbled a note, which, torn up and afterwards recovered from the battle-field, reads in the Green Book as follows:—

"Dear Dr.

"The rumour of massa . . . Johannesburg that started yo . . . our relief was not true. We a . . . right feeling intense. We have armed . . . a lot of men. I shall be very glad to see you. . . . not in possess . . . town. . . . men to . . . fellow . . .
"Yours ever,
"F. R."

"We will all drink a glass along . . . you
"L .."

"31st.

"11.30 Kruger has asked for . . . go over and treat armistice for . . . to . . . my view is that they are in a funk in Pretoria and they were *wrong* to agree from here.
"Dr. Jameson. "F. R."

The following is a correct restoration of the torn parts of this document:—

"Dear Doctor,—The rumour of massacre at Johannesburg that started you to our relief was not true. We are all right. Feeling intense. We

have armed quite a lot of men. I shall be very glad to see you. We are
not in possession of the town. Would you like me to send you some men
to show you the way? You are a fine fellow. Here's wishing you good
luck.

"Yours ever,
"F(RANK) R(HODES)."

"We will all drink a glass along with you.

"L(IONEL) P(HILLIPS)."

"31*st*, 11.30. Kruger has asked for some of us from here to go over
and treat for armistice. They have agreed to this. My view is that they
are in a funk at Pretoria, and they were wrong to agree from here.

"F. R."

Mr. Phillips' postscript was scribbled in pencil on Col. Rhodes' note. Col. Rhodes' second note, scribbled while the cyclists were waiting, reflects an impulse of the moment which events have turned into a thoughtful conclusion. Jameson's reply to these messages has been recorded in an earlier chapter. It, or rather the cyclists carrying it, were intercepted by the Boers.

Meanwhile, all was toil and moil this Wednesday in Johannesburg. Men were astir in the grey dawn, anxious for news of Jameson. No information was forthcoming. The Reform Committee knew nothing. Sixty hours had passed since Jameson set out on his march to the Rand, but the Reform Committee were utterly ignorant of his whereabouts. There was a vague idea, from the character of the man, that Jameson was "pushing on," and there was unbounded confidence that he would "brush aside," as it was termed, any attempt to arrest his progress. Absorbed in the colossal task of feeding, drilling and organizing Johannesburg, the Reform Committee was behindhand with any sort of Intelligence Department to bring in news from outside. Government remained in charge of the telegraph system of the country, and upon the outbreak of trouble had promptly sent confidential Hollander telegraph censors to scrutinize all messages sent to or from Johannesburg. Thus, the ordinary channels of intelligence were closed, and no effectual steps seem to have been taken to utilise, until almost too late, the splendid corps of cyclists which the Wanderers' Club might have furnished. But though news of Jameson's whereabouts was not at hand until late in the day, Johannesburg made up its mind very early to accept the situation—Jameson and all. The recall of Jameson by the High Commissioner had rather incited than discouraged the Reform Committee in adopting him. In their position of wretched impotence—for they had but 2,000 rifles, though more than ten times that number of men—the Committee determined to accept the man whom only the day before they had openly and formally repudiated. The assistance of the column must, it was given out, be accepted in defiance of all consideration, and international jurists might beat the air until they were blue in the face with exertion. Necessity knew no law, and Johannesburg's need was great and urgent. As the mouthpiece of the Reform Committee put it :—

"What was initially a grave crime on the part of Dr. Jameson, his gallant officers and brave men, becomes, by sheer stress of events, a magnificent achievement. Its success will silence all criticisms of his conduct. It will be justified by the event. He may fairly claim, if he gets through after repulsing every commando sent to stay his advance, to be the saviour of the situation, because we ardently believe that his presence here, his junction with our own forces, will end the campaign. It will compel an unconditional surrender. The Boer Government will go down, to be replaced by one of our own creation under the same flag. For the present, as desperate men, we have no time to consider the welter of international complications which may possibly arise. We have to establish ourselves in possession of the reins of Government first; reflection will have to come afterwards. There is no backward path and no returning."

It was determined to address the High Commissioner, blandly treating the Imperial Government as responsible for Jameson, and Jameson for the massing of Boers on Johannesburg, calling on Her Majesty's representative to intervene and make peace, and generally putting him, as local slang has it, "in the cart."

The following telegram was sent :—

" Lionel Phillips, George Farrar, Colonel Rhodes, J. H. Hammond, Percy Fitzpatrick, and other inhabitants, Johannesburg, to His Excellency the High Commisioner, Cape Town.

"*January 1st*, 1896.—Rumour prevalent that Doctor Jameson has crossed the border; we know nothing of this. The result of this report is massing of Boers, who are threatening Johannesburg. We presume, if Dr. Jameson has left, that it is on behalf of Imperial Government to avert bloodshed here. We invoke your immediate assistance to prevent civil war, and urge you to come up at once and establish peace."

No reply was received to this. It puzzled the recipient exceedingly, and well it might, for he had just had put into his hands a copy of the letter of invitation purporting to be signed by the very men who here denied any knowledge of Jameson's actions. Sir Hercules had not the clue to this puzzle, and he let the telegram alone.

Presently it was followed up by one still more urgent :—

" Percy Fitzpatrick, Secretary, Reform Committee, Johannesburg, to His Excellency the High Commissioner, Cape Town.

"*January* 1st.—We have absolute information that large numbers of Boers are commanded to attack Johannesburg at once, and are authorized by Commandant-General to shoot at sight all who are concerned in the present agitation. Matters are so critical that we call upon you again to intervene to protect the lives and properties of citizens who have for years agitated constitutionally for their rights."

It must be understood that the situation here depicted was fully known only to the inner circle of the Reform Committee, for, save when the full Committee were called together to impress Messrs. Marais and Malan, the direction of affairs was left in the hands of about a dozen men, who tired themselves out with perpetual session, sleeping, some of them, on the floor at the "Goldfields." The masses who thronged the streets were utterly ignorant at the time of the circumstances that had compelled the Reform deputation at Pretoria to agree to an armistice. The fiction that there were rifles sufficient to arm every man in the town was not yet exploded among the masses, and this, together with the implicit faith that Jameson would be "in" by the morrow, resulted in a great and continued rush to the several recruiting offices.

The pay was princely—10s. a day and all found. This revolution was not done "on the cheap" in any single particular. Some of the corps were billeted at the expense of the Reform Committee on the best hotels. During the morning the several corps paraded, and elected their officers, whilst bands played military airs to keep up the enthusiasm.

The scene which Johannesburg presented on this memorable New Year's day will not soon be forgotten by those who looked on at the strange medley.

By noon it was given out at the "Goldfields" that for the present no more recruits would be enlisted, or rifles served out. Then it was that the ugly truth—creeping outwards already from the inner circle—began to dawn on the people at large. The Committee were short of firearms! Attempts were made to reassure the people, but in vain.

The crowds that but now were all enthusiasm began to despond, and to throw blame on the leaders.

The temper of the crowd began to look ugly, when it was diverted for the moment by an incident which looked like "business." The outposts reported that about 150 Boers were approaching, and were likely to strike the camp at two o'clock. A strong detachment came into town and escorted a couple of Maxims out of town towards Langlaagte, in which direction everybody looked for signs of Jameson's approach.

With the arrival of the time for the evening meetings the spirits of the masses rose again. At seven o'clock that evening first definite news of the fighting was brought into town by cyclists, and a large body of the Uitlander forces, mounted and infantry, were despatched in the direction where Jameson was expected to show himself. Simultaneously it was known that the Boer forces were closing in on the town from various sides.

In the nick of time to reassure the Committee, Mr. Lionel Phillips and the other members of the deputation returned to Johannesburg. They arrived about seven in the evening. The Reform Committee met, and readily acquiesced in the terms the deputation had made with the Government at Pretoria. It had been agreed that a member of the Reform Committee should go out and convince Jameson that the armistice was no Government fiction. Accordingly Mr. Lace was sent on this not wholly grateful errand.

The stir at headquarters was not lost upon the packed street outside the "Goldfields," and in response to repeated calls Mr Lionel Phillips, shortly before ten o'clock at night, stepped out on to the balcony and addressed the multitude. He said he had just returned from Pretoria, where he had interviewed a Commission appointed by the Government to see if they could not arrange matters amicably. They were informed that Her Majesty's High Commissioner had been invited to come up in order to act as mediator. He had informed the commission that they intended to stand by Dr. Jameson—(immense cheering)—who had come all this way with his brave little band for their succour. If necessary, they were prepared to continue the movement they had seen fit to commence with their guns. (More cheering.)

These declarations were received with the utmost enthusiasm. In answer to shouts for Dr. Jameson, Mr. Phillips stated that he was within fifteen miles of Johannesburg. Mr. Phillips called for three cheers for Dr. Jameson, and Mr. J. W. Leonard called for three cheers for Mr. Phillips, and jubilation reigned in Johannesburg; while eighteen miles away the man they were cheering suddenly bivouacked beside the "pan" amid the dropping fire of the Boers.

Such irony of events does not need the bitter embellishment of the story that the ammunition sent from the Pretoria arsenal to replenish the Boers at Krugersdorp, who were running short, actually went through Johannesburg in the train which carried the Rand deputation back in apparent triumph from the capital. As a matter of fact, some ammunition went the day before, along with Messrs. Marais and Malan, Field-Cornet Van Wyk and others, sent from Krugersdorp to procure it.

It was thus the Government deputation, not the Rand one, that travelled in the ammunition train; and those who had guns covered them with their macintoshes, fearing that the presence of ammunition might be discovered.

The ammunition which really replenished the Boers when they were running short on Thursday was not taken through Johannesburg at all, but sent by wagon across country. So says the officer who took it.

And so that Wednesday evening, the first evening of 1896, the Uitlander cause was cheered in Johannesburg and lost at Krugersdorp, and nobody knew.

Chapter XIII

THE STORY OF THE PROCLAMATION

IN Cape Town, Monday, December 30th, was a day of strange, undefined tension of feeling, through the general expectancy strained towards Johannesburg, not towards the border, and although the actual news was known to nobody that day beyond some half-dozen people. So unromantic a person as Sir Gordon Sprigg confessed to " presentiments." But even Mr. Hofmeyr, who was presently to become counsellor-in-chief by telegram to the Pretoria Government, had as yet heard nothing. The writer had been pestering the leader of Dutch Cape Colony for an interview or utterance of some kind in sympathy with the Uitlander demand for citizenship ; and late on Monday evening, the town being full of vague rumours of action at Johannesburg, Mr. Hofmeyr was drawn to the *Cape Times* Office for news. Owing to the block on the wires the evening telegrams had not yet come in ; one of which, much later, brought the incredible information, and to this alone it was due that there could be pumped out of the reticent Bond leader even the few guarded words of sympathetic interest in the Uitlander grievances which duly appeared in print next morning as an interview, concluding as follows :—

His views on the franchise demand Mr. Hofmeyr has expressed years ago. He favoured a compromise then, but it found no support at Pretoria. Now it would be useless to offer the compromise which then might have satisfied legitimate aspirations.

On reading this over Mr Hofmeyr found the tone of it expressive only of one side of his feelings in this difficult question, in which he felt himself, he confessed, pulled both ways; and he desired the addition in clear terms that in spite of the manner in which his efforts on behalf of the Transvaal had been received, and though he regretted that no statesmanlike compromise had been arrived at, the Transvaal still kept his strong sympathies and affection. " Blood is thicker than water."

The point being put that the blood of many young Afrikander " Uitlanders " was closer to many Cape families even than the blood of the Boers, Mr. Hofmeyr admitted the fact. " But then," he said, smiling, " how if those Afrikander ' Uitlanders ' also found that blood was thicker than water?"

" But they are solid with the other ' Uitlanders,' that is just the point," it was rejoined to this; and the question added:

" Suppose war broken out, Mr. Hofmeyr, what would you yourself do?"

" God knows! . . . Try to get peace made as soon as possible, I suppose, like last time," said Mr. Hofmeyr.

And not one word could be got out of him.

Mr. Hofmeyr gone, enter one of the two Johannesburg emissaries, visibly excited, mysterious as to the reason, but urgent in the same question, " Have you any news? Enter later the Imperial Secretary, looking ill with anxiety, but constant even then to the habitual officialism which deems it a sin to tell a newspaper anything except what it already knows. His was the same question, " Have you any special news?" which, by now, it was possible to answer, and from him was eventually obtained the authority to state that the High Commissioner had repudiated and recalled Jameson, an item which accordingly accompanied the brief announcement in Tuesday's *Cape Times* of what was there called " the almost incredible fact, presumably due to a brave, wild, mad, foolish impulse," and to exaggerated rumours from Johannesburg.

These possible excuses for Jameson, by the way, for one must speak by the card in these matters, were no part of what Sir Graham Bower authorized or suggested. The author heard no word from him or any Imperial official during the crisis otherwise than deploring and disapproving of Jameson's action.

Enter again, still later on that well-remembered evening, the Johannesburg emissary aforesaid, who was provoked to passionate remonstrance by the tenor of a half-finished leading article begun at the very first receipt of the news, in which, while it was remarked that "the first shot fired in the Transvaal must needs make many people round its fringes, alike in Colonies and Republic, hard to hold," yet "through all such events the High Commissioner's duty is to stand high above the quarrels—even the just quarrels—of the Uitlanders, for it is to him that all South Africa will look to hold the balance even and to mould the united statesmanship of South Africa into the great settlement which must inevitably ensue upon the struggle." To this, and much more which need not be here repeated in the way of argument against the Imperial Power allowing itself to be in any way implicated in Jameson's mad attempt, the burden of the Johannesburg leader's answer was: "Then all I can say is—the Imperial Power will lose South Africa." Jameson, he admitted, had precipitated and upset the plans of Rhodes and the plans of everybody, but while admitting all this, the Johannesburg man declared that Jameson would undoubtedly carry the whole thing through if the Imperial Government would let him, and the policy of repudiation and recall would never, he declared, be forgiven by the Uitlanders.

It was hard to see anything clear in that first rush of surprise, but one thing did seem clear to the writer, and he clung to it accordingly. Though heart and soul with the Johannesburg Revolution if only the Uitlanders would make it, he could not see that the Imperial Government had the right to interfere and make it for them. The Johannesburg leader left the office unconvinced and fuming.

The story of how the news came to Cape Town, and how it was received by various people from various points of view is one which can best be illustrated by concrete example and personal reminiscences; hence these recollections of one night at a Newspaper Office, bringing across the stage as it does so conveniently a quick succession of figures typical of the different forces engaged in the crisis. Let me add that at the *Cape Times* Office this news, that is, the Jameson part of it, and the much later discovery of Mr. Rhodes' full relation to that part, was as much a surprise that evening as it was to Ministers and to Cape Town generally when it appeared in print next morning. Let me add also this, that the foregoing conversations, joined to the imperfect knowledge at the time of what might have led to Jameson's act, give all the key that any candid person will require to the following telegram which the writer addressed next day to the *Star*, Johannesburg, after hearing of the coming proclamation :—

"You must expect, and not misunderstand, a proclamation putting Jameson formally in the wrong. Imperial authorities have no other course. Don't let this weaken or divide *you*. This merely for your information."

It was merely a private reading of the situation exchanged between two journalists, perfectly understood by the recipient, and conveying a common-sense hint which proved of some small use in the confused brouhaha at Johannesburg. Why it should have been seized on by the Transvaal Government as a great find, and immortalized in a Green Book, and even debated in the Cape Parliament, is a mystery only to be explained by the epoch of suspicious unreason which the crisis produced. As all this was done, the matter is just mentioned here.

December 31*st*, 1895, *in Cape Town.* — At Government House a great part of Tuesday was occupied by the great fight about the proclamation. Abundant evidence came to hand during the morning to show what passion and indignation the news of the raid had evoked wherever it was known in Dutch South Africa. A message from the Acting President of the Free State referred to Jameson's cool reply to the Commandant of Marico, and expressed anxiety for the "peace and welfare of South Africa." The Free State, in fact, was up in arms. 1,600 burghers were commandeered to take up a position about sixteen miles on the Free State side of the Vaal, and mounted expresses scoured the country and the border, and it may be recalled as a significant fact that in one district twice the number of burghers commandeered responded to the call.

But it was in the person of Mr. Hofmeyr that Dutch South Africa really marched into Government House that Tuesday morning.

Mr. Rhodes had called and assured Sir Hercules that Dr. Jameson acted without his authority, adding something about the stopping telegram and the cut wires, and offering to resign if either Mr. Chamberlain or Sir Hercules thought it necessary.

Mr. Hofmeyr came up scarcely knowing what to think. He openly suspected the attitude of Mr. Rhodes towards Jameson, and covertly, perhaps, that of the Imperial Government. Indeed, he has since confessed that what cleared and composed his mind in this matter was simply the transparently candid personality of one man—Sir Hercules Robinson. Mr. Rhodes had said a year before that only one man had enough prestige with Dutch South Africa to be fit to cope with the coming racial crisis and save a war. This one man was now to make good the words—if not quite to the purpose their author had dreamed of.

It may be said that Lord Rosmead, in South African politics, is now a man of one idea. But the point is that that one idea was, for the beginning of 1896, the right one—the only feasible one. Mr. Chamberlain had to come to see it; Mr. Rhodes saw it before and probably sees it now again; perhaps it will dawn some day even on Lord Rosmead's own countrymen in the colonies, to whom to-day he is even as Mr. Gladstone once was in the Jingo Party.

The writer had the opportunity to see this old and ill man in the thick of the crisis. His was the coolest head there.

"It is almost impossible to know what to do next," he remarked to a visitor at almost the most puzzling moment of all; "but I have an old formula which I have always found come out well in the end—and that is, 'Don't trouble about a "policy," but do the thing that you see to be *right*.'"

The Right Honourable Sir Hercules George Robert Robinson, Bart., G.C.M.G., lately created Baron Rosmead of Rosmead in Ireland and Tafelberg in South Africa, has exceeded the Psalmist's limit of years, and spent more than half of it in viceregal functions. He has represented the Queen in the West Indies, Hong Kong, Ceylon, New South Wales, New Zealand, and South Africa, but his chief work has been done under the shadow of the grand old mountain from which he has chosen part of his title; and the distinctive note of that work has been to gain and keep for the Queen's Government the confidence of those Afrikanders to whose language that title pays a delicate compliment. He was Governor and High Commissioner during the stormiest years of South African history, and the Transvaal has never forgotten what a good interpreter he was of the spirit of fairness and magnanimity which dictated the retrocession of the Republic. As Mr. Rhodes became a power, and struck the self-same Afrikander note in his policy harmonising with the self-same British Colonial patriotism, the two men seemed to be working perfectly together. Both had a share in keeping open the north, though it was Mr. Rhodes who alone had the means and the impetus to add "Rhodesia" to the Empire. Both seemed at one for years in the policy which made this process of indirect Colonial expansion palatable to the Dutch, and indeed Sir Hercules Robinson got into sore trouble with Downing Street in 1889 by emphasizing, in a farewell speech after nine years of office, the half truth that there was only place left for the Imperial Factor in South Africa in its form of Colonialism, not in its form of direct Imperialism. In other words, it was the Rhodes kind of Imperialism, the kind implied in his great British-Colonial Company, that would be the real force to meet and conquer the force of Anti-British Republicanism on its own ground.

When Sir Henry Loch had to be replaced, the Colonial Office had come round to see what Sir Hercules meant in 1889, just as Mr. Rhodes and others have come, since that again, to see more clearly the other side of the shield, the direct Imperial side. But it was notorious that only the insistence of Mr Rhodes made the Colonial Office insist strongly enough to drag Sir Hercules back to South Africa, the "Grave of Reputations," from his well-earned leisure. There were obvious objections to the appointment, and it was Mr. Chamberlain, destined soon to become the new Governor's chief, and later his convert, who voiced them in Parliament. Sir Hercules having retired into private life had been elected to various boards of public companies, and of course all his South African directorships and interests had to be given up when he was thrust back into Government House. As it was Mr. Rhodes who pressed the Colonial Office to appoint him, so it was Mr. Rhodes who pressed his old co-worker not to decline. It is even whispered that Mr. Rhodes, fearing that he might now seem to have grown too masterful at the Cape since Sir Hercules and he had last worked together, wrote to Sir Hercules impulsively promising that if they ever came to loggerheads he would admit *ipso facto* that he must be in the wrong. They did come to loggerheads, for to Sir Hercules fell the hard task of remaining coldly consistent to Mr. Rhodes' own policy while Mr. Rhodes himself floundered in an impossible departure from it. "Don't altogether desert the Doctor" was Mr. Rhodes' cry, when once his friend had started on the perilous march. But that was just what Her Majesty's representative had to do.

Five minutes with Sir Hercules Robinson dissipated from Mr. Hofmeyr's mind the ugly dream of any complicity on his part. But Mr. Hofmeyr at once made it clear that the repudiation by the Imperial authority must be made far more public and unequivocal than by mere messages sent through Mr. Newton and Sir Jacobus de Wet. The Bond leader enforced this view with the trenchant decisiveness which he can show on critical occasions. He scouted the idea that Jameson would stop for the messages, and pointed out that the public would not know of these. There must be a proclamation repudiating Jameson in the name of the Queen, and calling on all British subjects to hold aloof from him. The moment such a proclamation was suggested it was seen to be a necessity, a logical sequel to the Imperial disavowal of the raiders. Sir Hercules called the Imperial Secretary, sat down with Mr. Hofmeyr, and proceeded to draft the proclamation. Mr. Rhodes had gone out of town again, but Mr. Schreiner, the Attorney-General, approved of the draft on behalf of the Colonial Cabinet. Meanwhile, however, representatives of English, as well as Dutch, Cape Colony had made their appearance. Mr. Hofmeyr had won ready hearing when he described what would be the feeling of *his* kindred; but it was impossible to ignore the somewhat different sentiments which the first news of Jameson's act had aroused among South African Britishers everywhere.

Remember that it was universally assumed at that time that Jameson had moved upon some definite intelligence which might justify him. Remember, too, that for weeks the provocation had been thought of as coming from Pretoria to Johannesburg, not from Jameson to Pretoria. Remember, too, that it was supposed that at that moment the Uitlanders had struck, were striking, or were about to strike, a blow for rights which commanded general sympathy. Even those Englishmen who most shook their heads over the immediate outlook, and who admitted that the Imperial Government could not back Jameson, were not prepared for such extreme action on the other side as the practical outlawing of the man in the Queen's name, accompanied by an injunction to the Queen's subjects to stand aside, and apparently abandon their own justifiable hostility to the Government, simply because of Jameson's action.

Dr. Harris, and subsequently Mr. Rhodes, whom he fetched post haste back to town from Rondebosch, urged on some such grounds as these that the proclamation should not be issued at all. Failing that, they set themselves at least to gain time. Mr. Rhodes exclaimed again and again, very much moved, "It's making an outlaw of the Doctor!" His line was, that since his friend had broken away and the deed was now past recall, he should be given a fair field, and perhaps all would yet be well. He took the same line with his colleagues in the Cabinet. But in arguing against the proclamation *in toto* these gentlemen went too far; for they cut at the whole position taken up by His Excellency. Repudiation of Jameson was an international, honourable obligation. Anything else would not only have implied complicity, it would have been complicity. And of repudiation by the Queen a Royal Proclamation, once suggested, was seen to be a logical *sequitur*. In spite of all that Mr. Rhodes could say, therefore, Sir Hercules remained firm, and the process of drafting, approving, copying, signing, sealing, publishing, and telegraphing the document proceeded as expeditiously as such things can in Government Offices.

A small part of the purpose in which these gentlemen made so little headway was achieved, as it happens, by another agency, acting quite independently of them. Naturally the journalists heard of the coming proclamation as soon as the publicists, and one journalistic caller, known to Sir Hercules Robinson, it may be said, as one who cared for the honour of England considerably more than for any conceivable interest of Mr. Rhodes or of Johannesburg, had the privilege of a conversation with him about the draft proclamation.

This caller's criticism was directed solely to that part of the proclamation which might be considered as interfering in the internal affairs of the Republic. It was one thing to proclaim Jameson's external intervention. It was quite another thing to use words tantamount to an internal interference between the Transvaal Government and certain Transvaal inhabitants. The Imperial policy towards the Johannesburg movement *per se* had been, so far, one of strict impartiality. It could neither promise the Uitlanders support nor could it officiously bid them sit down under their grievances. It might intervene to part the combatants, as the Power mainly responsible for the peace of South Africa; or to prevent whichever side won from proceeding to extreme action against the other; but the conversation of the Johannesburg leaders then in Cape Town sufficed to show how deeply Johannesburg would resent any act on the part of the Imperial Government that could fairly be described as first leaving the Uitlanders to work out their own salvation against an armed Government, and then stepping in to divide and paralyse their ranks the moment they began to do it.

Sir Hercules weighed the English side, as it may be called, as gravely and fairly as he had weighed the Dutch. Unfortunately, it was too late to keep raid and revolution wholly distinct, and the proclamation, as finally published, did to some extent discourage British subjects from abetting either. One sentence, however, which was especially obnoxious to this objection disappeared from the draft. It was the last, which called upon British subjects even to abstain from demonstrations or any action calculated to disturb public order. It was undeniable that an injunction which vetoed even the calling of a public meeting would be, in spirit, a breach of the Convention.

Perhaps, in practice, the alteration amounted to little, for Johannesburg would be less influenced by the exact wording than by the general tenor of the Bull issued against their rash ally. But, as it happened, it was this alteration which led to a delay, afterwards the subject of bitter controversy.

The idea of the proclamation was Mr. Hofmeyr's; the first draft had been approved by Mr. Hofmeyr, and it was its prospective issue that led him to co-operate with the High Commissioner in the advice which he was now proffering over the telegraph to Pretoria, particularly as regards the acceptance of the High Commissioner's mediation.

The Imperial Secretary, therefore, felt bound to give Mr. Hofmeyr an opportunity of objecting to the alteration, and as Mr. Hofmeyr could not be found for some little time a delay of about an hour and a half was caused.

That is the full explanation of an incident which has been

absurdly exaggerated. A verbatim copy of the proclamation was telegraphed at 4.20 p.m. to the Acting President of the Free State and to the British Agent at Pretoria. It was published in a *Cape Gazette Extraordinary* at a quarter to six. It was communicated by the British Agent to President Kruger some time after eight, and about the same time telegraphed to the Reform Committee, Johannesburg, who may be regarded as the persons mainly addressed by it. Sir Jacobus got a copy through to Jameson on Thursday morning.

When, late that evening, a telegram arrived from President Kruger, evidently acting on advice received from Mr. Hofmeyr earlier in the day, asking for a proclamation to be issued, and bringing to remembrance a proclamation of his own which helped "to damp the trek" to Mashonaland in April, 1891, the High Commissioner was able to reply that the President's wishes had been anticipated.

PROCLAMATION

By His Excellency the Right Honourable Sir HERCULES GEORGE ROBERT ROBINSON, Baronet, a member of Her Majesty's Most Honourable Privy Council, Knight Grand Cross of the Most Distinguished Order of St. Michael and St. George, Governor and Commander-in-Chief of Her Majesty's Colony of the Cape of Good Hope in South Africa, and of the territories and dependencies thereof, Governor of the territory of British Bechuanaland, and Her Majesty's High Commissioner, etc., etc., etc.

Whereas it has come to my knowledge that certain British subjects, said to be under the leadership of Dr. Jameson, have violated the territory of the South African Republic, and have cut telegraph wires, and done various other illegal acts:

And whereas the South African Republic is a friendly State in amity with Her Majesty's Government:

And whereas it is my desire to respect the independence of the said State:

Now, therefore, I do hereby command the said Dr. Jameson, and all persons accompanying him, to immediately retire from the territory of the South African Republic on pain of the penalties attached to their illegal proceedings.

And I do further hereby call upon all British subjects in the South African Republic to abstain from giving the said Dr. Jameson any countenance or assistance in his armed violation of the territory of a friendly State.

GOD SAVE THE QUEEN.

Given under my hand and seal this 31st day of December, 1895.
HERCULES ROBINSON,
High Commissioner.

By command of His Excellency the High Commissioner,
GRAHAM BOWER,
Imperial Secretary.

Owing to the extraordinary block and breakdown which, at this crisis, affected alike the wires in South Africa and the cables to England, it was not till Wednesday morning that Sir Hercules Robinson received a message sent by Mr. Chamberlain in the middle of the day before, which, repeating the warning to Mr. Rhodes about the Chartered Company paying the piper, is also interesting from the hint it gives as to what circumstances might have been taken to excuse the entrance of a force; a hint fully consonant with the attitude of the Imperial Government as explained in Chapter IV. Here is an extract:—

"You should represent to Mr. Rhodes the true character of Dr. Jameson's action in breaking into a foreign State which is in friendly treaty relations with Her Majesty, in time of peace. It is an act of war, or rather of filibustering. If the Government of the South African Republic had been overthrown, or had there been anarchy at Johannesburg, there might have been some shadow of excuse for this unprecedented act. If it can be proved that the British South Africa Company set Dr. Jameson in motion, or were privy to his marauding action, Her Majesty's Government would at once have to face a demand that the Charter should be revoked and the Corporation dissolved."

Sir Hercules read this message to Mr. Rhodes when the latter called at Government House during Wednesday morning. In doing so Sir Hercules was urgent with Mr. Rhodes that he should make a public disavowal of all complicity with Jameson, but to all such advances, whether from the High Commissioner, or from Mr. Hofmeyr, or from Cabinet colleagues, Mr. Rhodes was sullenly impenetrable; his note to the Imperial Secretary—"Jameson has gone in without my orders"—represented the utmost point of repudiation that he would go to either to save himself or his cherished Company, and in all the mutual recriminations which followed upon so many sides, it is refreshing to notice that Mr. Rhodes never yielded to the temptation to emphasize the long series of messages which, as we now know, were sent to stop the actual raid, nor could Jameson be led, on his side, to emphasize the degree of Mr. Rhodes' complicity in the plans originally made for a raid of some sort. The two friends have been strikingly true to each other.

Mr. Chamberlain was evidently not quite clear how to take Mr. Rhodes' somewhat meagre disavowal of responsibility. On Wednesday he cabled:—

"Glad to hear of Rhodes' repudiation of Jameson, who must be mad. I see no need for Rhodes to resign. . . . Of course the B.S.A. Company, however innocent, will have to make amends for this outrage. . . . Take all steps you may think necessary in this crisis. I have full confidence in your discretion. The chief things are promptitude and vigour."

At the same time Mr. Chamberlain was cornering the British South Africa Company on the same point, and by way of encouragement to the Directors to commit themselves, informed them that Mr. Rhodes had repudiated Jameson and offered to resign as Cape Premier, but that he appeared to him, Mr. Chamberlain, to have done his best to counteract the mischief. On Thursday Mr. Chamberlain cabled to Sir Hercules to "take strongest line with Jameson, whose continued refusal to obey would be an act of rebellion. Rhodes must send message to similar effect, otherwise B.S.A. Company will be held responsible for Jameson's action."

During all the time of suspense, while news was momentarily expected of a collision between the column and the Boers, the burden of Mr. Rhodes' representations to Sir Hercules Robinson was "Go up to Pretoria." As we have seen, much weight had been placed by the confederates on Mr. Rhodes' undertaking to press this advice. Events had not fallen out quite as had been counted upon, but there was all the more need for the High Commissioner to get his countrymen out of their pickle. Chief Justice Kotzé, of the Transvaal, an astute councillor in whom Afrikander patriotism and reform sympathies are subject to a passion for intrigue which seems to flourish on legal soil, strongly opposed the acceptance of such mediation by the Transvaal Government as a sign of fear, and it was some time before Mr. Hofmeyr committed himself at all strongly to the favourable view. However, he did so at last.

The High Commissioner received, in the course of Wednesday, two telegrams from the Reform Committee invoking him "to prevent civil war, and to come up at once to establish peace," and again calling upon him "to intervene to protect the lives and properties of citizens who have for years agitated constitutionally for their rights." The Reform Committee messages, however, were received by Sir Hercules with some reserve, as they were accompanied with expressions disclaiming any connection with Jameson's reported movement, and presuming that Jameson must be acting on behalf of the Imperial Government, an attitude which, at the moment, His Excellency was much puzzled how to reconcile with a copy of the historic letter of invitation which had just been put into his hands by the Cape Town confederates.[1]

However, whatever was the position of the Reform Committee, the duty of the High Commissioner to offer his services as peacemaker was dependent only on the discovery of a decent occasion. If Johannesburg would only do something, however small, on its own account, so that it could be treated as a threatening factor to the public peace!

As an onlooker at Cape Town cynically remarked: "Those Johannesburg fellows might at least shoot one Zarp" (*Anglice*,

[1] When Jameson "rushed," the Cape Town confederates cabled a copy of the letter to the *Times*, London, where it appeared January 1st. The date, left blank in original, was filled in as December 20th by Dr. Wolff.

policeman). The Johannesburg rebels did not shoot a Zarp, but their usurpation of the Government of Johannesburg became sufficiently overt to lead the special correspondent of the *Cape Times* to telegraph that the Reform Committee had declared itself the Provisional Government. As a matter of fact, the proclamation to this effect was set up, but never printed. However, it was upon this intimation on Wednesday morning that the High Commissioner directed Sir Jacobus de Wet to see the President at once, and ask if he would wish Her Majesty's representative to come to Pretoria and co-operate towards a peaceful settlement. At six o'clock that afternoon came the following reply :—

"I accept Your Excellency's offer, delivered to me by Sir Jacobus de Wet, to come to Pretoria to assist to prevent further bloodshed, as I have received information that Dr. Jameson has not given effect to your orders, and has fired on my burghers."

To any one who knew President Kruger this agitated message at once betrayed that he was by no means certain of the event. So far, indeed, his only messages from the Commandants engaged had a formidable ring about them. The column, spread out in the formation which has been described, looked larger than it really was, and the carts and artillery increased the threatening look. The burghers were still retiring before the column.

When Mr. Rhodes heard of Oom Paul's message it seemed as if the clouds lifted. Jameson, after all, was going to pull everything through ; the burghers were retiring before him ; he would reach Johannesburg, which would rise like one man, and then, when the lists were pitched, the High Commissioner would arrive to bid both sides lay down their arms and effect a settlement which would bring about all that had been counted on. "Kruger's in a tight place," he exclaimed. "He comes crying to the High Commissioner, 'Please come and help me; Jameson has been firing on my poor burghers.'" So he remarked to a friend. To the High Commissioner he urgently tendered the advice that he should start at once, should order a special train that very evening. Sir Hercules, however, decided to leave the following evening, and cabled for Mr. Chamberlain's approval.

Late the next morning official intimation reached Government House that Jameson had surrendered.

The writer remembers vividly seeing Mr. Rhodes issue from Government House just after this news had been received. In Cape Town it was still unknown.

His face was horribly changed from the exultant man of the night before.

He paused to speak, checked himself, jumped into a cart which was waiting to drive him to Rondebosch, then, as he started, turned the same dreadful face over his shoulder and jerked out in an odd, falsetto voice that he sometimes has:—
" Well, there is a little history being made; that is all."

It was a most mournful, characteristically English attempt to carry off lightly the sudden, crushing ruin of a career. The bitterest ingredient in the cup just then was the black uncertainty as to the fate of Jameson.

There was at first some idea of Mr. Hofmeyr accompanying the High Commissioner northwards. Mr. Hofmeyr's own attitude to the proposal was uncertain for some time. Sir Hercules had asked Mr. Hofmeyr on Tuesday. Local Afrikanders were anxious that he should have a hand in the settlement, and one at least of the Johannesburg emissaries in Cape Town evidently regarded his moderating influence as an Uitlander asset. The special train on Thursday evening was boarded by Mr. Charles Leonard, of the National Union, and Mr. Graaff, a prominent Bondman, member of the Legislative Council and friend of Mr. Hofmeyr. They begged Sir Hercules to press Mr. Hofmeyr to come, declaring that he would yield to pressure. Sir Hercules did telegraph to Mr. Hofmeyr, *en route*, inviting him to come up by next night's mail train, remarking that he had never doubted the loyalty and peaceful co-operation of the Afrikander population, and adding that his own desire from the first to have Mr. Hofmeyr's help was strengthened by finding that he enjoyed the confidence of the Chairman of the National Union. Mr. Hofmeyr's answer was as follows :—

"Thanks kind wire. Owing to physical complaint I shall go only when supreme necessity arises, which is not yet. Am preparing reply to Chamberlain's wire, which I will send you, and in which intend pressing for searching inquiry into working of Charter and genesis Jameson expedition."

In announcing his departure the High Commissioner telegraphed to President Kruger :—

"I earnestly entreat Your Honour, for the sake of humanity, as well as for the sake of South Africa in general, to arrange for a suspension of hostilities till my arrival."

This, as we have seen, was done. Having spent Friday and Saturday in the train, Sir Hercules Robinson arrived at Pretoria on the evening of the 4th January. What state of things he found there we shall see presently. But meanwhile we must return to Johannesburg. We have only seen the "boom in revolutions": we have to study the "slump."

Chapter XIV

A "SLUMP" IN REVOLUTIONS

THURSDAY, January 2nd. — The town was early astir on the following day, Thursday, January 2nd. This was the day when Jameson was to enter the beleaguered city like a conquering hero. And Johannesburg was going to give him a reception that would thrill a continent. All the brigades and all the corps such as were not on duty at the various camps on the outskirts had been ordered to muster at nine a.m. Besides the Town Bodyguard, a thousand and more strong, there were the Afrikander Corps, 1,100 strong, to which Mr. F. Eckstein had presented a flag—Transvaal colours—the previous night; there was the Scottish Brigade, reported to be 1,300 strong, and corps and brigades representative of the Irish, the Welsh, Australians, Americans, the Natal Horse, West Countrymen, North Countrymen, and so forth and so on.

All were to assemble at nine a.m.; the Reform Committee were to take formal control and the bands were to play Jameson and his heroes in. The ladies got ready bouquets to shower on them. It should be "roses, roses all the way." That was the programme.

Men were up early, and such as were not attached to the military organization betook themselves to the rise at Fordsburg, which commands a magnificent view of the undulating country stretching out towards Krugersdorp. The position was in charge of a troop of Horse, and a Maxim gun scientifically placed gave a business-like appearance to the scene.

Alas! during the morning hours when Jameson's triumphal pomp was a-preparing, he was fighting for dear life under the ridge of Doornkop; his men had strayed into a rat-trap, and the Boers were "potting" the rats at pleasure. Soon the Hottentot "tanta's" apron would go up at Farmer Brink's out house, and all be over.

Very early on Thursday morning there did reach the "Goldfields" offices an authentic word from Jameson. His second message, the verbal one sent by a trooper after the miserable night bivouac under fire, was successfully brought in between six and seven. Colonel Rhodes, who was sleeping on the floor, was the only man in authority on the premises.

"*The Doctor's all right, but he says now he would like some men sent out to meet him.*"

Such was the message.

It might be wrong; it might be a breach of the armistice; it might be bad policy; it might be madness; but Colonel Rhodes could only send one answer.

He jumped up, found Bettington, and in as short a time as was needed to get the men together Bettington's Horse—meaning in this case some hundred and twenty mounted men with rifles—started off westward in the general direction where the firing was supposed to be located.

Meanwhile the Reform Committee was being got together, and Colonel Rhodes reported what he had done. Immediately there was a tremendous outcry. Johannesburg had made an armistice. It was not really in a position to resist attack. Jameson was responsible for exposing it to that risk before it was ready. A member of the Reform Committee had gone out, and was perhaps even now meeting Jameson with a copy of the proclamation and a distinct explanation why the Committee could not openly assist him. His messenger did not clearly say that he required assistance. Evidently he was fighting his way in. The small number of men who had been sent could be of no real help to the column, while Johannesburg would be damned with the Boer Government as much by the sending of 120 as by the sending of 2,000. The idea of sending a larger force, on the other hand, and thus taking away the defences of the town at the very time that they were defying the Boer Government by breach of the armistice, was equally untenable.

Either now Jameson was coming in without their help, in which case their arrangement with Pretoria made their leaders hostages for his harmless return, while the Government had practically promised to give them all they wanted; or in the alternative, if Jameson could not come in, the proclamation and the Reform Committee's messenger gave him a way out of the dilemma. He could surrender honourably to the proclamation. There was a vague idea that the hostage arrangement with the Government would operate in this case, equally as in the case of Jameson's success, to secure him a safe conduct outside the country. The upshot of it all was that twenty minutes after the troop had started a mounted messenger rode after it and stopped it by order of the Committee. The troop was then among the mines at the outskirts of the town, and though the Government got wind of its having sallied forth, the incident was successfully passed off as a measure for keeping order among the Kaffirs at one of the mines, and in the trials which followed the one tentative effort or impulse of Johannesburg to send out help to Jameson was, of course, the one thing above all others which the prisoners could not afford to avow.

Jameson, the reader will bear in mind, surrendered between eight and nine o'clock. It may well be argued that if Bettington's troop had known just exactly where to go, and had successfully evaded the vigilance of the Boers in reaching a point within earshot or eyeshot of the column, that surrender would not have taken place when it did. They would just have been in time to save it. What the after result would have been is another question. Here the fact is merely put on record that Jameson did, at the eleventh hour, ask help from Johannesburg, that the decision to give that help was countermanded, and that the Reform Committee is responsible for this decision. It should be added that Mr. Lionel Phillips and other prominent leaders readily assume the burden of justifying the decision, and indeed of showing that no other decision could have been justified for a moment in the difficult circumstances; while one of those clearest upon the point was Jameson's own brother, whose message telling the Doctor to wait for the signal had been the most emphatic, and whose sense of duty to Johannesburg and to his colleagues first and foremost rose above every other consideration at that painful juncture.

The rumour that ammunition had been run out to Krugersdorp by the railway to be fired against Jameson, being bruited about on Thursday morning, caused great excitement. A Reform Committee deputation represented to the "Government Commission"—a few officials who now alone represented the Govern-hierarchy in the town—that "unless Government stop the use of the railway line in the direction of Krugersdorp they cannot restrain their people any longer, and they will not be answerable for the consequences." Government made no response.

It has often been asked why Johannesburg had not even the enterprise to break up this line, and so interfere with the Boer connections. No armistice need have stopped *that*!

As a matter of fact, an attempt was made, but, as with so much else, not soon enough and not thoroughly enough. A man went out and put a dynamite cartridge on the line, but bungled the job, and the little damage done was soon repaired.

The hours wore away, and still no sign of Jameson. The most powerful field-glass could detect nothing in the far distance save three rising wreaths of smoke, such as battery-house chimneys might send up. As no batteries were working, but one construction could be placed upon this. Jameson had, of course, beaten the Boers off, and was resting his men preparatory to riding into town. One report, which was repeated with great authority, and purported to be the result of a reconnaissance, said that Jameson had lost 100 men, including Sir John Willoughby, but was forcing his way through all opposition.

News, as it happened, was more obtainable in town than

towards Langlaagte. Having the invaders completely hemmed in and at their mercy, the Government had no objection to driblets of news going along the wires to Johannesburg; and the telegraph agencies published scraps as rapidly as received. The afternoon wore on, however, before anything beyond scraps about the earlier incidents of the fighting had come credibly to hand. However, those scraps were enough to change eager hope to anxiety.

The populace clamoured around the " Goldfields " building, and demanded that word should be given for the town forces to go out to the relief of Jameson, who, as belated rumour had it, was surrounded and in dire peril. In response to the angry demand the Hon. J. W. Leonard stepped to the balcony of the building, and declared that the report that Dr. Jameson was surrounded by Boers was not correct. " He was not surrounded " (the newspaper report continues), " neither had he surrendered, and he was sure that if his hearers were the men he took them to be, they would believe his statement."

One irresistibly recalls " Much Ado ":—

" *Second Watch.*—How if they will not?

" *Dogberry.*—Why, then, let them alone till they are sober; and if they make you not then the better answer, you may say they are not the men you took them for."

" The announcement " (continues the report) " was received with unbounded enthusiasm. Mr. Leonard further stated that Dr. Jameson was within an hour and a half from Johannesburg."

It would be cruel to recall some of the details of the fighting as issued from Reform Committee sources on the fatal day, and passed on, some of them, to anxious inquirers at Cape Town and elsewhere. Here are a few extracts from the records of the hour:—" Dr. Jameson is fighting his way into town against heavy odds. Report after report has been brought in by the despatch riders showing that Dr. Jameson is very much nearer Johannesburg than last night, the latest account stating that he is at Roodepoort, and coming in very fast indeed, fighting all the time. The Boers are massing behind him, and not in front of nim, as stated, and it looks as if the gallant Doctor will be able to fight his way into town." This was the news which purported to come from the battle-field, and which was published in Johannesburg at two o'clock in the afternoon—three hours after the completion of the surrender.

To show in what perfect good faith the Reform Committee passed on these rumours, the question which was now exercising their minds was what action the Committee should take when Jameson joined forces with the Uitlander outposts at Langlaagte. That the Committee were thoroughly competent to hold the town of Johannesburg by their own resources and dispositions did not, for official purposes, admit of doubt. But suppose Jameson fought his way up to the town outposts, and wanted aid—what then? It was maintained that there would be no alternative but to lend him all the support possible, and accept the situation in all its entirety. This, of course, would be very improper in view of the armistice agreed upon at Pretoria the day before, but how could desperate men discuss points of international law at the cannon's mouth? Johannesburg, as represented by the Reform Committee, abundantly recanted its earlier repudiation of Jameson. This was the knotty point which was under discussion when the Committee learnt beyond the possibility of further doubt that Jameson had surrendered hours before, and, report pitilessly added, had cursed the Johannesburg leaders for a lot of cowards. For, to some one who got a few words from him at Krugersdorp immediately after his surrender, Dr. Jameson said he failed "owing to lack of support expected when the Krugersdorp railway terminus from Johannesburg was reached." There had been no *arrangement* for a junction, there or elsewhere, as has been seen in earlier chapters.

The fact of the surrender was known to the Government officials at Johannesburg and their Hollander friends by two o'clock, and several wine parties were instantly organized amongst this exclusive set.

They soon hastened to crow over the Reform leaders.

The naked truth was, however, withheld from the masses until very late in the afternoon.

When it came out, it was a black hour for Johannesburg. Happily, the mob was unarmed. All the firearms at the disposal of the Reform Committee were in the possession of the forces encamped at the Waterworks plantation, the Simmer mine, the Robinson mine, Colonel Bettington's, Colonel Wollaston's, and the Bonanza Corps. The thousands of men who composed the brigades and corps before mentioned carried no more murderous weapons than walking-sticks. All day long the people wandered to and from the Fordsburg eminence. Some camped out there, and others rode out a few miles further, but returned quickly and in haste, lest Jameson should have taken another route to town and they would have lost the opportunity of witnessing the heroes' triumphal entry into the city. It was weary waiting, and as the hours sped on the fear began to seize the patient watchers that Jameson had not, after all, found it such an easy thing to break the Boer obstruction.

By five o'clock in the afternoon the report had got well abroad that Jameson had surrendered.

An indescribable whirlwind of frenzy seized the mob.

All the magnificent order and restraint of the few preceding days gave way to a wild delirium of rage against the leaders of the movement. Ten thousand excited persons clamoured around the headquarters of the Uitlander Organization, venting their rage and shame, and, in the manner of mobs, seeking scapegoats. Why were the forces held in town, when Jameson wanted relief only a few miles away? First one, then another of the Reform Committee was called on by name to come out and speak. Presently Mr. Lionel Phillips appeared on the balcony and appealed for silence.

"In reply to cries of 'Where's Jameson?' Mr. Phillips said, 'I'll tell you about that presently.' Continuing, he said many citizens had applied for enrolment, but the Committee were now considering that question.

With regard to Dr. Jameson, he said that a despatch containing the High Commissioner's proclamation had been sent by special messenger to Krugersdorp yesterday. That despatch had been delivered to Dr. Jameson, and he had surrendered to the authority of the proclamation."

Later, Colonel Rhodes spoke. It is painful to think of a gallant and popular British officer in such a cruel position. Neither then nor since did he save himself at the expense of his colleagues by trading on the Bettington's Horse incident.

"As to the relief of Jameson, they would believe him when he said that if anything could have been done it would have been done. It was only at the last moment Jameson was known to be in the position he was. He thought that with the force Jameson had he would have come in without the slightest difficulty. If they thought that he (Colonel Rhodes) behaved like a cur he was prepared to take the penalty of their resentment. The moment he heard of the news of the Jameson disaster was the bitterest of his life. Dr. Jameson and his men had been promised safety."

The bitter truth was out at last! Shouts of derision went up from the crowds in the street. They demanded to be taken out, and declared that they would rescue Jameson. It was the case of the Tiber bridge over again:

"Those behind cried 'Forward!' And those in front cried 'Back!'"

All doubt as to what course the Reform Committee would take was set at rest by the following official notice which was issued later in the evening:

"The Committee recognise that at this juncture the interests of Dr. Jameson are paramount, and that any ill-considered or aggressive step taken by this Committee will grievously complicate the situation.

"Her Majesty's High Commissioner will arrive on Saturday, and the Committee urge upon the inhabitants of Johannesburg the absolute necessity for preservation of order. The Government has given an assurance that the marching of troops on Johannesburg is not contemplated, and further states that it will give no cause for conflict.

"Meanwhile, the Committee have taken all necessary steps for the public safety.

"By order of the Committee,
"J. PERCY FITZPATRICK."

And again official assurances were repeated of the extent and thoroughness of the dispositions for the town's defence: the total number of men who could be put under arms, and who were mostly at present under arms, publicly and privately, being boldly announced as about 25,000. And thus appearances were kept up. But it was not against the Boers that the guards on duty at the "Goldfields" buildings were doubled that night.

Were the leaders indeed cowards they would have been trembling within. But they were not really cowards, as they were soon to show under sentence of death. They were only men put by a series of blunders and a dead-set of circumstances into a horrible appearance of cowardice. So, exhausted and miserable, but sleepless, they waited out the night.

What an end to the day that had risen in such fine colours!

Friday, January 3rd.—Morning broke in Johannesburg upon a scene vastly different from those that had ruled during the previous four or five days. There was an ominous absence of the crowds in the streets, of the six o'clock demand for newspapers, and of the bustling to and fro that had been the features of the week. Agreeably to the order of the Reform Committee, the various corps and brigades paraded on Marshall Square, and drilling proceeded. The idea was a good one, since it prevented that demoralization that would inevitably have set in had the men been left to their own resources.

The general public recovered somewhat from the shock of the day before, and crowded into the streets. A demagogue or two mounted a cab and addressed the crowd, denouncing the Reform Committee, and declaring the time had come to depose them, and elect a People's Committee. There could be no mistaking the fact that a strong feeling existed against the Reform Committee for consenting to any armistice which did not include Jameson. Members of the Committee explained that they considered Jameson well able to look after himself. The town was so much upset that the Stock Exchange went into recess, mining magnates' offices and hotel bars were closed, merchants and tradesmen strengthened the guards on duty at their various stores and shops, and, generally, the town and every business house therein was put into a condition of defence. The enemy thus provided against was not the Boer forces, though burghers were pretty thick on the ground outside, and some even came into town to have a look round. Johannesburg was being protected against itself, for no one knew what course the public disappointment would take. Happily, as events proved, there was no need for these precautions, Trimble's special police force of one thousand men kept splendid order.

Jameson received popular canonization. Even the Government and Robinson organs joined the chorus, the latter calling him "lion-hearted," and his march a "glorious possession of the Anglo-Saxon race." Mr. J. B. Robinson dismissed his editor and staff by cable—but in Johannesburg that week no man could or would write otherwise.

People awaited with much concern the publication of the afternoon paper, which throughout the crisis had been the recognised mouthpiece of the Reform Committee. Commenting on the previous day's disaster, the journal said:

"A brilliant career has ended in glorious ignominy. The ignominy will be but a fleeting shadow; the lurid glory of Dr. Jameson's epic march and surrender will be held in passionate remembrance so long as the hearts of Englishmen —nay, so long as the hearts of all who are men—continue to beat true to their best traditions. Dr. Jameson was a hero before; he is ten times a hero to-day, and if it can be any consolation to him and his gallant officers and men in their bitter captivity, they may receive the proud though heartbroken assurance of this city that their names are enshrined for ever in the pages of history; the fault redeemed, obliterated, and forgotten; the motive transfigured with a radiance which will never die."

So far the vanquished; now the victors :

"Happily for the country, happily for the armistice which now endures, ay ! happily for the Government itself, which has thus vindicated its authority, that no stern, revengeful order for the actual annihilation of the column was taken into the field. The forces of the Government kept well within the dictates of humanity and what are recognised as the laws of war. The consideration shown to these heroes of a forlorn hope after their surrender will go far to redeem the bitter obloquy which has too often been cast upon the Boer name for unnecessary cruelty in the field; and this attendant incident of the pitiable story has done much to restrain a distracted community from an excess of dangerous frenzy. Government in its wisdom will continue to exhibit, in the custody of its prisoners of war—for in that light are they honourably regarded—that same humanity and consideration; and by such an attitude it may be possible to appease public feeling and smooth the way to successful mediation between us by the High Commissioner."

As far as one could gather by moving amongst huge masses of men in the street "dangerous frenzy" did not prevail against the Boer; what ill-humour there was was directed against the Reform Committee for failing to succour Jameson. The Committee's organ had little difficulty in finding a scapegoat. Listen to this :

"We blame the paralyzing intervention of the High Commissioner; we blame the departure from all implied by the original resolution to raise the Transvaal flag. The offices of the High Commissioner should have been declined, although such steps as he might have deemed necessary as representing the predominant Power in South Africa for the preservation of peace, even by pouring in Imperial troops to keep both Boer and Uitlander down, we could not have resisted. But the High Commissioner, if the intention were for the Imperial authority to come in at all, should have intervened at an earlier stage. It is another illustration of the lamentable ill-fortune which seems so consistently to overtake the overt exercise of Imperial influence in South Africa. Fortune pursues it with a peculiar malignity."

Still, it was authoritatively given out that the Cause remained. Johannesburg was lying prostrate at the feet of the Boer; the Committee had an army of 25,000 men, and guns sufficient for 2,000 only, but yet "the Cause remained!" It was further declared that any one who abandoned his post was a traitor to the Cause. The city was pronounced to be, beyond doubt, in a position of adequate defence. The doubt was rather, Defence against what?—as was shown by the following notice posted at the "Goldfields" early in the morning:—

"From Her Majesty's Agent, Pretoria.
"To the Secretary of the Reform Committee,
Johannesburg.

"Upon the request of your deputation, I waited upon His Honour the President, and he has given me the assurance that, pending the arrival of the High Commissioner, who has left Cape Town this evening, Johannesburg will not be invested or surrounded by burghers, provided that no acts of hostility against the Government, or breaking of the law, is committed by the Johannesburg people, or anything leading to hostilities or breaking the law.

"(Signed)   A. DE WET,
"Her Majesty's Agent."

The deputation referred to in Sir Jacobus de Wet's message consisted of Messrs. W. E. Hudson and Van Halsteyn (partner of Mr. Chas. Leonard), who had been sent over to Pretoria the night before to confer with the British Agent on the security of the town.

By way of further calming public feeling the Reform Committee issued the following notice at noon:—

"Resolved: That in view of the declaration by the Transvaal Government to Her Majesty's Agent that the mediation of the High Commissioner has been accepted, and that no hostile action will be taken against Johannesburg pending the results of these negotiations, the Committee emphatically direct that under no circumstances must any hostile action be taken by the supporters of the Reform Committee, and that in the event of aggressive action being taken against them a flag of truce be shown and the position explained.

"In order to avoid any possibility of collision definite orders have been given. The matter is now left with the mediation of the High Commissioner, and any breach of the peace in the meanwhile would be an act of bad faith.

"By order of the Committee."

These various notices had, on the whole, a soothing effect. It seemed that something was being done, somebody was in charge of affairs, some danger was being averted. As the day wore on it was apparent that no excesses in any direction would be committed by the mobs who thronged the streets. In the fitness of things the military display of the last few days was greatly curtailed. The Reform Committee began the disarmament of the forces not actually engaged on outpost duty. Business was resumed in a tentative, half-ashamed fashion, and in likewise the railway contractor recommenced the delivery of goods. Prices on morning market were thus : forage, £15 per 100 bundles ; boer meal, 60s per bag ; mealies, 50s per bag ; potatoes, 40s. per bag. A quiet night succeeded a quiet day. Stagnancy after storm : an apathetic reaction ruled. After the habit of Johannesburg, the "boom" had brought forth the "slump."

Chapter XV

JOHANNESBURG PUTS ITS COAT ON AGAIN

SATURDAY, *Jan. 4th.*—When Saturday arrived all eyes were turned towards Pretoria, where the High Commissioner was expected to arrive in the course of the afternoon. A project to interview His Excellency, as he passed through Elandsfontein Junction, seven miles out of town, had to be abandoned, the intimation having been conveyed that it would be more convenient that His Excellency should see the President before communicating with the Uitlanders. The Reform leaders hoped much from the negotiations thus preparing, and took comfort in the reflection that the moral position of the Cause in Government eyes had been, or should have been, immensely strengthened by the fact that no attempt had been made to effect a junction with Jameson's column. Government was also reported to be painfully anxious to avoid civil war; and altogether the fiction was very tolerably supported that something like parity existed between the Government and the revolution—the burghers and the Uitlander forces. The Government, however, was not as tender with this fiction as could have been wished. At an early hour of the morning its representatives at Johannesburg were preparing for the first act in the drama of the Great Humiliation. The Commandant of Police notified that he intended drafting 500 burghers into the town. Instantly the Reform Committee telegraphed the news to the British Resident and claimed protection. Sir Jacobus de Wet could only pass on somewhat dry assurances from Government that it was with no menacing intent that this was done, and that no apprehension need be entertained. The men came in before long—a lot of unkempt-looking fellows, on shaggy ponies, very distressing to the eye of the townsmen. These uncouth warriors carried their rifles, and rode about the streets at pleasure, seeming to enjoy the novelty of the large crowds and bustle of the town. If the Government's one pre-occupation had been to avoid all risks of collision, the step showed little discretion. However, nothing happened.

Gradually, the Government officials picked up the dropped reins, and resumed direction of affairs. During the day a civic bodyguard of 800 Germans, Hollanders, and other Continentals were sworn in, the temptation to join being a sort of half promise of the franchise. Swaggering and exultant, these creatures of the winning side made themselves as offensive as the Government could have wished, and rubbed in the bitterness of defeat.

In the various camps on the outskirts of the town, however, quite a bellicose spirit was kept up. There were plenty of men here who, maddened with the course of events, had the wish, as well as the means, to shoot. They were at once quieted down and buoyed up with the belief that Imperial troops were coming up from the Cape and Natal. This idea must have been diligently circulated by somebody, for the same language was used about it at camps distantly situated one from the other. There was real need of inducements to keep the Reform troops playing the dull, waiting game without retaliating for the petty annoyances levied by the burgher forces who were hanging about more and more openly. The Boers looted cattle, commandeered meat at the slaughter-houses, lifted wash clothes from Kaffir boys, and, however stern were the orders which came from Pretoria, it was patent that the ordinary burgher felt it more than human nature could do to resist the golden occasion for tweaking the Uitlander's nose. These little amenities nearly resulted in an engagement. The Bonanza Corps located at the Robinson mine saw a mob of burghers steal towards a troop of cattle, which were being kept for Sunday's dinner, evidently with the object of lifting them. Quick as lightning the Bonanza Corps were off to the rescue. The Boers outnumbered the troop by ten to one. A blow or a shot might have lit a flame. Fortunately, the officers on both sides were able to check the men in time, and the risk passed by.

The marvel of the day was the *volte face* of the leaders of the Reform movement about " the Imperial factor." Execrated and jeered at till now, to-day the High Commissioner's intervention was the only hope. Johannesburg, as represented by the Reform Committee, was again British to the finger-tips, and would have sung " Rule Britannia," but that nobody had the heart to sing that day.

Sunday, January 5th, brought little relief from the excitement of the times. No news was forthcoming from Pretoria. Sermons bearing on the situation were preached in the various churches. Some pleaded for peace at any price, but the general burden was " peace with honour—or quit yourselves like men." The Rector of the English Church delivered his soul in a diatribe, hitting out all round, which provoked much discussion. The newspapers refused to publish the sermon. The Church militant had to consume its own smoke.

Monday (it seemed strange to remember) was to have been the day of the great adjourned mass meetings, when, according to the Leonard Manifesto of a week before, having decided what it wanted, Johannesburg was to declare further " how to get it." How, indeed? The day found the town more ready to ask than answer anything, while a meeting was the last thing anybody felt inclined for. The oppression of failure, of unaccountable disgrace, hung over the town like a thundercloud. The war party was again in the ascendant, but there were no recognised leaders. The Reform Committee, conscious of a weakness it could not publish to every follower, was all for conciliation and compromise. Any straw was caught at if happily out of the drowning swirl of disaster some solid concession might be won. The *Star* again declared that Imperialism had no place in the movement for reform; it was given out with every show of authority that "Johannesburg would gladly surrender that diplomatic fiction, the London Convention, in return for full burgher rights." The Reform Committee, having chosen pacification as the only policy, carried it out with logical consistency and thoroughness. Notices were issued requesting that all miners and employees of mining companies should return to their duties, as work was being resumed. Amongst the miscellaneous notices posted outside the Reform Committee's office was the following :—

"The Reform Committee desire to make it known that negotiations between the Government and the High Commissioner will be opened to-day. It is believed that the negotiations will necessarily take some considerable time, and the Committee therefore warns the public against accepting any rumours that may be put about. In the meantime, the Committee promises to use every endeavour to obtain and publish authentic news, and appeals to those not directly employed in maintaining order and protecting life and property to resume their usual occupation, which course will greatly facilitate negotiations. The Committee has neglected no means to lay before the Government and the High Commissioner the facts of the situation.

"By order of the Committee,
"J. PERCY FITZPATRICK."

This was the first occasion during the crisis that the Committee had shown any disposition to take the public into their confidence.

What next? On this the mind of the Reform Committee was now made up for them without further choice by the following cogent message, which was received shortly before noon :—

"PRETORIA, 6*th January*, 1896.
"*From H.M. Agent to Reform Committee, Johannesburg.*
"I am directed to inform you that the High Commissioner met the President, the Executive and the Judges to-day. The President announced

the decision of the Government to be, that Johannesburg must *lay down its arms unconditionally, as a condition precedent* to a discussion and consideration of grievances. The High Commissioner endeavoured to obtain some indication of the steps which would be taken in the event of disarmament, but *without success*, it being intimated that the Government had nothing more to say on that subject than had already been embodied in the President's proclamation. The High Commissioner inquired whether any decision had been come to as regards the disposal of the prisoners, and received a reply in the negative. The President said that, as his burghers, to the number of eight thousand, had been collected and could not be asked to remain indefinitely, he must request a reply—yes or no—to this ultimatum within twenty-four hours."

Note the words here italicized. Such was the ultimatum which the 6th January brought forth, instead of the ultimatum proposed a week before to be formulated on this day by a citizen army to the Government.

"What would Kruger do with the Reform Committee?" That was the question which now dominated public attention, and especially certain members' attention. The man in the street canvassed it with a merely philosophical curiosity. An ultimatum requiring the disarmament of the town and the arrest of the Reform Committee was regarded by the saner minds as certain. But it was by no means assumed in the street that it would be meekly received. Even the Reform Committee itself cherished lingering hopes from the presence of the High Commissioner at Pretoria, and seemed to think that the Imperial Power would, after all, step in to pull them out of the mess, and prevent any undue humiliation.

Unfortunately, the fiction that the "paralyzing intervention of the High Commissioner" was holding Johannesburg off the throat of the burghers, not the burghers off the throat of Johannesburg, was not one which could be maintained either to the High Commissioner himself or to the Pretoria Government.

Tuesday, January 7th, was the day of the Great Humiliation News of the Government ultimatum was not published until this morning. Sir Sidney Shippard, who, as an old Imperial official who happened to be in Johannesburg, had been sent to Pretoria to explain the Uitlander position to the High Commissioner, returned with the news of the ultimatum, and was followed by Sir Jacobus de Wet, sent as British Agent by the High Commissioner.

Now to recall the situation for a moment. The hard, cold fact, admitted by Johannesburg emissaries to the High Commissioner, was that the leaders could not but accept the Government ultimatum; while the followers, led away by "bluff" meant for the edification of the Government, were ready to cry, "*Nous sommes trahis,*" like a French mob, if not to add, "*A la lanterne !*" and proceed to lynching. The High Commissioner's task, as he conceived it, was simply to provide a golden ladder for a climb-down. Probably he would have failed, for a thousand or two of men in the camps, armed and angry, and no more cowards than others of their race or races elsewhere, were undoubtedly ready to "go and have a bang at the Boers," where or to what end they cared not, if a leader had started up to lead them. But now came into play, as against the fiction which overlay hard fact in the camps at Johannesburg, another fiction from Pretoria—the misunderstanding or misrepresentation about the life of Jameson. Not a soul, as has been seen, knew that Jameson's life (though not his liberty) was technically secured by Cronje's unreported word. It was, of course, really in danger; for a whole day the War Council clamoured for it, till shrewd old Oom Paul adjourned them; and had hostilities begun again, Jameson would probably have been shot, officers and all, and neither the world, nor Sir Hercules Robinson, nor, perhaps, the Pretoria Government, ever heard that terms of surrender had been so much as discussed. But whether or no, all these implicitly believed Jameson's life to be now hanging by a thread; Sir Hercules seized the golden ladder; the climb-down at Johannesburg became a foregone conclusion; a flood of generous emotion swept all other considerations away.

The British Agent informed the Committee that he had had

several interviews with the Executive Council, and had been greatly impressed by their desire to meet the people of Johannesburg in a conciliatory spirit. It must at the same time be remembered that Dr. Jameson's life was in danger. The Executive had, however, intimated its intention of handing the Doctor and all his men over to the High Commissioner, provided Johannesburg immediately disarmed.[1] Sir Jacobus then read the following telegram which he had received from Her Majesty's High Commissioner:—

"It is urgent that you should inform the people of Johannesburg that I consider that if they lay down their arms they will be acting loyally and honourably, and that if they do not comply with my request they will forfeit all claim to sympathy from Her Majesty's Government and from British subjects throughout the world, as the lives of Jameson and the prisoners are now practically in their hands."

Sir Jacobus (adds the *Star*):—

"Further impressed upon the Committee that the disarmament was a condition precedent to all negotiations between the High Commissioner and the Government, and that any delay would only have the effect of prejudicing those negotiations, besides prolonging the position, which was pregnant with serious possibilities. The Government, he added, was prepared to guarantee the preservation of law and order.

"The Committee decided to accept the advice of the High Commissioner, and comply with the terms."

Various members of the Committee have stated since that Sir Jacobus said to them many other things which he had certainly no authority to say, guaranteeing that "not a hair of the Committee's heads should be touched," that the Government would "grant" reforms as well as "consider" them, etc., etc. Probably Sir Jacobus, among his anxious questioners, went further than he remembers in reassuring them as to what he thought was the outlook; but the contemporary reports of

[1] The Government denied afterwards having treated this as provisional; but then it even disputed the "armistice" made in writing with the Reform deputation, which, as Sir Hercules pointed out, was mere verbal hair-splitting.

the Committee's official organ, here quoted, mention no such promises as are now talked of.

Accordingly at noon the following notice was issued :—

IMPORTANT NOTICE.

THE REFORM COMMITTEE
Notify hereby that
ALL RIFLES ISSUED FOR THE DEFENCE OF LIFE AND PROPERTY,
IN TOWN AND ON THE MINES,
Are to be returned
AT ONCE TO THE CENTRAL OFFICE,

In order to enable the Committee to carry out the agreement with the Government, upon the faithful observance of which so much is dependent.

By order of the Committee,
J. PERCY FITZPATRICK,
Secretary.

In further notices the Committee did full justice to the basis of the High Commissioner's appeal, and, in short, invited Johannesburg to a competition in magnanimous self-denial with the Government. Johannesburg could rescue Jameson with its rifles—by giving them up. All it had to do was to surrender the Lee-Metfords served out by the Reform Committee seven days before, for which, of course, there were no permits, and which were thus contraband by law. His own proper rifle any man might keep.

To one notice about "arms and the man," the rifles and Jameson, signed by the Committee's Secretary and the British Agent jointly, this was appended :—

"The Committee can add nothing to the above, and feel that there will not be one man among the thousands who have joined the Reform movement who will not find it consistent with honour and humanity to co-operate loyally in the carrying out of the Committee's decision.

"By order of the Committee (7th Jan.),
"J. PERCY FITZPATRICK, Secretary."

But all did not go without a struggle. It was understood that the Reform Committee had been given until three o'clock in the afternoon to decide upon the question of the disarmament. In view of possible refusal, or trouble during the process, the Netherlands Railway Company had been instructed to get everything in readiness to remove by train from Johannesburg all who wished to leave, giving preference to the women and children.

Meanwhile preparations were being made at the Police Barracks on Hospital Hill, where a detachment of the Staats Artillery and the burgher forces were massed, to carry out the ultimatum, if necessary, by shelling the town.

The Government, fleshed on the raiders, was in earnest: the roused burghers still more. Indeed, the High Commissioner had presently to use very firm language. But the Reform Committee was powerless to do more than advise, and their request for rifles fell on deaf ears—and abusive mouths.

Early in the afternoon it was decided that a public appeal should be made to the people by the agents of the High Commissioner, Sir Jacobus de Wet and Sir Sidney Shippard, from the balcony of the Rand Club. Notice given, a crowd of several thousands of people assembled in no time. This crowd proved very intolerant of anything like impartiality in the references to Jameson, the Government, and the Reform Committee. Sir Jacobus spoke of " Dr. Jameson and his brave little band, misguided though they might have been, but brave they were."—(Loud cheers) :—

"A terrible mistake had been committed undoubtedly by Dr. Jameson, which had placed all of them in a most awkward and painful position. (Uproar.) It had also placed Her Majesty's Government in a most painful position. He rejoiced, however, to be able to announce to them officially that Dr. Jameson and his men would be honourably handed over to Her Majesty's Government, to be dealt with at the latter's discretion. But before that could be done the men of Johannesburg must lay down their arms. (Loud cries of 'Never,' 'Who to?') As their friend, as an official pledged to Her Majesty's Government from the time of his manhood up to the present moment, he appealed to them as Britons with large hearts and with brave hearts, as men of sense, not to act idiotically, but to give up their arms. (Renewed cries of 'Who to?') . . . Though they might fight as bravely as lions, as Englishmen always did—(cheers and uproar)—it was utterly impossible for them to hold their position against the forces opposed to them. With all their valour, with all their determination, with all their pluck, they would have to die, and what was the good of dying?"

This very direct appeal to the first of instincts Sir Jacobus proceeded to reinforce by reference to the women and children, the horrors of a siege, starvation, Johannesburg in ashes, etc. "Don't frighten us!" shouted a voice; but "We shall have to 'take it' now!" was the dry comment of another. Sir Sidney Shippard, after much more to the same effect, took up the tale, answering the persistent and pertinent, if ungrammatical "*Who to?*" by "Give them up to your High Commissioner." Sir Sidney struck a wrong note when he reinforced the plea of Jameson's safety by adding "and of the leaders"—(interruptions)—and another wrong note when he insisted on the magnanimity and even generosity that the Government was showing. But it was evident that the speeches had the expected effect, and would duly work.

Sir Sidney concluded:—

"I, whose heart and soul is with you, say again that you should follow the advice of the High Commissioner, and I beg you to go home and to your ordinary avocations, deliver up your arms to your High Commissioner, and if you do that you will have no occasion to repent it." (Cheers.)

It must be understood that the crowd which heard these speeches was practically unarmed. But the word went round to the armed outskirts of the town, and disarming began in a very practical way shortly after the break-up of the meeting. Men in the camps, on hearing the orders of the Committee, threw their rifles away in disgust; some smashed the weapons, and others bent the barrels so as to render them useless. The whole force showed signs of disbandment and demoralization.

The guns were collected and taken to the Reform Committee offices, most of this work being done under the kindly cover of the night. Later on the rifles and Maxims were handed over by the wagon-load to a commission, consisting of Mr. J. C. Krogh, Administrator of Swaziland, and Mr. Joubert, Landdrost of Ermelo, who came over for the purpose. Before midnight the Reform Committee formally reported that the disarmament was complete. All the corps on outpost and camp duty were recalled, the defences were abandoned, and the Reform Committee disappeared as a militant factor in the situation.

The town passed a quiet night, save for one extraordinary incident. Lieutenant Eloff, with thirty Boers from Krugersdorp in uniform, rode through the main thoroughfares firing blank cartridge. The young man was arrested and escorted to Krugersdorp, and the Government War Commission publicly apologised for his tomfoolery.

The worst over, Johannesburg lost no time in getting back into the groove of every-day life. The town settled down with extraordinary quickness after the wild scenes of the last twelve days. On Wednesday morning, January 8th, most of the disarmed brigades paraded, were paid for their services—from 15s. to £1 per day—for the past week, and were dismissed with the injunction that the individual members would resume their normal avocations without delay. Before noon the town had got back something of its old aspect; work was resumed in some of the Government offices; men bought and sold as usual " between the chains "; the vicinity of the " Goldfields " building was no longer the great rallying-place; barricades were generally removed from shops and stores, and assistants smoothed their faces to the wonted smile; hotel bars reopened, and the thirst of the parched was quenched at the usual, not at siege, prices; the boom of the " hooters " signalled that the mines were making up arrears in the " output "; butchers' and bakers' carts rattled on their rounds again; the market on the square was once more in swing; fugitives returned; women and children were no more rare in the streets; there was a renewal of confidence in the banks—more deposits than withdrawals; while the Government police, no more "withdrawn to avoid possible collisions," stalked along the thoroughfares on their accustomed beats.

The Reform Committee began to tumble to pieces. Members resigned, discovering that they had never been made acquainted with the real nature of the business in hand, and

Mr. J. H. HOFMEYR.
From a Photograph by J. HAACK, *Cafetown.*

that the first intimation they had of armed force was the distribution of rifles and the parading of the Maxims, from which they now thought well to dissociate themselves.

Meanwhile, a veritable riddle of the Rand had presented

itself. Up to two o'clock in the afternoon 2,100 Lee-Metfords, three Maxims, and 300 boxes of ammunition only had been delivered up to the Special Commission. The Reform Committee gave the assurance that that comprised the sum total of the arms and munitions of war in the possession of the organization; but the Commission were not satisfied, and left for Pretoria to report the matter to Government. A large number of the rifles were damaged, and the principal screws of two of the Maxims were missing. During the night a dozen detectives searched the "Goldfields" building from ceiling to cellar for arms, but without avail. Sir Jacobus de Wet again came over from Pretoria to reason with the Committee, and to represent the difficulty in which the High Commissioner was placed by the keeping back of arms. The Committee, in reply, assured Her Majesty's Agent that there never were more than 2,100 rifles at the disposal of the organization. Government remained sceptical, and early in the evening a proclamation by the President was published, stating that, as the Government was aware that all the arms and ammunition illegally held without special permit from the Government in Johannesburg had not been handed over by the Reform Committee, it was notified that, unless such handing over was completed before six o'clock on Friday night, steps would be taken to enforce the law of the land. Further, a pardon was granted to all who took up arms against the Republic in Johannesburg with the exception of the leaders, the members of the Reform Committee, and captains of troops and drill instructors and all engaged in the training of the men.

The explanation of this discrepancy about the rifles—which nearly shelled Johannesburg, for the order to attack in a few hours was only withdrawn on the High Commissioner's plain threat of war—is one of the humours of the crisis. It came of the policy of "bluff." The Committee had advertised, for Government edification, 25,000 rifles, and Maxims by the half-dozen, and two worthy old gentlemen, Government officials, had been induced to take a drain pipe in a cart for a large piece of ordnance. Now the Government insisted on those 25,000 rifles and batteries of ordnance being produced! And for weeks afterwards went on, at all sorts of times and absurd places, the comedy of the search for those "bluff" rifles.

Throughout the day there was a big scramble to get out of town. The deadlock between the Government and the Reform Committee respecting the disarmament was magnified into a matter of grave importance, and trouble was freely prophesied. With a view to preventing the departure of what the Government proclamation described as "the principal criminals, leaders, instigators, or perpetrators of the trouble at Johannesburg," a rigorous passport system was instituted. Exit from town by road was prohibited, and some people who ventured beyond the three mile radius were shot at. The only way out was by rail, but none were permitted to leave even by that means save upon the presentation of a return half of a railway ticket. This was the certificate of *bonâ fides* upon which a passport was granted, this and none other. Passports being in demand, the normal business instincts of the Johannesburger impelled him to "make a bit." A trade in passports sprang up, and the price ruled as high as £4 apiece.

Having used the Committee to disarm Johannesburg, the Government could now afford to come down on the Committee. Thursday, 9th January, is the date of the following :—

"PROCLAMATION by HIS HONOUR STEPHANUS JOHANNES PAULUS KRUGER, State President of the South African Republic, with the advice and consent of the Most Honourable the Executive Council.

"WHEREAS, according to the resolution of the Government of the South African Republic, dated Monday, January 6th, 1896, by which to all persons at Johannesburg and suburbs twenty-four hours were granted, within which time they had to lay down, unconditionally, all arms and ammunition for which no permit could be produced, and unconditionally to hand them over to the Government, and whereas the said term of twenty-four hours had already elapsed at 4 o'clock p.m. on Tuesday, January 7th, and

"Whereas, the so-called Reform Committee and other British subjects have intimated their willingness and resolution to comply unconditionally with the decision of the Government, and considering that several persons already have given up and surrendered their arms and ammunition as aforesaid, and whereas the laying down and surrendering still continues, and whereas it is desirable and serviceable that this shall take place as soon as possible in a satisfactory manner, and a period shall be fixed for that purpose; so it is that I, Johannes Stephanus Paulus Kruger, State President of the South African Republic, with advice and consent of the Executive Council, do command and proclaim according to Article 5 of their Minutes, that up to Friday, January 10th, 1896, at 6 o'clock in the afternoon, time shall be given for that purpose.

"All persons or bodies who after that time are found in possession of guns and ammunition for which no permit from the Government can be produced by them shall be dealt with according to law.

"And considering that the laying down and surrendering of arms and ammunition should take place unconditionally,

"So it is that I further proclaim, that all persons who have already laid down and surrendered the arms and ammunition as aforesaid, or shall do such before 6 o'clock of Friday afternoon, January 10th, 1896, will be exempt from all prosecution, and will be pardoned for, and on account of, all that has been committed at Johannesburg and suburbs, with the exception of all persons and bodies that may appear to be principal criminals, leaders, instigators, or perpetrators of the troubles at Johannesburg and suburbs.

"Such persons or bodies as the last mentioned shall have to justify themselves before the legal and competent courts of this Republic. Further, I do proclaim, that I will address the inhabitants of Johannesburg and suburbs to-morrow by a particular proclamation.—GOD SAVE LAND AND PEOPLE!"

The anticipated action against the Reform Committee took place on the 9th and 10th, when the Government effected a *coup d'état* in a prompt and business-like way. As many of the members of the Committee as could be found at their houses and resorts were quietly, politely, but firmly escorted to Doornfontein gaol by a motley crowd consisting of members of the State Artillery, mounted and foot police, and detectives. Excellent arrangements had been made for their reception. They were to eat, though they were also to be eaten; for, like all Transvaal gaols, the town prison is "alive with vermin." One batch safely deposited, the police scoured the town in search of others, till all had been collected. The prisoners—sixty-four

THE MOST RECENT PORTRAIT OF
PRESIDENT KRUGER.

in number—were conveyed to Pretoria, and thus severed, for the time being, their connection with the Rand and its political affairs.

The following final notices were issued on this day, Friday, January 10th :—

"NOTICE.

"It is hereby requested any who have goods or other articles of whatsoever nature, the property of the above Fund, or moneys, will kindly return the same to Tattersall's Bar. Those also who have horses belonging to the Fund, please communicate at the above address without delay.

"By Order."

"RELIEF FUND.

"It is hereby desired that all Tradespeople and other Persons who have Accounts against the above will at once render the same for examination to Tattersall's Bar, so that a settlement can be effected as soon as possible.

"By Order."

"REFORM COMMITTEE.

"All Accounts against the Commissariat must be filed immediately, as all affairs are being wound up. The temporary offices are in Tattersall's Buildings."

In short, the members of the Reform Committee were in gaol, the affairs of the Committee were being wound up, and the headquarters were removed from the lordly "Goldfields" building to Tattersall's. At noon the final prosaic touch was given to the dream of a Johannesburg Government by a proclamation in which the President, with tears in his voice, offered the town—a non-elective Burgomaster!

"TO ALL THE RESIDENTS OF JOHANNESBURG.

"I, S. J. P. Kruger, State President of the South African Republic, with the advice and consent of the Executive Council, by virtue of Article 6 of the Minutes of the Council, dated January 10th, 1896, do hereby make known to all the residents of Johannesburg and neighbourhood that I am inexpressibly thankful to God that the despicable and treacherous incursion into my country has been prevented, and the independence of the Republic saved, through the courage and bravery of my burghers.

"The persons who have been guilty of this crime (misdryf) must naturally be punished according to law, that is to say, they must stand their trial before the High Court and a jury, but there are thousands who have been misled and deceived, and it has clearly appeared to me that even among the so-called leaders of the movement there are many who have been deceived.

"A small number of intriguers in and outside of the country ingeniously incited a number of the residents of Johannesburg and surroundings to struggle, under the guise of standing up for political rights, and day by day, as it were, urged them on, and when in their stupidity they thought that the moment had arrived, they (the intriguers) caused one Dr. Jameson to cross the boundary of the Republic.

"Did they ever ask themselves to what they were exposing you?

"I shudder when I think what bloodshed could have resulted had a merciful Providence not saved you and my burghers.

"I will not refer to the financial damage.

"Now I approach you with full confidence; work together with the Government of this Republic and strengthen their hands to make this country a land wherein people of all nationalities may reside in common brotherhood.

"For months and months I have planned which changes and reforms could have been considered desirable in the Government and the State, but the loathsome agitation, especially of the Press, has restrained me.

"The same men who have publicly come forward as leaders have demanded reforms from me, and in a tone and a manner which they would not have ventured to have done in their own country, owing to fear for the criminal law. For that cause, it was made impossible for me and my burghers, the founders of this Republic, to take their preposterous proposals in consideration.

"It is my intention to submit a Draft Law, at the first ordinary session of the Raad, whereby a municipality, with a Mayor at the head, would be granted to Johannesburg, to whom the control of the city will be entrusted. According to all constitutional principles, the Municipal Board will be elected by the people of the town.

"I earnestly request you, laying your hands on your hearts, to answer me this question: After what has happened, can and may I submit this to the representatives of the people? My reply is, I know there are thousands in Johannesburg and the suburbs to whom I can entrust such elective powers. Inhabitants of Johannesburg render it possible for the Government to go before the Volksraad with the motto:

"'FORGOTTEN AND FORGIVEN.'"

Chapter XVI

SCENES AT PRETORIA, CAPE TOWN, AND ELSEWHERE

THE excitement at Pretoria during the critical week was scarcely less than at Johannesburg itself.

Pretoria, it must be remembered, though the seat of Government, is a town of merchants, shopkeepers, and professional men, largely Uitlander in sympathy; and a person of Uitlander sympathies, living under the very nose of Dr. Leyds and in daily touch with the Hollander bureaucracy, is apt to become a Jingo outright. The general division is between the Government set and the Hollanders on the one hand, and on the other hand the Afrikanders and the Jingoes. At the beginning of the crisis these last two classes were driven together by their common hatred of the Hollander and sympathy with the Uitlander.

A revulsion of feeling came with the news of Jameson that drove the Afrikanders into the Government camp at once. Men who had been in the warmest sympathy with Johannesburg volunteered to go out against Jameson, and, in fact, while the effect of the Jameson news in Johannesburg was mixed, its effect at Pretoria was almost unanimously damning to the cause. That uncertain and sometimes vanishing quantity, the progressive Boer, especially the progressive Raadsman, who, a day or two before had taken his cue of tempered sympathy with Johannesburg from General Joubert, the leader of the party, now saw its hopes of making head against the Krugerites swamped by the wave of reaction certain to be conjured up by Jameson's act among the burghers at large. There are many stories like the one which is told of a number of men sulkily declining to be commandeered to watch Johannesburg just before the irruption, and the same men eagerly rushing to arms the moment after against the invader of their country. In Pretoria itself the feelings aroused were complicated by two strong impressions. "'There is intense indignation here," telegraphed Sir Jacobus de Wet to the High Commissioner on the Tuesday. "There is a strong suspicion that Her Majesty's Government countenanced the movement, or, at all events, must be cognizant of what was intended." That was one idea, and the other was the rooted conviction that Jameson was marching on Pretoria, and that it was the Capital, rather than Johannesburg, which would be the scene of battle, murder, and sudden death. The crowding of trains, the bivouacking in back gardens, and frantic precautionary measures about wives and families were, therefore, incidents of the crisis at Pretoria as much as at the great mining town thirty miles off.

One scene is worthy of commemoration from its personal interest and from its historic value as showing that the Pretoria Government, and even the hard old man at its head, had their moments of panic apprehension just before the turn of the tide. It is a Watch Night incident, the scene of it being the stiff, farmhouse-parlour-like reception-room in the President's villa in the outskirts of Pretoria. The time, the witching hour when 1895 was merging into 1896.

About one o'clock of that New Year's morning the slumbers of the British Agent were broken by the urgent hand of Commissioner of Police Van Niekerk, whose name, by the way, recalls a previous South African raid, the Boer one of Stellaland. The Commissioner begged Sir Jacobus de Wet to get up and come to the Presidency at once. The British Agent, Sir Jacobus, dressed and went. He found His Honour *en déshabillé*, surrounded by all the Members of the Executive save General Joubert, and, of course, Dr. Leyds, who was in Europe, together with three judges of the High Court, and a number of Raad officials. All of these gentlemen seemed to labour under strong excitement and alarm, and the President, who seemed with difficulty to control his feelings, told Sir Jacobus with that wealth of gesture and force of emphasis which he commonly uses when in animated talk, that he had just received reliable information from Johannesburg that large armed forces, 2,000 at least, with Maxims and cannons, were then marching upon Pretoria, undoubtedly with the object of taking possession of the seat of Government.

Sir Jacobus expressed his incredulity, and assured the President of his willingness to assist him in any possible way to stay the onward march of the 2,000.

An escort to conduct Sir Jacobus through the Boer lines was suggested, but the President, after considerable discussion, remarked : "No; my burghers might take you for a spy, and shoot you." So that idea was abandoned, and Sir Jacobus bade the imaginary 2,000 halt in the Queen's name by telegram to the Reform Committee.

Everything was made ready for the President's escape from the supposed invaders. A horse stood at his door ready saddled—"and he not been across a horse for twenty years," as Mevrouw Kruger put it afterwards.

The old man himself sat up, all on the *qui vive*, and the Chief Justice sat up with him.

Where were the Nachtmaal burghers now? Alas! mostly gone to the front, to meet Jameson or threaten Johannesburg, leaving Church Square once more empty. Even next day, when a strong guard was stationed at the Presidency, a heterogeneous guard of volunteers and burghers, the good wife's suspicions were still alert. Among them were many young Afrikanders, whose medium of conversation was English. She overheard some of them on guard duty chatting together, and at once despatched a messenger to His Honour, who was then in the Government Buildings, ordering that the volunteers should be removed "als hulle Engelse praat." The change was speedily made, and the burgher guard increased in numbers.

The panic of that Tuesday night spread from the Presidency in widening circles. Acting Field-cornets, who had been making themselves ingratiatingly officious for the past few days, were on the alert, and went from house to house warning all and sundry to repair to the camp, alleging that the town was going to be stormed. Women and children, scared out of bed, were to be seen scurrying towards the artillery camp, clasping a few of their dearest possessions in their hands. One philosophical Dutch dame, however, after hearing all, remarked testily that "whatever else the English might be going to do, confound them! she supposed they would let the women alone." And so went back to bed.

The acting manager of the *Press*, the Robinson-cum-Government organ at Pretoria, declared that its offices would be the first place sacked—the angry crowds at Cape Town and Johannesburg did threaten the *Telegraph* and *Diggers' News* offices during the crisis—and he actually gave the hands orders to destroy the machinery and "pye" the type on the first alarm.

Then there was the great joke of the "Vigilants," a set of special constables for the occasion. "Among this motley crew," wrote the *Cape Times* Pretoria correspondent, "were parsons and painters, actors and attorneys, masons, 'free' and otherwise, and many strange fowl. It was not till after the surrender at Doornkop, however, that the Vigilants became a strong body. *Then* there were many valiant men enrolled. A Vigilant's was generally a thankless billet, but it was not without its humorous side. To see a brother 'Vig,' a Raad Member, 'running in' a provoking Kaffir, or another in the loving embrace of a French milliner who had taken too much stimulant to fortify herself in the terrors of the hour, was amusement sufficient to relieve the monotony of one night's guard. Luckily many Vigilants, although provided with guns, had no ammunition, and in consequence those over whom they kept guard slumbered peacefully. The Government buildings, too, were considered to be a likely object of attack, and hasty entrenchments, excavated by the entire strength of the convicts in gaol, were thrown up during the course of the day. A strong guard of Hollanders and others, many of whom had never before handled a rifle, but who were on this occasion little walking arsenals, were stationed inside the building."

Great difficulty (the same correspondent adds) was experienced in feeding the burghers in Pretoria, and every little canteen and large hotel were requisitioned to supply them with meals. As much as £4 per 100 bundles was paid for forage, and a wagon-load that happened to reach Pretoria was snapped up by the Landdrost, who at first was in serious doubt as to whether he should buy at the price, but on a well-known, shrewd Pretorian remarking, " De Engelse zal daarvoor betaal " (the English will have to foot the bill), the thrifty Landdrost quickly made up his mind and bought the lot.

Even a crisis, thank Heaven! has its humours. But to more serious matter. On the High Commissioner's first day in Pretoria, on the Sunday following the Sunday of Jameson's start, he could only exchange polite greetings with the Sabbatarian President. But from the Rand and the Reform Committee came messengers urgent and confidential: Sir Sidney Shippard and Mr. Seymour Fort. They told the High Commissioner shortly that Johannesburg could not stand attack. The crowds and the Committee's posters kept up the fiction of an armed community straining at the leash of the armistice. But the leaders wished His Excellency to know the fact that, while provisioned for a month's siege, the town had no means of preventing its water supply being cut off, while—consideration which made all else a detail—the stock of ammunition would not outlast a general attack of half an hour's to an hour's duration. Jameson had moved when they were all unready: they had not been able to help him, and they could not now help themselves with 8,000 exultant Boers surrounding their show of half-armed earthworks.

The only thing for Sir Hercules to do was to keep these facts locked in his bosom, make the best terms he could, and enable the inevitable disarmament to take place with as good a grace as might be.

However, in cabling to Mr. Chamberlain the state of affairs, Sir Hercules fully represented that the Johannesburg crowd, as apart from the Reform Committee, were ready to "elect their own leaders and fight it out," if they could not get promises of reform, as well as of Jameson's safety, as the price of disarmament.

Early on Monday (6th January), Sir Hercules met the President and the Executive Council. His illness had increased on the tedious train journey and under the wear and tear of anxiety; but he lay on a sofa, and the President and Council, who have a great respect for Sir Hercules, sat round him.

"The judges (he writes), the chief officials, and the delegates from the Orange Free State were also present. The Government ultimatum was that Johannesburg must surrender its arms and submit unconditionally as a precedent to any discussion and consideration of grievances. The promises in the President's proclamation of 30th December, 1895, would be observed, and grievances put forth constitutionally would be carefully considered and brought before the Volksraad without delay. No decision had been come to up to that time as to disposal of Dr. Jameson and other prisoners. I at once communicated terms of this ultimatum to the Reform Committee at Johannesburg, through Her Majesty's Agent, and advised their acceptance of them. It appeared to me the case of the Johannesburg people would have been hopeless in the event of an appeal to arms."

That afternoon, the Council, through Sir Jacobus de Wet, promised to hand over Jameson and the officers, but "not until Johannesburg had complied with the terms of the ultimatum." Sir Hercules at once sent Sir Jacobus to Johannesburg to make the people, "who were infuriated with the Reform Committee," see the true state of the case, and on Tuesday morning helped him by telegraphing the message which (as we have seen) practically disarmed Johannesburg. Armed with the Committee's acceptance of the ultimatum (7th January), and with a brief but able summary of the Johannesburg grievances cabled by Mr. Chamberlain on January 4th, Sir Hercules thought he could "now confer with President and Executive as to prisoners and redress of grievances." Unfortunately, hitches arose as to "prisoners," and Sir Hercules was not destined to get to "grievances" at all.

On the 7th and 8th Sir Hercules was engaged in checking the impulse of his chief to make a demonstration and despatch troops to South Africa, first on the pretext of preventing any further raid from Bulawayo, such as the Pretoria Government still professed to anticipate, and secondly, to "provide for all eventualities." Mr. Chamberlain's ardent desire to be doing something eventually led the harassed High Commissioner to entreat him rather sharply to "leave the matter in my hands," which Mr. Chamberlain then did. Sir Hercules, however, could be firm when occasion required. On the 8th came the hitch about the disarmament, when the Government calmly announced that they were not satisfied with the number of arms given up, and that unless many more came to hand an attack on Johannesburg would be ordered that evening. Sir Hercules at once told the Government that if any such hostile step were taken he would regard it "as a violation of an agreement for which he had made himself personally responsible, and would place the issue in the hands of her Majesty's Government." The effect of this language was immediate and sufficient. The disarmament satisfactorily over, arrangements for taking over the raiders and sending them to England took till the 14th of January, on which day Sir Hercules left for Cape Town, after having only one other direct interview with the President and Council, making two in all,—the rest of the negotiations having had to be carried on through the Imperial Secretary and British Agent, while Sir Hercules was more or less in bed. The fact was that the collapse of Johannesburg, the defeat of Jameson, and the discovery of the startling evidence as to the details of the recent plot had entirely changed the situation since the moment when, just in the nick of time, Sir Hercules had obtained the President's assent to mediation. One mediates between combatants. A mediator is handicapped when one combatant is already practically sitting on the other's head. Sir Hercules saw plainly enough that to expect to get anything really done about reforms at this juncture was idle. No sensible person, indeed, had expected anything more than vague promises in this direction even when he set out from Cape Town. He had to return with scarcely even that; the Government, indeed, having politely intimated to him that, while much obliged for his assistance, they, as he puts it, "found no further inducement to request me to lengthen my stay." "I thought it more politic," he adds, "to rest content meanwhile with the concession of Municipal Government which the President had promised, and with the statement in his proclamation of the 30th December, 1895, that all grievances advanced in a constitutional manner would be carefully considered and brought before the Volksraad without loss of time."

Cape Town folk will not easily forget the look of St. George's Street during the week of the crisis: a recurrent sea of heads, waiting on the slips that the papers issued as the confused and broken news came in, hours late, over the blocked wires; leading politicians jostling the man in the street and showing the alternations of joy, anxiety, and despair in their faces. Turning back to the file of the *Cape Times* for that week, the scene comes vividly back as in a mirror. It is like turning up an old diary, jotted down in days of *Sturm und Drang*. Here are a few extracts from the hurried leading articles of those days and nights:—

"*Tuesday, December* 31*st.*—(With news of Jameson's start, 'due to a wild—brave—mad—silly impulse,' but fraught with most 'solemn issues':) —'God defend the right.' Which is the right in this quarrel from the standpoint of the Afrikanders of the Cape Colony? We know well that many of them, as Mr. Hofmeyr says in the interesting talk reported in another column, will find their hearts sorely pulled both ways. In the War of Independence the farmers of Cape Colony sympathised deeply with the farmers of the Transvaal. It was that sympathy, more than any other factor, which moved England to give back the country; and

England knows well that the same feeling to-day would be as strong as ever against re-annexation. But there is no question of re-annexation. England asks nothing of the Transvaal to-day for herself; only one or two things for South Africa. England is not in this quarrel at all—unless she is dragged in simply as peacemaker. But, in one sense, the struggle to-day is the same as the struggle of 1881 : only the parts are reversed. What did the burghers fight for then ? For the right to govern themselves, to be free men, not to have to obey the laws of other people. And what are the 'Uitlanders' fighting for to-day—if to fight they are forced ? For that very same right to govern themselves, to be free men, to have laws of their own, not of other people's. The burghers called God to vindicate a right in 1881. The 'Uitlanders' can call God to vindicate the very same right in 1895. The 'Uitlanders' are struggling for their freedom, ay, and for their country, for they feel that it is their country. The Boer began the making of it, but they are finishing it ; it is their work that has added all that power, and prosperity, and wealth, all those outward and visible signs of a great Republic, of which the Boer is as proud as anybody when he outspans his wagon at Nachtmaal in the square at Pretoria and looks at the splendid Raadzaal. . . . For, never forget, it is the South African cause for which these men are fighting. South Africa for the South Africans, and not for Hollanders, might be their motto. Take the programme which they have put out in their manifesto and think what it will mean to the Cape Colony if they are ever in a position to carry it out. All that we have been struggling for, all that Paul Kruger in his fatuous hatred of the Cape has so strenuously denied us, a Railway Union, a Customs Union, a South African labour policy based on the application of a general Glen Grey principle throughout these territories, the free exchange of all South African commodities—the very boon which the Paarl farmers looked to get when they had helped Paul Kruger back into the saddle, and out of which he has cynically cheated them ever since. Afrikanders are in the forefront of this movement, with men bearing such names as Wessels and Auret, familiar in our colonial countrysides as household words. There can be few Cape families that have not a son, a nephew, a cousin, among the men whom the Transvaal Government degrades as unfit to be citizens. These are the men whom the immediate clique of the President hates worse than the *rooinek*. And these frowning arsenals of the Government's are an allegory. It is upon South Africa at large, us as well as them, that the Government's Hollander clerk and German officers turn the guns of their Continental policy, in maniac hatred of that Government under which the Afrikanders of the Cape Colony live in contented freedom. The Krugerites have been selling the birthright of the Afrikander to every Hollander that would give a mess of pottage for it. If blood be shed as the result of this policy, no matter who fires the first shot, heavy will lie the responsibility on the head of one obstinate old man."

The above, entitled "To all Afrikanders," was got out in Dutch as well as English; a novelty, however, which it proved too great a strain to keep up throughout the crisis.

"*Wednesday, Jan 1st.*—(No news of Column. Proclamation. *Title*, 'ONE MAN'S MADNESS.')—'I am no longer pulled two ways,' Mr. Hofmeyr remarked, yesterday, with reference to a phrase in the interview we published. 'Jameson has decided me.' There is no cloaking the fact that this is the general verdict of Afrikanders. Dr. Jameson's colossal blunder, in taking the aggressive, instead of helping the political revolution in the Transvaal, has checked the rising sentiment of sympathy with the 'Uitlanders.' Had the act not been disowned promptly and fully by the Chartered Company and the Imperial Government (and the same will apply, no doubt, to the rumours from Bulawayo), the situation in South Africa to-day would be very serious. As it is, the question is reduced to the dare-devil impulse of one man; and as that man is now in so critical, so isolated, perhaps so tragic a situation, we spare further comment, and try simply to conceive the frame of mind in which he and his companions may have gone to work. . . .

"In the case of trouble at Johannesburg every man of them individually would be burning to join his friends. To expect them to stay twiddling their thumbs on the border a couple of days away, while those friends were being shot down by Mr Kruger's quick-firing guns, would be expecting too much—or two little—of human nature. They would not wait on the slow and uncertain chances of an Imperial pacification: they would not stop for niceties of international law. In one form or another —in twos or threes, or as a specially recruited column of volunteers— they would make a rush for the Rand. And if at this moment Mr. Kruger's German guns, under German officers, were shooting Afrikanders down, we take it most colonists would wish them Godspeed. In some such sense as that, we doubt not—though we have no direct authority for saying—that Mr. Rhodes himself would have been willing to turn a blind eye on his young men's indiscretion. And we think he would have carried, on the whole, Colonial feeling with him, even if 'Dr. Jim' had gone in in official capacity. But unluckily, Dr. Jameson did not wait for an actual break-out. He received, probably, an appeal or a report, or something which was too much for his hot-head temper. . . .

"And now what of the amazing Doctor and his men? In the dearth of news and stoppage of wires they seem to have disappeared under an impenetrable black storm-cloud, charged with lightnings and with thunders.

When the dark pall lifts, who will emerge? What wild work will have been done under its mantle? Will it be:

> "'Then they rode back : but not,
> Not the six hundred'?

"It was a black responsibility that Dr. Jameson took when he crossed the border ; but it was a still blacker risk ; and they knew it. They flung careers and commissions to the winds, took their lives in their hands, and went in : Ishmaels of the desert. Their one haste was to get beyond recall : and if they had meant to turn back for a recall, they would never have started. They rode lightly in, with a price upon their heads, a mark that every man who lists may shoot at. There is something in the sheer audacity of the thing that disarms. But it will not disarm the Boer commandoes. To-day, if uninterrupted, Dr. Jameson should be effecting a junction with any forces which Johannesburg may push out to meet him ; and nobody supposes that the Boers will allow that junction to be made without bloodshed. It is a grisly thought that for that blood Dr. Jameson is liable to be hanged like a felon. Never, surely, was such a gamester's throw, with the peace of half a continent trembling in the balance. All we can do is to wait for news, and hope for the best, most of us with sympathies painfully divided."

"*Thursday, January 2nd.*—(Contradictory news of column. Belief that Johannesburg effecting junction. Kruger has accepted High Commissioner's mediation.) '*Peace-making: Thanks to ——?*'— Dr. Jameson's men may not be out of danger yet ; but clearly Johannesburg is. We hear no more of the commandoes which, according to yesterday's positive statements, had been ordered to close upon the town now for some days in open, if passive, rebellion. The Government have had enough to think of with Dr. Jameson. There is no disguising the fact that, however wrong he was in taking the initiative, he has carried the cause of the revolution which we all sympathise with. Bloodshed, according to his evident belief, which subsequent news has done so much to justify, was imminent on the Rand. He has stopped it, at the cost of other bloodshed, perhaps less than would have flowed in the revolution. For none of us doubt that if once that teeming town began it must needs carry on the contest till it won. Yet the struggle might have been prolonged. The community on the Rand, in spite of these packed trains, still consists of men, women and children. There are but a few thousand arms among the lot, and the possibilities of indiscriminate shooting among the streets are terrible to contemplate. Half-armed, unorganized, undrilled, inexperienced, and hampered with non-combatants—that is a fair description of the Rand revolutionists. Dr. Jameson's compact little force was just the opposite.

"In practice, then, this proclaimed invader may have economized in bloodshed; and he has won the cause which South Africa admits that others, at least, had some sort of right to shed their blood for. For what means this sudden gush of promises of sweeping reforms? What this acceptance of mediation which cannot but recognise the justice of nearly all the revolutionary committee has formulated? We see the President actually proffering the franchise to all who refrain from joining in the demand for it. What has brought him to this pass? A sudden conviction of the soundness of arguments long familiar even to staleness? We trow not. The arming of Johannesburg is the argument that has converted President Kruger and his Hollanders; and this audacity of Dr. Jameson's, in taking sides in a civil war prematurely, has made the President accept the very settlement which would have averted everything, without putting the arms of the townsman to actual test.

"Matters still hang in the balance. It was a wild New Year's Day this : Cape Town half pale with suspense, eager knots discussing news in the streets, and the noisy mirth of some of our perambulating coloured friends jarring terribly on strained nerves. But we have hopes now of a less dark sequel to it. The Paramount Power has held the scales firmly even."

"*Friday, January 3rd.*—(News of surrender resolutely disbelieved.) The *Cape Times* could get no news though; nor could the *Argus*; and Cape Town utterly refused to accept the real news, which came from a Transvaal Government source to Mr. J. B. Robinson's *Telegraph*. Drawbacks of an official Censorship! Cape Town was now feverishly Jingo, and resented even the moderate censures of the *Cape Times* on Jameson. One article of to-day was headed 'In Suspense.' A second dealt with 'The dead-set against Mr. Rhodes': 'Save us from the horrors of a race war in South Africa.' There is not one of us so light-headed or so callous-hearted as not to breathe that prayer. By a spite of fate, this struggle has come to have the race-war look; but remember, it was no race war as it stood a few days back, it is no race war now in its essence. Dutch against English? No! It is Progressive Colonists throughout South Africa against Retrogressive—Unionists against Disunionists, free government against corrupt oligarchy. There are monopolists and capitalists on both sides, Dutch Afrikanders and English Afrikanders on both sides, working-men and Republicans on both sides. We are glad to note that general disgust has been excited by the attempt to rouse race-hatred against Mr. Rhodes in Cape Colony over this unhappy business. Perhaps it is bound to come. But it is time to point out that those who are combining to foster it, and are making one supreme dead-set to hound the Prime Minister out of public life, are a big combination of his financial and political rivals, operating largely through the Press. . . ."

Saturday, January 4th.—Dismal certainty about Jameson: but Johannesburg?—The article headed "Revolution by Proxy," given here as a faithful record of the feeling of that black hour, was preceded by a sort of prophetic forenote, which fuller knowledge has since brought to fulfilment. *Then* Cape Town, and the world, had not the clue to the "desertion":—

Revolution by Proxy.

[" We know there must be brave men on the Rand. We feel that we do not yet know all. We shall always uphold the rights of the 'Uitlanders' to free government, and we rejoice that more blood has not been shed to win them, so long as they are won. But on what we know we feel impelled to express the intensely bitter disappointment of the following article: which, though struck off at heat, certainly voices a feeling universal in the capital. Some day, perhaps, we may be enabled to take back some of our reproaches."]

" THERE is a saying that one cannot make a revolution with rosewater. Johannesburg is to be congratulated on an even more luxurious *tour de force*. It has made a revolution by proxy. 'I am not one of those tame moralists,' said one of the most eloquent of Irish rebels in a famous peroration, 'who hold that liberty is not worth the spilling of one drop of blood.' The revolutionists of the Rand agree with Meagher. They have found that their emancipation from political servitude was quite well worth the cost of blood—other people's. For weeks past we have been edified by columns of eloquence upon the wrongs, intolerable to manhood, under which they smarted. Their ultimatum to the Government was declared to represent a charter of freedom for which ten thousand men were ready, if forced, to take up arms. With the irony of coincidence, it is to-day that a *Times* article is telegraphed declaring that while Mr. Leonard's manifesto asked for little more than the programme adopted by the National Union last year, there was this important difference, 'that those who endorse the manifesto of 1895 will take the responsibility of enforcing it.' In reality, it appears, the extent of the stern resolve of the citizen army of ten thousand was to invite a handful of other men to enforce it for them. We owe an apology to the Kruger Government and to its organs for refusing for a whole night and day to believe their statements of this plain, simple fact. We simply laughed away, as a fantastic fiction, the news that Johannesburg had sat inactive for four-and-twenty hours within earshot, ay, almost within eyeshot, of the stubborn struggle of a few hundred lads to push their way into town through two or three thousand Boers; that they had refrained, with a 'calm restraint,' perhaps unparalleled in the records of philosophy, from so much as sending out a patrol to reconnoitre. Before this, when an armistice was suggested to them by the Boer commandant, it does not seem to have occurred to them that an armistice which excludes the only fighting part of your belligerents leaves something to be desired. So they made their armistice, saw the Boers massing at their convenience in Jameson's path, and—made speeches. That was all the support 'Dr. Jim' got from those 'principal residents' who, as he wrote in his characteristic little scrawl to the Commandant of Marico, had invited him to 'assist them in their demand for justice.'

"The streets of Cape Town yesterday were a curious sight. People's faces were as gloomy as if everybody had lost a near friend—as, indeed, not a few must have done. The abstract rights of the people of Johannesburg are the same as ever, no doubt—and the revolutionists by proxy say now that they are all to be conceded. But while the cause is the same, and all Cape Colonists support it, you cannot to-day conjure out of Cape Town the ghost of a cheer for the 'Uitlanders' of Johannesburg. It may be wrong, but it is well that Johannesburg should know it, should feel that it lies under a great and grievous need to clear itself before the world.

"The whole business is simply incomprehensible. The Reform Committee puts the blame on the High Commissioner's proclamation. Since the Imperial Government disavowed Jameson, they must, of course, follow suit. Did they really expect the Imperial Government to personally conduct their revolution? The way the average Johannesburger talks over his drinks never led us to suppose that his political judgment was so fettered by the proprieties of Downing Street. These people, whose representatives invited Jameson in, can they not see that while it was inevitable for us to disavow him, it was grotesque for them? It was for us to deplore civil war—which is always deplorable. *They* had declared themselves ready, if forced, to make it. Yet a proclamation addressed to British subjects when they had just sworn allegiance to the Transvaal flag suffices to make them coldly repudiate their ally. The *Star*, which has been preaching sedition bravely for a week, actually congratulated the forces of the Government on having defeated him, and the whole of Johannesburg looks on unmoved while the Boers draw on the ammunition in the town for those supplies which might have saved Jameson. And then, when the mass of people suddenly realized their disgrace, and in a passion of shame and anguish turn on the Committee, one of these gentlemen looks out of a window and declares, like Mrs. Micawber, 'that it is no use asking him, the Committee will never desert Dr. Jameson.'

"We say nothing as to whether Jameson had the right to take a contract for somebody else's revolution. We do not care at this moment to repeat our original verdict upon that. The one thing now left for Johannesburg, before it finally lay down its arms, is to put the release of Jameson with full honours of war before any other claim that it presses on the President. For, as is written above the petition for which we bespeak our readers' signatures, Cape Colony 'had rather the " Uitlanders " went voteless for ever than that a hair of Jameson's head should be touched.'"

The petition referred to ran as follows (addressed to the High Commissioner at Pretoria) :—

"We, the undersigned Cape Colonists, desire earnestly to represent to Your Excellency that in the interests of the general reconciliation and peaceful settlement now happily in progress, after the late deplorable bloodshed, Your Excellency should treat the release of Dr. Jameson and his comrades as of more importance than any other conditions which the Government of the South African Republic is asked to grant."

Part of every copy of the *Cape Times* one day was made into a form for this petition, and in a few days 10,000 signatures, in twos, and tens, and fifties, had come in ; and the Mayor telegraphed the fact to the High Commissioner. The *Cape Times* Petition ran through the Colony : Kimberley, Port Elizabeth, and East London did the like ; there were many Afrikander names among the signatures ; and the united voice found an echo in the watchwords of the negotiations then in progress.

In London the suspense of those days was aggravated by a cable breakdown, which kept them over a week without any detailed news, and then things came to hand in the wrong order ! At Bulawayo a mass meeting was ready to send 1,000 men if Mr. Rhodes or Dr. Jameson held up a finger.

It was indeed wired that the Rhodesia Horse had started, but that, as seized papers show, was part of the pre-arranged "complot," a mere announcement for effect. It would take the Horse weeks to reach the Transvaal.

Of the two Johannesburg emissaries whom the crisis left stranded at Cape Town, one, Mr. Hamilton, of the *Star*, went honourably back to face arrest ; the other, the chairman, the chief, the manifesto man, left for England. His nerves gave way in the crash, and he sailed for London, as it was assumed, to unmask Mr. Rhodes as the villain of the Johannesburg piece, Mr. Rhodes being already off on a flying visit to the Colonial Office, *en route* to Rhodesia. Eager anti-Rhodes Afrikanders appear to have helped Mr. Leonard off on his mission—to have worked on his fears to make him go, instead of returning to share his comrades' durance, helped him to disguise himself at a Cape Town barber's (the disguise was never needed), and were woefully "sold" when Mr. Leonard, recovered by the voyage, turned up in London an "Uitlander" renewed, though retired. Whether or no the remissness of the Transvaal Government was designed and prompted by what its friends at Cape Town had gathered as to the National Union Chairman's attitude to Mr. Rhodes[1] cannot be said. But while it got all the smaller fish extradited, it left Mr. Leonard hanging about Cape Town for weeks, though twice reminded by the Cape Attorney-General that he had as yet no warrant to arrest on. As soon as Mr. Leonard was a day at sea—lo! the warrant. No traitor, but an honest, well-meaning man, Fate cast the National Union Chairman for a part he could not play. It was his eloquent brother, by the way, not he, who in a wild moment drafted a Provisional Ministry of the Transvaal, with the portfolios elaborately distributed among the Reform leaders, which was printed and very nearly published in the thick of the crisis at Johannesburg.

Mr. Hofmeyr, who ordered the proclamation and wired to President Kruger on the 31st, "hoping that his burghers would play the man when they met Jameson's filibusters"—an odd, anxious note in that, by the way—struck one good blow for

---

[1] The idea was that Mr. Rhodes must have sent Jameson a private hint to go in. Mr. Rhodes at first thought the Johannesburg leaders must have done so. It has been ascertained both from Holden and Heany that they duly gave their "Stop!" messages to Jameson, and no contrary hint from either Cape Town or Johannesburg. An alleged diary of "Bobby" White's, with the entry, "Sun., Dec. 29th.—Received orders from Rt. Hon. C. J. Rhodes to cross the Border" (a discovery first published in *Cape Times*, May 10th), is admitted by Transvaal State Attorney (who bought it) to be a forgery.

English as well as for Dutch, a few days later. This rambling chapter shall end with it, and with the memorable episode of the Kaiser's telegram. The blunder of one hot-head had cleft a chasm between Dutch and English South Africa. The blunder of another hot-head was the one lucky stroke in those disastrous first few days of 1896 that for a moment closed the chasm up again. In pursuance of the subterranean intrigue with Germany, referred to in Chapter I., Dr. Leyds was, at the very moment when the crisis came, hanging about the Court of Berlin on a mission diplomatically described as "consulting German specialists about his throat." His state of mind when the cable reported the raid may be imagined. Had the revolution succeeded there was an end of him and his Hollanders in the Transvaal. If it failed there were fine times coming. The moment offered a supreme chance of completing the German entanglement. Exactly what passed between Dr. Leyds and the Kaiser is not known. What is known is that on Monday, the 30th December, a Member of the Executive Council of the Transvaal solemnly informed the British Agent at Pretoria that assistance had been asked from Germany, he added also from France. President Kruger has since stigmatized this statement of one of his own officials as a dastardly lie, and the only plausible explanation of it must be one which removes the onus of making the request from official Pretoria to the State Secretary's unofficial pranks at Berlin. However this may be, the German Consul and the German Foreign Office did agree by cable on the landing of certain German marines from Delagoa Bay, of course only "for protection of German interests," interests which have lately been expanded officially into a veto *inter alia* on any South African federation. The German Government did apply for leave to pass these troops through Portuguese territory, and the Portuguese Government did refuse that leave. Lastly, no sooner was Jameson defeated than there was given to the world this telegram :—

"Received *January* 3rd, 1896.
"From "To
Wilhelm I.R., President Kruger,
Berlin. Pretoria.

"I tender you my sincere congratulations that without appealing to the help of friendly Powers you and your people have been successful in opposing with your own forces the armed bands that have broken into your country to disturb the peace, in restoring order, and in maintaining the independence of your country against attacks from without.

"WILHELM I.R."

The publication of this officious message, with its hint about the help of other Powers being available in a matter where the Paramount Power had intervened, coming at a moment when feeling was very sore and tender, aroused a storm of anger. The Emperor was amazed at the fire he had kindled. It was only for a moment, if at all, that Dutch opinion wavered. *Ons Land*, a mischievous Dutch organ at the Cape, alone had an article palliating the attempt of Germany "to look after her own interests" in the Transvaal, and the Transvaal policy of playing off Germany against England. The *Cape Times* at once drew attention to this, and appealed to Mr. Hofmeyr, as the recognised leader of the party of which *Ons Land* aspires to be the organ, to speak out and disown the heresy, and Mr. Hofmeyr at once addressed this letter to the Editor :—

"Allow me, in connection with your leader of this morning, to say publicly what I have repeatedly stated to friends privately ever since Kaiser Wilhelm's blundering utterances on recent South African occurrences became known.

"I took his interference as mere bluster, not deserving any serious consideration, except in so far as it was calculated to create misleading impressions, or to raise false hopes in the Transvaal. Nobody knows better than His Imperial Majesty that the first German shot fired against England would be likely to be followed by a combined French and Russian attack on 'das Vaterland,' and by the acquisition by England of all German colonies, Damaraland included, which would not be an unmixed evil for the Cape."

From that moment the attitude of Dutch South Africa was beyond a doubt, and Dutch and English united in Mr. Hofmeyr's imperative "Hands off!"

This was the bitterest pill of all that were prescribed for the Kaiser's telegram. It was not till some months afterwards that speeches of the German Foreign Minister, and a published White Book, revealed the fact that Germany's half-avowed denial of British Paramountcy in South Africa included a claim to object to any such South African Customs Union as has been the avowed ideal of South African and British statesmen for many years! In January the practical reply to the Leyds-Berlin intrigue and the vapourings of the German Press was the prompt commissioning of a special service squadron (" for Delagoa Bay," was the popular guess) in readiness to reinforce any of the fleets already in commission or to constitute a separate force to be sent in any direction where danger might exist. The new squadron, which was placed under command of Rear-Admiral A. T. Dale, was composed of two first-class battleships, the *Revenge* and *Royal Oak*, the two first-class cruisers *Gibraltar* and *Thesus*, and the two second-class cruisers *Charybdis* and *Hermione*—all vessels of recent design and powerful armament, together with a flotilla of torpedo boat destroyers; all duly assembled at Spithead on the 18th January, in complete readiness to proceed to sea. The ease and rapidity with which the dockyard authorities at Portsmouth and Chatham fitted out this squadron without any fuss or special preparation was regarded at the time as showing that our resources in officers and men are larger than some critics have contended, and was quoted as a proof of a vast improvement in naval organization of recent years. At the same time the staff of artisans in Her Majesty's dockyards was largely augmented, and tenders were invited from private shipbuilding firms for the construction and immediate commencement of ten additional cruisers. The diplomatic situation soon simmered down, but popular excitement continued long after the slightest danger of a rupture had passed away, and the scenes in the London theatres and music halls, where jingoism of a very pronounced type held high carnival, forcibly recalled the popular frenzies about Russia and Constantinople.

Chapter XVII

PICKING UP THE BROKEN CROCKERY

THE pre-occupation of British Transvaal diplomacy for the first few months of 1896 was with an invitation to President Kruger to come to England in state in a British man-o'-war, and have a square talk with Mr. Chamberlain. The invitation arose from the usual "authorized" misunderstandings about the President's own wishes, and the answer to it was for months regarded as the battle-ground of Afrikanders *versus* Hollanders, the former wanting the President to go, the latter resisting a step which might lead to a friendly settlement. Finally, when the Government had kept the matter hanging on to an insulting length of time, Mr. Chamberlain insisted on "Yes" or "No," and, Dr. Leyds having returned in the nick of time from Germany and Holland, the Hollanders won and the answer was "No."

The following was, in brief, the course of the negotiations:—

"The original invitation to the President in January distinctly mentioned the condition that Article IV. of the London Convention (making Transvaal treaties with foreign States subject to British veto) was to be excluded from the discussion. This Mr. Chamberlain reiterated. 'You should,' he telegraphs a week later to the High Commissioner, 'in order to prevent the possibility of any mistake, repeat the statements . . . that we cannot consent to modify the terms of Article IV., . . . but other matters are open to friendly discussion.' The President was inclined to accept the invitation, if he could get the *non possumus* about Clause IV. made not quite as absolute, and if a number of questions of his choice were allowed to enter into the discussion, and assurance being given that they would be maturely considered 'with an earnest desire to comply with his wishes.' Of these questions he sent on the 25th February a portentous list. His first item was:—

"'The superseding of the Convention of London, with the eye, amongst others, on the violation of the territory of the South African Republic: because in several respects it has already virtually ceased to exist; because, in other respects, it has no more cause for existence; because it is injurious to the dignity of an independent Republic; because the very name and the continual arguments on the question of suzerainty, which since the conclusion of this Convention no longer exists, are used as a pretext, especially by a libellous Press, for wilfully inciting both white and coloured people against the lawful authority of the Republic; for intentionally bringing about misunderstanding and false relations between England and the Republic, whereby in this manner the interests of both countries and of their citizens and subjects are prejudiced, and the peaceful development of the Republic is opposed.'

"To this he added a new plea that Article IV. should not be excluded 'on account,' as he surmises, 'of false representations and lying reports spread by the Press and otherwise to the effect that the Government of the Republic has called in or sought the protection of other Powers.' He denied that he had ever sought 'or would ever seek' any such thing. He was prepared to 'give the necessary assurances.' (It was not the Press, by the way, but a member of the Executive Council, who 'spread' this particular calumny by telling the British Agent. It is easy to reconcile the statement and the denial when it is remembered that Dr. Leyds was at Berlin at the time). (2) The second item was the replacing of the Convention by something vaguely described as a treaty of amity and commerce, in which, however, England was to get guaranteed on the most favoured nation footing only her '*existing*' privileges . . . of commerce.' (3) Guarantees against any future raid, also against 'unlawful' military or police or even private movements on the border of the Republic. (4) Compensation for the raid. (5) Swaziland to be made part and parcel of the Republic. (6) Ditto as regards Zambaan's land. (7) Ditto as regards Umbegisa's land. (8) Revocation of the B.S.A. Company's Charter. This modest little bill President Kruger thought should be footed without grumbling because he is such an old man: 'considering especially my advanced age,' etc. But he was careful to leave an opening for adding a few more dishes to his Barmec de *menu*, if he should happen to think of anything later. 'The contents of this letter are without prejudice to an eventual statement in detail of lawful rights.'

"When Mr. Chamberlain got this remarkable draft agenda for the little 'friendly discussion' that he had so innocently proposed, his comment was evidently 'Phew!' What Oom Paul wanted to *get* was clear indeed but he scoured it in vain for any hint of what Oom Paul proposed to *give*. All that Mr. Chamberlain had suggested on this side was the consideration of the 'Uitlanders'' grievances; and this the letter ruled out—save for a guarded willingness to receive 'private hints'—as absolutely as Mr. Chamberlain had ruled out Article IV. So Mr. Chamberlain steeled his heart even against the President's 'advanced age,' as a consideration hardly relevant to the diplomatist, however interesting to the biographer. He observed drily that the President's letter 'refers only to the concessions which he desires to obtain from Her Majesty's Government, and that he offers nothing in return, except what they already possess under the existing Convention.' He felt sure that His Honour did not 'contemplate discussion on so one-sided a basis.' But that is exactly what His Honour did contemplate. 'President remarks,' the High Commissioner reported to Mr. Chamberlain soon afterwards, 'that it is not clear to him what is meant by the giving of concession from his side.' That is just it. 'Giving too little and asking too much' is a characteristic which an English versifier observed in the President's ancestors at an earlier period of their history, and commemorated as a national foible. Having got at last the definite answer he was pressing for, and finding it still 'one-sided,' Mr. Chamberlain, on April 27th, 'withdrew the invitation, which it appears was given under a misapprehension' (of the President's attitude)."

An incident of the prolonged wrangle was Mr. Chamberlain's "Home Rule" despatch, suggesting a scheme of modified autonomy for the Rand, which was accepted by nobody. The original idea of this was Mr. Merriman's. Some fuss was caused by premature publication of the despatch.

In March and April, when the delays of the Pretoria Government in answering Mr. Chamberlain were amounting to a grave slight, and it dawned on that "pushful" gentleman that they had merely been gaining time, and had no intention of even discussing reforms with him, the diplomatic situation became for a short time strained, almost to breaking point, and the Jingo part of the Press in London and South Africa poured forth war-talk. Some excitement (and loud cries of "turncoat" from the pavement politicians of Cape Town) were caused by a series of articles in the *Cape Times*, in the last days of March and early days of April, entitled, "A Fool's Paradise," "A Word to Mr. Chamberlain," etc., in which it was said :—

"Mr. Chamberlain may offer good advice and point out dangers as emphatically as he likes; but if once he tries to force the Transvaal Government about internal reforms by the threat of war, of which his mentors speak so glibly, we tell him plainly that he will have either to fulfil the threat—which is a wicked folly that we do not contemplate—or else to take a humiliating rebuff—which will be less wicked, but scarcely less foolish and mischievous. We hear that the Pretoria Government is very restive under some recent despatches. If Mr. Chamberlain is allowing himself to be pushed over the precipice, it is the duty of the High Commissioner, and the Colonial Government, too, for that matter, to pull him up before he gets any nearer the edge. We value the influence of the Paramount Power too highly in the present chaos of South African units to care to see that influence imperilled by a blunder. . . . As we have pointed out over and over again, even while the negotiations for the Kruger visit and the Big Deal seemed still practicable, the ' Uitlander ' must not expect that much can be done for his political status at the present moment. The Boer would have to be either a fool or a supreme statesman—and he is neither ; he is a Boer.

"Rumour says that in his impatience to get something to show before the Transvaal debate, the Colonial Secretary has been writing himself into a tone of ultimatum. Common sense says that, if he has, he is simply preparing for himself a crushing rebuff, to which the only effective rejoinder would be one which no responsible person dreams of."

Mr. Chamberlain soon afterwards explained away the language which the Pretoria Government had taken for that of ultimatum, and the air soon cleared, but not before the Governments of Cape Colony and of Natal had added their protest, and no doubt, though the Blue Books do not seem to reproduce this, the High Commissioner also. The latter was now summoned home to confer with Mr. Chamberlain over the situation created by the refusal of the Transvaal Government to negotiate reforms with Great Britain, and from the date of his visit the Imperial authorities at home and in South Africa have seemed to be at one in accepting a watchful patience as the only possible policy until the crisis of 1896 shall have been obliterated.

The Cape Ministry firmly resisted the attempt to get a special session called while race feeling and the personal issue about Mr. Rhodes were at fever-heat. The Colonial Parliament met in May, and the debate on the raid began in the House of Assembly on the 12th on a motion of Mr. Merriman's, a leading member of the Opposition, pointing at revocation of the B.S.A. Company's Charter—a formula adopted by both Republican Raads. Owing to a tedious notion that each individual member was bound in duty to his constituents to say something about the crisis, the debate lasted nearly three weeks. Mr. Merriman led the attack in a speech of unusual warmth and brilliant declamation, in which he directed every dialectic weapon against the continuance of the sovereign rights of the Charter. As to the *trading* rights, Mr. Merriman contemptuously disclaimed any idea or wish of interfering with them; but he must have the administrative scalp as well as the military one. He concluded by moving "That in the opinion of this House the exercise of sovereign rights by a trading and financial company such as the British South Africa Company is not consistent with the peace and prosperity of South Africa. That the Queen be requested, by respectful address, to take this matter into her most gracious consideration, and by the revocation or alteration of the terms of the Charter granted to the said Company to make such provision for the government of the territories embraced therein as may seem to her advisable."

The practical effect of this resolution would have been to ask Downing Street to assume the direct responsibility of administering the Chartered Company's territories, a proposal which markedly ignored the opinions and wishes of the colonists in the new country itself. What was more to the purpose, it made no allowance for the keen traditional prejudice against direct Downing Street rule which prevails among the Afrikander majority in the Cape Parliament. Mr. Merriman's effort was generally dismissed, in the formula usual in his case, as "brilliant, but—erratic." As the debate went on it became increasingly evident that many a country member who felt angry with Mr. Rhodes and the Chartered Company nevertheless shrank from the grave impolicy of banning altogether the only agency which had won the north for Colonial South Africa. In the result Mr. Merriman's sweeping resolution was negatived (May 27th) by sixty votes to eleven, and a judiciously worded amendment by Mr. Schreiner—which deplored and repudiated the raid, expressed a hope that it would be made the subject of a searching Imperial inquiry, and of steps making the recurrence of such an incident impossible in the future, and resolved on a Cape inquiry by Select Committee—was agreed to without a division.

Before Parliament met, the reaction stirred by attacks on Mr. Rhodes in Mr. J. B. Robinson's Cape Town paper, with which Mr. Sauer was closely connected, had led to Mr. Sauer's deposition from the leadership of the Opposition—as since then it has led to the cessation of the journal. Mr Rose-Innes, the new leader, than whom nobody more deplored the raid, took a line nearer to Mr. Merriman's than Mr. Schreiner's; but his amendment referred (in the most delicate manner possible) to Uitlander grievances and the need for their redress. It was lost by forty-five to twenty-eight. Mr. Schreiner evidently represented the "mixed emotions" of the Cape majority more nearly than any other leading member.

The surprise of the debate was its moderation. Marked tact and self-restraint was shown by most of the speakers who followed Mr. Merriman, and especially by Mr. Schreiner, in handling a subject which had caused so lately so much bitter racial feeling. Still there were one or two grievous lapses; *e.g.*, when Mr. Van Wyk casually expressed his conviction that 50,000 British troops would only provide a breakfast for those brave Republican burghers, and again, when Mr. Merriman lost his temper and stigmatized some provocative reminiscence of Mr. Orpen's as a "deliberate lie." This un-Parliamentary language the Speaker—perhaps because he was new to the work—allowed to pass at the moment, but the *amende* afterwards offered by Mr. Merriman was all the more gracious as it was spontaneous and voluntary. An incident of the debate which was keenly resented, and helped the pro-Rhodes and pro-Charter reaction, was the reading by Mr. Sauer of a telegram from the Chief Justice of the Transvaal urging exemplary steps against Rhodes and the Charter to satisfy Transvaal feeling.

At a later date in the session, the Jameson affair cropped up afresh in an indirect way in connection with Mr. Rhodes' leave of absence, which the House granted by a large majority, though subsequently refusing the same privilege to Dr. Harris.

In accordance with Mr. Schreiner's resolution, the Raid Select Committee began its sittings shortly after the conclusion of the debate, and the report—a bulky document of some 700 pages—was laid on the table of the House on the 21st July. There were two reports—one signed by everybody, including the Attorney-General (Chairman), subject to his own minority report, and another signed only by the Attorney-General. The majority report established as against Mr. Rhodes nothing beyond what the *Cape Times*, for instance, had publicly assumed from the time when the crisis disclosed the plot;[1] but so much it showed very clearly and ably. The report was Mr. Merriman's composition. It made it clear that Mr. Rhodes made some efforts to stop Jameson going in when he did, though he had connived at the earlier preparations; and the Committee found this, briefly and simply, "inconsistent with his duty as Prime Minister of this Colony." Everybody was prepared for so much, and more, but hardly for Sir Thomas Upington's rather special pleading and rather too legal exceptions in Mr. Rhodes' favour. Sir Thomas did not defend his minority report in the subsequent debate, and the other was adopted by the House practically without discussion on a moderate speech by Mr. Schreiner, which referred with sorrow to Mr. Rhodes' high aims in his wrong-doing, and which was left by the House to serve as a sufficient expression of its feeling.

Shortly after their arrival in England Jameson and his officers were quietly smuggled to Bow Street, where on the 25th February they were arraigned before Sir John Bridge on charges framed under the Foreign Enlistment Act, and re-

[1] Further :—See, for instance, issue of January 6th.

manded on bail until the 10th March, when the Attorney-General (Sir Richard Webster) opened the case at length for the prosecution. The examination of witnesses, many of whom had been summoned from the South African Republic, proved a long and tedious process, and public interest in the proceedings had largely waned when at length on the 15th June, after several intermediate adjournments, the preliminary examination was brought to a close. Jameson, Sir John Willoughby, Major Coventry, and the two Whites were committed for trial, the remainder of the accused being discharged by the magistrate.

The trial "at bar" of the raid leaders opened in the Queen's Bench Division on the 20th July, before the Chief Justice (Lord Russell of Killowen), Baron Pollock, and Mr. Justice Hawkins, with a special jury. The Attorney-General led for the Crown; Sir Edward Clarke, aided by Mr. Lockwood and a galaxy of legal talent, watched the interests of the accused. The trial lasted seven days. Sir Edward Clarke, in a brilliant address to the jury, made the best of what, from a legal point of view, was an intrinsically bad case; but Lord Russell's masterly summing-up brushed all technicalities aside, and left the accused no loophole of escape. It was, however, with evident reluctance that the jury returned a verdict of guilty. The sentences, pronounced by the Chief Justice, were as follows:—

Jameson, fifteen months; Willoughby, ten months; "Bobby" White, seven months; the others five months each, without hard labour.

One passage of the stern and masterly summing-up aroused much comment. The Chief Justice told the jury that an offence against the Foreign Enlistment Act has been committed whenever any one has equipped or fitted out or in any way taken part in preparing on British soil an expedition intended to operate against a friendly State. It is not even necessary, he added, that the expedition should actually start; the offence is complete when the intention is present. Then he laid it down that any subject of the Queen aiding, abetting, or procuring such an expedition, even from a place outside of Her Majesty's dominions, is equally an offender against the law—a *dictum* which Mr. Labouchere *cum suis* has caught at as flinging the net wide enough to take in Mr. Rhodes, Dr. Harris, and even "Herr Beit," who, however, is not yet a naturalized Briton. Whether the evidence is legally sufficient for this has yet to be seen. Seemingly not, unless by means of Mr. Rhodes consenting to incriminate himself at the London inquiry.

Mr. Rhodes' name, by the way, was barely mentioned once in the whole course of the Jameson trial, but on the following day a letter was published from Mr. Hawksley in the London papers, stating that Mr. Rhodes (who was then romantically risking his life away in Matabeleland, where he brought the harassing rebellion to an end at the famous "indaba" in the Matoppo Hills) was ready to surrender, come home, and take his trial whenever Her Majesty's Government might think fit to call upon him to do so.

The prisoners, in strict accordance with the terms of their sentence, were at first placed under the ordinary convict *régime*, and for a day or so public opinion was inflamed by the idea of these eminently political offenders sitting cropped and clad in the "broad arrow." But by the exercise of the Queen's prerogative an order was issued from the Home Office in a few days directing their removal to Holloway, where quarters were provided for them as first-class misdemeanants. Major Coventry's health being endangered by confinement, owing to the troublesome nature of the wound near the spine which he received at Krugersdorp, he was a few weeks later released from gaol. In December Dr. Jameson's release was also forced by his slow recovery from a painful operation, the cause aggravated largely by the effects of confinement on a man used to open-air activity.

The five Chief Officers, as the sequel to their sentence, were also retired from the Army, as was Colonel Rhodes.

While the raiders were standing trial in England, the eyes of South Africa were steadily fixed on Pretoria, where the spectacle of a great State prosecution—the arraignment of the leaders of a movement which enjoyed in some sense the sympathy of a majority of the people in the Republic—was being gradually unfolded. The preliminary examination of the Reformers began before Mr. Zeiler, the Judicial Commissioner, on the 3rd February. The chief features of this long-drawn function were that no witness could remember anything, and that the State Attorney seemed hardly to know what evidence to offer. It was not concluded until the 8th April, when the accused were formally committed.

The actual trial opened on the 24th April, before Mr. Justice Gregorowski, a Free State advocate, who, as the Transvaal judges had been made to act along with the Executive Council in many of the New Year doings, was specially imported to relieve them of an ambiguous position. Though known for severe sentences, one on a Kaffir being notoriously brutal, Mr. Gregorowski was then taken to be an enlightened lawyer. His position, however, was anomalous, as the necessary confirmation by Volksraad of his appointment was arranged to come after this trial, instead of before it. He was thus "imported on approval." At the eleventh hour the whole of the prisoners decided to plead guilty, four to high treason, the rest to *lèse majesté*, subject to certain reserves which were not objected to by the State Attorney, and evidence being led in as brief and perfunctory a manner as possible, the closing scene was not long delayed. On the 28th the four co-signatories with the absent Leonard of the letter to Jameson—George Farrar, Lionel Phillips, Colonel Rhodes, and John Hays Hammond—were sentenced to death, while the rank and file were ordered to be imprisoned for two years, to pay a fine of £2,000 each, or an extra year's imprisonment, and to be banished from the Republic for three years.

These were the heads of the Republic's one great industry; the men whom their able counsel, Mr. Wessels, could describe as "employers of half its population"; the men whose co-operation the Government had bargained for and made use of after Mr. Phillips's admission of their dealings with Jameson.

An indescribable wave of feeling swept the packed court, and then the streets. The condemned four kept a right English bearing.

The surprise occasioned at first by the plea of guilty ceased with the publication by the Pretoria Government of the mass of cipher telegrams laying bare to an astonished world the whole plot which led up to Jameson's march, according to the description of the earlier chapters of this number. It was an early private view of these astounding messages which had led Mr. Fischer, of the Free State, to go back to his Rand soon after the crisis and talk about "the bloody complot"[1] in terms which made all South African flesh creep. At that time, in the first flood of suspicion and sweeping inferences, the Pretoria Government declared that the plot included various heinous elements which there has never been an attempt to prove and which have since been abandoned—such as the arming of Kaffirs on the Rand, the stirring up of the native chiefs to attack the Transvaal or the Free State, and the charge that the raid was in some mysterious and unexplained way intended to rehabilitate the finances of the Chartered Company by what Mr. Austin calls "the crushings of all the Rand."

Despite the shock of the cipher telegrams, the severity of the Gregorowski sentences aroused great public excitement in England and throughout South Africa. It was repeated how the new Judge had asked one of his colleagues for a black cap before the trial even began. It was asserted, even by sober lawyers, that the sentences were simply designed for the Government to make political capital by remitting them in the piecemeal way which was eventually adopted. One of Gregorowski's colleagues cut him in private life, and there were

[1] The actual phrase itself was an embroidery upon Mr. Fischer's Dutch wrought by the fervid pen of the Free State *Express*.

many other signs of the extraordinary feeling created. Mr. Chamberlain lost no time in informing the Commons (April 29th) that he had telegraphed to President Kruger, expressing his confidence that the death sentences would be commuted, and adding that he had assured Parliament to this effect. The tension of public feeling was relieved in South Africa on the same day by the news that commutation had actually taken place. Some further intimation of the intentions of the Executive was now eagerly awaited; but as day after day, and week after week passed without any sign being given by President Kruger or his advisers, the public grew anxious and impatient. Meantime, the Reformers were herded together, with every circumstance of discomfort, in a corrugated iron shed, hastily improvised for their accommodation within the precincts of Pretoria gaol. The district surgeon warned the Government regarding the unsanitary condition of the place and the hardships suffered by the prisoners under its baking roof; but his representations passed unheeded, and on the 16th May one of the prisoners, whose mind had become unhinged, was discovered to have committed suicide. The tragedy of poor Gray, deepened as it was by the despair of a young wife hopefully awaiting her husband's release at the prison gates, cast a gloom over the whole of South Africa, and was not without its effect on the Transvaal Government. Hollander influences, which had, it was believed, been prolonging as far as possible the period of suspense,[1] recoiled before the genuine sentiment of concern which the Reformer's death aroused among the kindly burghers; and a few days later (May 19th) it was made known that the Executive had commuted the sentences of the leaders to fifteen years' imprisonment, and that three sick prisoners, Lionel Phillips being one of them, had been sent to the Volks Hospital. The

---

[1] When the prisoners were being marched off to gaol, and also while those under death sentences were driven past the Government Buildings, Dr. Leyds stood conspicuous with his hands in his pockets and ostentatiously laughed at them.

sentences on the other prisoners, with eight exceptions, were reduced on the following day to terms of twelve, six and three months, or rather, they were given to understand that the question of their release would be favourably considered if they petitioned the Executive at the expiration of those periods; and the eight referred to were set free at once on payment of their fines.

Still public sentiment was by no means satisfied, it being too evident that the policy of the Transvaal Executive was to dole out magnanimity by inches, whereas the interests of South Africa required that there should be a speedy amnesty. On the 23rd May the *Cape Times* declared that the policy of silence had failed, and that the Government would make the releases then and then only when it was shown that they would lose more political capital by keeping the prisoners on tenterhooks than they could possibly make out of them. The *Cape Times* therefore proposed a plan, set forth in an article entitled, "To the Towns of South Africa: An Historical Opportunity," of which the following is an extract :—

"What we want to see, then, is that all the towns of South Africa—for they are all at one, they only wait for the signal—should, on this subject of the prisoners, speak out and speak together. Suppose that a simultaneous and unanimous vote were passed by large and orderly gatherings at Cape Town, Durban, Bloemfontein, Pretoria, Johannesburg, Port Elizabeth, Kimberley, East London, Queen's Town, King William's Town, Graham's Town, Bulawayo and Salisbury. We have communicated inquiringly with each of these towns, and with others, and the answers already received indicate that a great movement is beginning through the length and breadth of the country, and that, if action be not taken unitedly, it will be taken sporadically.

"We plead for united action. Let a day be chosen—say, to-day week, next Saturday. For that day let meetings be called by the Mayors or by influential public leaders. Let these secure that the tone set from the beginning is sober and responsible. Let a form of resolution be chosen expressing in general terms the public sentiment in favour of a spirit of amnesty in dealing with the still imprisoned Reformers, and let this be submitted to each of the simultaneous meetings, subject only to such local alterations as may be necessary to secure genuine unanimity. We would suggest that the resolution itself should stick strictly to the question of the prisoners, and the effect would be strengthened if there were a general tacit consent that the discussion should not stray off more than is necessary into the detail of 'Uitlander' grievances, the franchise question, the merits or demerits of Rhodes and Jameson. The feeling on the actual issue will be there and to spare—it is for chairman and leading speakers to keep it to the right channel. If all goes well in this respect, if only a great part goes well, is it easy to believe that such a simultaneous and unanimous vote of all the towns of South Africa—representing nowadays, after all, not much less than half the entire white population of the country—can be wholly without effect? Let the towns make themselves spokesmen for the country on the side of freedom, as towns did in the middle ages. It may prove an historical opportunity. If our voice fails, the voice of the townsmen, if there is to be more suspense, more chaffering, more gaol tragedies, more lasting embitterments, till, perhaps, some chance explosive lights the smouldering embers of hatred into war, at least our action, the action of the towns at this critical juncture, will be on record. On other shoulders will rest the unenviable responsibility."

This article evoked immediate response from many centres. On the following Monday a letter from Mr. Rose-Innes, the most respected of Cape politicians, proposed a capital amendment to the *Cape Times* plan: viz., that the "uniform resolution" should take rather the form of a uniform petition, which the Mayor should be authorized by each town's meeting to sign and carry to Pretoria as its delegate. Mr. Innes' name gave the movement fresh impetus. The Political Association of Cape Town (May 27th) set to work to organize the other centres. On the 29th of the same month the Cape Town meeting under the scheme was held in the Good Hope Hall, and in the course of the ensuing week the rest of the towns followed suit. The example thus set told in other directions. The Cape and Natal Governments, as soon as they saw that the movement was going to be a universal one, addressed friendly representations to the Transvaal Government, recommending amnesty, while the Bond itself, and the Associated Chambers of Commerce determined to send delegates of their own to Pretoria. The first fruits of the agitation were soon gathered.

The day after the great Cape Town meeting, the whole of

the prisoners, with the exception of the four leaders and Messrs. Sampson and Davies, were released on payment of their fines and entering into a bond not to meddle with Transvaal politics for a term of years. It was explained that as Messrs. Sampson and Davies had refused to sign a petition to the Executive, their cases had not been considered, and they still remain in prison.

If it was believed that these releases would nip the amnesty movement in the bud, and that the leaders would be left to their fate, the anticipation was ill-founded.

On the 10th June the great deputation of over fifty Mayors or other municipal officials, having a large additional number of petitions from unrepresented centres, mustered in Pretoria. And on the following day came the news that the four leaders were to be released immediately on payment of a fine of £25,000 each. The decree of banishment was waived on an agreement being entered into by each of the four not to be mixed up in Transvaal politics again for the space of fifteen years. The fines were at once paid, and the prisoners set free. Colonel Rhodes, refusing to sign the bond required, was conducted to the frontier, whence he speedily found his way to Rhodesia.

The trials of Jameson and the Reformers do not, however, exhaust the list of prosecutions arising out of the famous raid. The Colonial Government, in pursuance of their policy of conciliation towards the South African Republic, set inquiries on foot regarding the smuggling of arms over the Cape Railways, and on the 4th March Mr. Gardner Williams, general manager of De Beers, was arrested at Kimberley on a charge of removing rifles and other warlike munitions without a license. The arrest of Mr. F. F. Rutherfoord, a well-known Cape Town merchant and agent, on a similar charge followed two days later. In the case of Mr. Williams, great care had been observed in concealing the arms in course of transit, and also in putting the railway authorities off the scent; in the case of Mr. Rutherfoord there was no concealment whatever, and it was actually at the request of the Customs authorities that he sent the offending consignments forward. The law requiring a license, it was shown, had been allowed to fall into desuetude. Under these circumstances Mr. Rutherfoord's offence was treated as a merely technical one, and he was mulcted in a penalty of £20 (April 15th); Mr. Gardner Williams was committed to take his trial, but the case was remitted to the magistrate, who (May 27th) imposed a fine of £30, with the alternative of three months' imprisonment.

It is only natural that the Jameson Raid should have left the back-country Transvaal burghers uneasy and suspicious. For months the reinforcement of the South African garrisons and the movements of troops consequent on the outbreak of the Matabele rebellion gave rise to many absurd rumours in the Western Transvaal. On the 20th April the State Secretary reported that there was unrest among the burghers owing to troops being assembled and kept at Mafeking, instead of being sent through to Matabeleland as expected, and that officers and men were spreading the rumour that they were destined to march into the Republic. The High Commissioner replied on the same day, assuring President Kruger that the alleged detention was not in accordance with fact, as the troops were being sent forward as fast as practicable, and adding that he need hardly repeat assurances so frequently given that Her Majesty's Government had no hostile intentions against the South African Republic. During the next week or two the military wags seem to have been at work on the border, for on the 2nd May Sir Jacobus de Wet sent a breathless despatch to the High Commissioner, mentioning fresh disquieting rumours and urging the appointment of a joint Commission to convince the Transvaal burghers of the true position. This suggestion was too much for Lord Rosmead, after his repeated denials and assurances, and he administered to Sir Jacobus the severe snubbing which proved the prelude to the discovery by Mr. Chamberlain that the British Agent had "earned his rest." The State Secretary on the same day, however, apprised Lord

Rosmead of affidavits by burghers testifying to the presence of six thousand troops at Aasvogelkop and Mafeking, "and similar bodies everywhere along the frontier," getting ready for a fresh invasion of Transvaal territory. These were the rumours which had made such a deep impression on the British Agent, and His Excellency, in rebuking President Kruger for noticing such a tissue of absurdities, suggested that proceedings for perjury should be taken against the authors of the affidavits.

Side by side with the concern displayed at the most trivial military movements on the British side of the frontier, warlike preparations on a very large scale have been in progress in the Transvaal since the beginning of the year. New forts are in course of erection in Pretoria, the whole of the burghers have been armed, and the importation of warlike munitions has been on a scale altogether without precedent in the history of South Africa. These preparations have naturally been much discussed, and the rumour has more than once been revived that the Transvaal Government were preparing the way for the declaration of the absolute independence of the Republic. Whether owing to the rinderpest, or to the prevalence of wiser counsels, or to the fact that no such *coup* was ever contemplated by the Transvaal Government, it is fortunate that nothing has occurred since the raid to disturb the good relations between the South African Republic and the Paramount Power.

The following figures culled from the Transvaal Estimates for the current financial year will furnish some idea of the scale of magnificence on which Transvaal warlike preparations have been conducted:—

War Office Salaries	£52,462
War Purposes	943,510
Johannesburg Revolt	160,000
"Public Works"	730,000
	£1,885,972

Public works, it may be noted, is largely a Hollander euphemism for forts and their appurtenances; so that the total outlay on military preparations amounts to over a million and a half sterling, or more than a quarter of the whole estimated expenditure for the year.

The Transvaal Volksraad during a prolonged session turned out the expected lot of retrogressive and coercive legislation. As against one good thing done for the mining industry (a Liquor Law not yet operative), there have been an almost Russian Press Law, and an Uitlander Expulsion Law and Uitlander Immigration Law, which both look like violating the London Convention. In December, however, the President at a banquet made a speech, warmly protesting his intention to uphold that instrument as a bulwark of the Republic: a *volte face* which, despite the busy warlike preparations, made the year close in a feeling of greater serenity.

In January, 1897, Mr. Rhodes returned to England, which he had visited for a week just after the crisis, in order to face a Select Committee of the House of Commons, re-appointed from the last session to enquire into the origin of the raid, and the administration of the Chartered Company, and report on its future.

Since such an enquiry was first promised, early last year, Mr. Rhodes' star had come once more into the ascendant. So far, the steps taken against him had been confined to accepting his resignation of the Managing Directorship of the Chartered Company, and sending an Imperial officer, Sir Richard Martin, to take over the Company's police and military administration. But Mr. Rhodes "in his shirt," as Mr. Stead put it, was still Mr. Rhodes. The man who, as Mr. Chamberlain had reminded a sympathetic House, "could not move a single policeman," when he went back to the veld shorn of all his offices, nevertheless rallied the settlers and made peace with the rebel Matabele at the famous *indaba*. Wherever he passed through in the Colony on his way home, Mr. Rhodes had an unprecedented popular reception, in which, strange to say, a distinct Dutch element took part; and he now confronts the inquiry with British South Africa solidly at his back in an enthusiasm which has created a new South African situation.

APPENDICES

APPENDIX I

THE "LETTER OF INVITATION"

A.   JOHANNESBURG,
                                         20*th Dec.*,[1] 1895.

DR. JAMESON,

DEAR SIR,—The position of matters in this State has become so critical that we are assured that at no distant period there will be conflict between the Government and the Uitlander population. It is scarcely necessary for us to recapitulate what is now matter of history. Suffice it to say, that the position of thousands of Englishmen and others is rapidly becoming intolerable. Not satisfied with making the Uitlander population pay, virtually, the whole of the revenue of the country, while denying them representation, the policy of the Government has been steadily to encroach upon the liberty of the subject, and to undermine the security for property to such an extent as to cause a very deep-seated sense of discontent and danger.

A foreign corporation of Hollanders is, to a considerable extent, controlling our destinies, and, in conjunction with the Boer leaders, endeavouring to cast them in a mould which is wholly foreign to the genius of the people. Every public act betrays the most positive hostility, not only to everything English, but to the neighbouring States as well. In short, the internal policy of the Government is such as to have roused into antagonism to it not only, practically, the whole body of Uitlanders, but a large number of the Boers; while its external policy has exasperated the

---

[1] Date left blank in original. Filled in by Dr. Wolff.

neighbouring States, causing the possibility of great danger to the peace and independence of this Republic.

Public feeling is in a condition of smouldering discontent. All the petitions of the people have been refused with a greater or less degree of contempt, and, in the debate on the franchise petition, signed by nearly 40,000 people, one member challenged the Uitlanders to fight for the rights they asked for, and not a single member spoke against him.

Not to go into detail, we may say that the Government has called into existence all the elements necessary for armed conflict. The one desire of the people here is for fair play, the maintenance of their independence, and the preservation of those public liberties without which life is not worth having. The Government denies these things and violates the national sense of Englishmen at every turn.

What we have to consider is, what will be the condition of things here in the event of conflict?

Thousands of unarmed men, women, and children of our race will be at the mercy of well-armed Boers; while property of enormous value will be in the greatest peril. We cannot contemplate the future without the gravest apprehension, and feel that we are justified in taking any steps to prevent the shedding of blood, and to ensure the protection of our rights.

It is under these circumstances that we feel constrained to call upon you to come to our aid should disturbance arise here.

The circumstances are so extreme that we cannot avoid this step, and we cannot but believe that you, and the men under you, will not fail to come to the rescue of people who would be so situated. We guarantee any expense that may reasonably be incurred by you in helping us, and ask you to believe that nothing but the sternest necessity has prompted this appeal.

We are yours faithfully,

(Signed) CHARLES LEONARD.
FRANCIS RHODES.
LIONEL PHILLIPS.
JOHN HAYS HAMMOND.
GEORGE FARRAR.

APPENDIX II

THE NATIONAL UNION MANIFESTO[1]

IF I am deeply sensible of the honour conferred upon me by being elected Chairman of the National Union, I am profoundly impressed with the responsibilities attached to the position. The issues to be faced in this country are so momentous in character that it has been decided that, prior to the holding of a public meeting, a review of the condition of affairs should be placed in your hands, in order that you may consider matters quietly in your homes. It has also been decided that it will be wise to postpone the meeting which was to have taken place on the 27th December until the 6th day of January next.

On that day you will have made up your minds on the various points submitted to you, and we will ask you for direction as to our future course of action. It is almost unnecessary to recount all the steps which have been taken by the National Union, and I shall, therefore, confine myself to a very short review of what has been done.

THE THREE PLANKS.

The constitution of the National Union is very simple. The three objects which we set before ourselves are : (1) The Maintenance of the Independence of the Republic ; (2) The Securing of Equal Rights ; and (3) the Redress of Grievances. This brief but comprehensive programme has never been lost sight of, and I think we may challenge contradiction fearlessly when we assert that we have constitutionally, respectfully, and steadily prosecuted our purpose. Last year you will remember a respectful petition, praying for the franchise, signed by 13,000 men, was received with

[1] Given as it appeared in a *Cape Times'* telegram of 27th December, 1895, retaining the newspaper paragraph headings.

contemptuous laughter and jeers in the Volksraad. This year the Union, apart from smaller matters, endeavoured to do three things.

Three Efforts: (1) The Raad Elections.

First we were told that a progressive spirit was abroad, that twelve out of twenty-four members of the First Volksraad had to be elected, and we might reasonably hope for reform by the type of broad-minded men who should be elected. It was, therefore, resolved that we should do everything in our power to assist in the election of the best men who were put up by the constituencies; and everything that the law permitted us to do in this direction was done.

The result has been only too disappointing, as the record of the debates and the division list in the Volksraad prove. We were, moreover, told that public speeches in Johannesburg prevented the progressive members from getting a majority of the Raad to listen to our requests, that angry passions were inflamed, and that if we would only hold our tongues reform would be brought about. We, therefore, resolved in all loyalty to abstain from inflaming angry passions, although we never admitted we had, by act or speech, given reason for legislators to refuse justice to all. Hence our silence for a long time.

(2) The Railway Concession.

We used all our influence to get the Volksraad to take over the railway concession; but, alas! the President declared, with tears in his voice, that the independence of the country was wrapped up in this question, and a submissive Raad swept the petitions from the table.

(3) The Franchise Petition.

Our great effort, however, was the petition for the franchise, with the moderate terms of which you are all acquainted. This petition was signed by more than 38,000 persons. What was the result? We were called unfaithful for not naturalizing ourselves, when naturalization means only that we should give up our original citizenship and get nothing in return, and become subject to disabilities. Members had the calm assurance to state, without any grounds whatever, that the signatures were forgeries, and, worst of

all, one member, in an inflammatory speech, challenged us openly
to fight for our rights, and his sentiment seemed to meet with considerable approval. This is the disappointing result of our honest
endeavours to bring about a fusion between the people of this
State and that true union and equality which alone can be the
basis of prosperity and peace. You all know that, as the law now
stands, we are virtually excluded for ever from getting the franchise, and, by a malignant ingenuity, our children born here are
deprived of the rights of citizenship unless their fathers take an
oath of allegiance, which brings them nothing but disabilities.

The Bitter Cry of the "Uitlander."

We are the vast majority in this State. We own more than
half of the land, and, taken in the aggregate, we own at least ninetenths of the property in this country ;-yet, in all matters affecting
our lives, our liberties, and our properties, we have absolutely no
voice. Dealing now first with the legislature, we find taxation is
imposed upon us without any representation whatever, that taxation is wholly inequitable : (*a*) because a much greater amount is
levied from the people than is required for the needs of government ; (*b*) because it is either class taxation pure and simple, or,
by the selection of the subjects, though nominally universal, it is
made to fall upon our shoulders ; and (*c*) because the necessaries
of life are unduly burdened.

Abuse of Public Expenditure.

Expenditure is not controlled by any public official independent
of the Government. Vast sums are squandered, while the Secret
Service Fund is a dark mystery to everybody. But, essential as
the power to control taxation and expenditure is to a free people,
there are other matters of the gravest importance which are
equally precious. The Legislature in this country is the supreme
power, apparently uncontrolled by any fixed constitution. The
chance will of a majority in a Legislature elected by one-third of
the people is capable of dominating us in every relation of life,
and when we remember that those who hold power belong to a
different race, speak a different language, and have different pursuits from ourselves, that they regard us with suspicion, and even
hostility, that, as a rule, they are not educated men, and that

their passions are played upon by unscrupulous adventurers, it must be admitted that we are in very grave danger.

Tribute to the Moderates.

I think that it is but just to bear tribute to the patriotic endeavours of a small band of enlightened men in the Volksraad who have earnestly condemned the policy of the Government, and warned them of its danger. To Mr. Jeppe, Mr. Lucas Meyer, the De Jagers, Mr. Loveday, and a few others in the First Raad, leaving out the Second Raad, we owe our best thanks, for they have fought our battle, and confirmed the justice of our cause. But when we look to the debates of the last few years, what do we find? All through a spirit of hostility; all through an endeavour not to meet the just wants of the people; not to remove grievances; not to establish the claim to our loyalty by just treatment and equal laws; but to repress the publication of the truth, however much it might be required in the public interest; to prevent us from holding public meetings; to interfere with the Courts, and to keep us in awe by force.

The Powers of the Executive.

There is now threatened a danger even graver than those which have preceded it. The Government is seeking to get through the Legislature an Act which will vest in the Executive the power to decide whether men have been guilty of sedition, and to deport them and confiscate their goods. The Volksraad has, by resolution, affirmed the principle, and has instructed the Government to bring up a Bill accordingly next session. To-day this power rests justly with the courts of law, and I can only say that, if this Bill becomes law, the power of the Executive Government of this country would be as absolute as the power of the Czar of Russia. We shall have said good-bye finally to the last principle of liberty.

President Kruger Indicted.

Coming to the Executive Government, we find that there is no true responsibility to the people. None of the great departments of State are controlled by Ministerial officers in the proper sense; the President's will is virtually supreme, and he, with his unique influence over the legislators of the House, aided by an able if hostile State Secretary, has been the author of every Act directed against the liberties of the people. It is well that this should be recognised. It is well that President Kruger should be known for what he is, and that, once for all, the false pedestal on which he has so long stood should be destroyed. I challenge contradiction when I state that no important Act has found a place on the Statute book during the last ten years without the seal of President Kruger's will upon it; nay, he is the father of every such Act. Remember that all legislation is initiated by the Government, and, moreover, President Kruger has expressly supported every Act by which we and our children have been deprived by progressive steps of the right to acquire franchise; by which taxation has been imposed upon us almost exclusively, and by which the right and the liberty of the Press, and the right of public meeting have been attacked.

The Judges and the Liberty of the Subject.

Now we come to the judicial system. The High Court of this country has, in the absence of representation, been the sole guardian of our liberties. Although it has, on the whole, done its work ably, affairs are in a very unsatisfactory position. The judges have been underpaid, their salaries have never been secure, the most undignified treatment has been meted out to them, and the status and independence of the Bench have on more than one occasion been attacked. A deliberate attempt was made two years ago by President Kruger and the Government to reduce the Bench to a position subordinate to the Executive Government, and only recently we had in the Witfontein matter the last of the cases in which the Legislature interfered with vested rights of action.

No Real Trial by Jury.

The administration of justice by minor officials, by native commissioners, and by field-cornets, has produced, and is producing, the gravest unrest in the country; and, lastly, gentlemen, the great bulwark of liberty, the right to trial by jurymen who are our peers, is denied to us. Only the burgher or naturalized burgher is entitled to be a juryman, or, in other words, any one of us is liable to be tried upon the gravest charge possible by jurymen who are in no sense our peers, who belong to a different race, who regard us with a greater or lesser degree of hostility, and whose passions, if inflamed, might prompt them, as weak human creatures, to inflict the gravest injustice, even to deprive men of their lives. Supposing, in the present tense condition of political feeling, any one of us were tried before a Boer jury on any charge having a political flavour about it, should we be tried by our peers, and should we have a chance of receiving even-handed justice?

THE SECRET SERVICE FUND.

When we come to the administration we find that there is the grossest extravagance; that Secret Service moneys are squandered, that votes are exceeded, that the public credit is pledged, as it was pledged in the case of the Netherlands Railway Company, and, later still, in the case of the Selati Railway, in a manner which is wholly inconsistent with the best interests of the people.

SQUANDERING THE PUBLIC REVENUE.

The Delagoa Bay festivities are an instance of a reckless disregard of a Parliamentary vote. £20,000 was voted for those useless festivities—about £60,000 was really expended, and I believe certain favoured gentlemen hailing from Holland derived the principal benefit. It is said that £400,000 of our money has been transferred for some extraordinary purpose to Holland. Recently £17,000 is said to have been sent out of the country with Dr. Leyds for Secret Service purposes, and the public audit seems a farce. When the progressive members endeavoured to get an explanation about large sums of money they were silenced by a vote of the majority prompted by President Kruger. The administration of the public service is in a scandalous condition.

A CORRUPT LEGISLATURE.

Bribery and corruption are rampant. We have had members of the Raad accepting presents of imported spiders and watches wholesale from men who were applying for concessions, and we have the singular fact that in every instance the recipient of the gift voted for the concession. We have the President openly stating that such acceptance of presents was wholly moral. We have a condition of affairs in which the time of the meeting of the Volksraad is looked upon as the period of the greatest danger to our interests, and it is an open secret that a class of man has sprung up who is in constant attendance upon the members of the Volksraad, and whose special business appears to be the "influencing" of members one way or the other. It is openly stated that enormous sums of money have been spent, some to produce illegitimate results, some to guard against fresh attacks upon vested rights. The Legislature passed an Act solemnly denouncing corruption in the public service. One man, not an official, was punished under the law, but nothing has ever been done since to eradicate the evil.

AND A TAINTED CIVIL SERVICE.

I think thousands of you are satisfied of the venality of many of our public servants. I wish to guard against the assumption that all public servants are corrupt. Thank God there are many who are able and honourable men, and it must be gall and wormwood to these men to find the whole tone of the service destroyed, and to have themselves made liable to be included under one general denunciation. But there can be no health in an administration, and the public morals must be sapped also, when such things as the Smit case, and the recent Stiemens case, go unnoticed and unpunished.

TWO GLARING CASES.

I think it right to state openly what those cases are. N. J. Smit is the son of a member of the Government. He absented himself for months without leave. He was meantime charged in the newspapers with embezzlement. He returned, was fined £25 for being absent without leave, and was reinstated in office. He is now the Mining Commissioner of Klerksdorp. He has been charged in at least two newspapers—one of them a Dutch newspaper, *Land en Volk*, published within a stone's-throw of the Government Offices—with being an "unpunished thief," and yet the Government have taken no notice of it, nor has he thought fit to bring an action to clear himself. In the Stiemens case, two officials in the Mining Department admitted in the witness-box that they had agreed to further the application of a relative for the grant of a piece of public land at Johannesburg, on condition that they were each to receive one quarter of the proceeds. A third official, the Landdrost of Pretoria, admitted that he had received £300 for his "influence" in furthering the application; yet no notice had been taken by the Government of their scandalous conduct, and sad to say, the judges who heard the case did not think it their duty to comment strongly upon the matter. I have in my possession now a notarial deed which proves that the Railway Commissioner, the Landdrost, and the Commandant of Pretoria are members of a syndicate whose avowed object is, or was, to wrest from the companies their right to the "bewaarplaatsen." This shows what is going on, and what is the measure of safety of title to property. Those who should guard our rights are our worst enemies. In a law introduced by the present Government, the Government, instead of the Courts, are the final judges in cases of disputed elections. No Election Committees are allowed. This operates against candidates opposed to the Government, because the Government has virtually a vast standing army of committee men, henchmen, officials being allowed openly to take part in swaying elections, and the Government being in a position, by the distribution of contracts, appointments, purchase of concessions, the expenditure of Secret Service money, and otherwise, to bring into existence and maintain a large number of supporters who act as canvassers always on the right side in times of elections.

NATIVE AFFAIRS.

The administration of native affairs is a gross scandal and a source of immense loss and danger to the community. Native Commissioners have been permitted to practise extortion, injustice, and cruelty upon the natives under their jurisdiction. The Government has allowed petty tribes to be goaded into rebellion. We have had to pay the costs of the "wars," while the wretched victims of their policy have had their tribes broken up, sources of native labour have been destroyed, and large numbers of prisoners have been kept in gaol for something like eighteen months without trial. It was stated in the newspapers that, out of sixty-three men imprisoned, thirty-one had died in that period, while the rest were languishing to death for want of vegetable foods. We have had revelations of repulsive cruelty on the part of field-cornets. We all remember the Rachman case and the April case, in which the judges found field-cornets guilty of brutal conduct to unfortunate natives; but the worst feature about these cases is that the Government has set the seal of its approval upon the acts of these officials by paying the costs of the actions out of public funds, and the President of the State a few days ago made the astounding statement in regard to the April case, that, notwithstanding the judgment of the High Court, the Government thought that Prinsloo was right in his action, and therefore paid the costs. The Government is enforcing the "plakkerswet," which forbids the locating of more than five families on one farm. The field-cornets in various districts have recently broken up homes of large numbers of natives settled on "Uitlanders'" lands, just at the time when they had sown their crops to provide the next winter's food. The application of this law is most uneven, as large numbers of natives are left on the farms of the Boers. Quite recently a well-known citizen brought into the country, at great expense, some hundreds of families, provided them with land, helped them to start life, stipulating only that he should be able to draw from amongst them labour at a fair wage to develop his properties. Scarcely had they been settled when the field-cornet came down and scattered the people, distributing them among Boer farms. The sources of the native labour supply have been seriously interfered with at the borders by Government measures, and difficulties have been placed in the way of transport of natives by railway to the mines. These things are all a drain upon us as a State, and many of them are a burning disgrace to us as a people.

THE EDUCATION SCANDAL.

The great public that subscribes the bulk of the revenue is virtually denied all benefit of State aid in education. There has been a deliberate attempt to Hollanderise the Republic, and to kill the English language. Thousands of children are growing up in this land in ignorance, unfitted to run the race of life, and there is the possibility that a large number of them will develop into criminals. We have had to tax ourselves privately to guard against these dangers, and the iniquity of denying education to the children of men who are paying taxes is so manifest that I pass on with mingled feelings of anger and disgust.

RAILWAYS.

This important branch of the public service is entirely in the hands of a corporation domiciled in Holland. This corporation holds a concession, of course, under which not only was there no adequate control over expenditure in construction, but it is entitled to charge, and is charging, us outrageous tariffs. How outrageous these are will be seen from the admission made by Mr. Middelberg that the short section of 10 miles between Boksburg and Krugersdorp is paying more than the interest on the cost of the construction of the whole line of railway to Delagoa Bay. To add these to its general revenue, of which 10 per cent. is set aside as a sinking fund, and then to take for itself 15 per cent. of the balance, the Company reports annually to the Raad from Amsterdam in a language which is practically foreign to it, and makes up its accounts in guelders, a coinage which our legislators, I venture to say, know nothing of, and this is independence. We are liable as guarantors for the whole of the debt. Lines have been built entirely on our credit, and yet we have no say and no control over these important public works beyond the show of control which is supposed to be exercised by the present Railway Commissioner. The Company, in conjunction with the Executive Government, is in a position to control our destinies to an enormous extent, to influence our relations internally and externally, to bring about such friction with the neighbouring States as to set the whole of South Africa in tumult. Petitions have been presented to the Raad, but the President has constantly brushed these aside with the well-worn argument that the independence of the State is involved in the matter. It is involved in the matter, as all who remember the recent Drifts question will admit. I have been told that it is dangerous for the country to take over the railway, because it would afford such an immense field for corruption. Surely this is the strongest condemnation of the Government by its friends, for, if it is not fit to run a railway, how can it be fit to manage a whole State? The powers controlling this railway are flooding the public service with Hollanders to the exclusion of our own people, and I may here say that in the most important departments of the State we are being controlled by the gentlemen from the Low Country. While the innocent Boer hugs to himself the delusion that he is preserving his independence, they control us politically through Dr. Leyds, financially through the Netherlands Railway, educationally through Dr. Mansvelt, and in the Department of Justice through Dr. Coster.

CUSTOMS AND TRADE.

The policy of the Government in regard to taxation may be practically described as protection without production. The most monstrous hardships result to consumers, and merchants can scarcely say from day to day where they are. Twice now has the Government entered into competition with traders who have paid their licences and rents, and who keep staffs. Recently grain became scarce. The Government were petitioned to suspend the duties, which are cruelly high, in order to assist the mining industry to feed its labourers. The Government refused this request, on the plea that it was not in a position to suspend duties without the permission of the Volksraad, and yet within a few days we find that the Government has granted a concession to one of its friends to import grain free of duty, and to sell it in competition with the merchants who have had to pay duties. I do not attempt to deal with this important question adequately, but give this example to show how the Government regards the rights of traders.

Monopolies.

It has been the steady policy of the Government to grant concessions. No sooner does any commodity become absolutely essential to the community than some harpy endeavours to get a concession for its supply. There is scarcely a commodity or a right which has not been made the subject of an application for the grant of a concession. We all remember the bread-and-jam concession, the water concession, the electric lighting concession, and many others, but I need only point to the dynamite concession to show how these monopolies tend to paralyse our industries. There may be some of you who have not yet heard, and some who have forgotten, the facts connected with that outrage upon public rights.

Story of the Dynamite Concession.

Some years ago, Mr. Lippert got a concession for the sole right to manufacture and sell dynamite and all other explosives. He was to manufacture the dynamite in this country. For years he imported dynamite, under the name of Guhr Impregne, duty free. He never manufactured dynamite in the country, and, upon public exposure, the Government was compelled to cancel the concession, the President himself denouncing the action of the concessionnaire as fraudulent. For a time we breathed freely, thinking we were rid of this incubus, but within a few months the Government granted virtually to the same people another concession, under which they are now taking from the pockets of the public £600,000 per annum, and this is a charge which will go on growing should the mining industry survive the persistent attempts to strangle it. How a body charged with the public interests could be parties to this scandalous fleecing of the public passes comprehension. Then, the curious feature about the matter is that the Government gets some petty fraction of this vast sum, and the concessionnaires have on this plea obtained enormous advances of public moneys from the Government, without security, to carry on their trade. Shortly, the concessionnaries are entitled to charge 90s. a case for dynamite, while it could be bought, if there were no concession, for about 30s. a case. It may be stated incidentally that Mr. Wolmarans, a member of the Government, has been for years challenged to deny that he is enjoying a royalty of 2s. on every case of dynamite sold, and that he has up to the present moment neglected to take up the challenge. Proper municipal government is denied to us, and we all know how much this means with regard to health, comfort, and the value of property. The Statute books are disfigured with enactments imposing religious disabilities; and the English language, the language spoken by the great bulk of the people, is denied all official recognition. The natural result of the existing condition of things is that the true owners of the mines are those who have invested no capital in them—the Government, the railway concessionnaires, the dynamite concessionnaires, and others. The country is rich, and under proper government could be developed marvellously, but it cannot stand the drain of the present exactions. We have lived largely upon foreign capital, and the total amount of the dividends available for shareholders in companies is ridiculously small as compared with the aggregate amount of capital invested in mining ventures. Some day the inevitable result upon our credit and upon our trade will be forced upon us.

HATRED OF THE SAXON.

There is no disguising the fact that the original policy of the Government is based upon intense hostility to the English-speaking population, and that even against the enfranchised burgher of this State there is the determination to retain all power in the hands of those who are enjoying the sweets of office now, and naturally the grateful crowd of relations and friends and henchmen ardently support the existing *régime*; but there are unmistakable signs, and the President fears that the policy which he has hitherto adopted will not be sufficient to keep in check the growing population. It seems the set purpose of the Government to repress the growth of the industry, to tax it at every turn, to prevent the working classes from settling here and making their homes and surrounding themselves with their families, and there is no mistaking the significance of the action of the President when he opposed the throwing open of the town lands of Pretoria on the ground that "he might have a second Johannesburg there," nor that of his speech upon the motion for the employment of diamond drills to prospect Government lands, which he opposed hotly on the ground that "there is too much gold here already."

THE POLICY OF FORCE.

We now have openly the policy of force revealed to us. £250,000 is to be spent upon the completing of a fort at Pretoria, £100,000 is to be spent upon a fort to terrorise the inhabitants of Johannesburg, large orders are sent to Krupp's for big guns, Maxims have been ordered, and we are even told that German officers are coming out to drill the burghers. Are these things necessary, or are they calculated to irritate the feeling to breaking point? What necessity is there for forts in peaceful inland towns? Why should the Government endeavour to keep us in subjection to unjust laws by the power of the sword, instead of making themselves live in the heart of the people by a broad policy of justice? What can be said of a policy which deliberately divides the two great sections of the people from each other, instead of uniting them under equal laws, or the policy which keeps us in eternal turmoil with the neighbouring states? What shall be said of the state-craft every act of which sows torments, discontent, or race hatred, and reveals a conception of republicanism under which the only privilege of the majority of the people is to provide the revenue, and to bear insult, while only those are considered Republicans who speak a certain language, and in greater or less degree share the prejudices of the ruling classes?

A STIRRING PERORATION.

I think this policy can never succeed, unless men are absolutely bereft of every quality which made their forefathers free men; unless we have fallen so low that we are prepared to forget honour, self-respect, and our duty to our children. Once more, I wish to state again, in unmistakable language, what has been so frequently stated in perfect sincerity before, that we desire an independent republic, which shall be a true republic, in which every man who is prepared to take the oath of allegiance to the State shall have equal rights, in which our children shall be brought up side by side, as united members of a strong commonwealth, that we are animated by no race hatred, that we desire to deprive no man, be his nationality what it may, of any right.

The Charter of the Union.

We have now only two questions to consider : (*a*) What do we want ? (*b*) how shall we get it ? I have stated plainly what our grievances are, and I shall answer with equal directness the question, "What do we want?" We want : (1) the establishment of this Republic as a true republic ; (2) a Grondwet, or Constitution, which shall be framed by competent persons selected by representatives of the whole people and framed on lines laid down by them—a constitution which shall be safeguarded against hasty alteration ; (3) an equitable franchise law, and fair representation ; (4) equality of the Dutch and English languages ; (5) responsibility of the Legislature to the heads of the great departments ; (6) removal of religious disabilities ; (7) independence of the courts of justice, with adequate and secured remuneration of the judges ; (8) liberal and comprehensive education ; (9) efficient civil service, with adequate provision for pay and pension ; (10) free trade in South African products. That is what we want. There now remains the question which is to be put before you at the meeting of the 6th January, viz., How shall we get it ? To this question I shall expect from you an answer in plain terms according to your deliberate judgment.

CHARLES LEONARD,
Chairman of the Transvaal National Union.

APPENDIX III

STATEMENT OF THE REFORM LEADERS AT THE TRIAL

For a number of years endeavours have been made to obtain by constitutional means the redress of grievances under which the Uitlander population labours. The new-comers asked for no more than is conceded to immigrants by all the other Governments in South Africa, under which every man may, on reasonable conditions, become a citizen of the State, whilst here alone a policy is pursued by which the first settlers retain the exclusive right of government. A petition supported by the signatures of 40,000 men was ignored, and when it was found that we could not get a fair and reasonable hearing, that provisions already deemed obnoxious and unfair were being made more stringent, and that we were being debarred for ever from obtaining rights which in other countries are fully granted, it was realized that we should never get redress until we should make a demonstration of force to support our claims. Certain provision was made regarding arms and ammunition, and a letter was written to Dr. Jameson, in which he was asked to come to our aid under certain circumstances. On December 26th the Uitlanders' manifesto was published, and it was then our intention to make a final appeal for redress at the public meeting which was to have been held on the 6th of January. In consequence of matters that came to our knowledge, we sent on December 26th Major Heany by train *viâ* Kimberley, and Captain Holder across the country, to forbid any movement on Dr. Jameson's part. On the afternoon of Monday, the 30th December, we learnt from Government sources that Dr. Jameson had crossed the frontier. We assumed that he had come in good faith to help us, probably misled by some of the exaggerated rumours which were then in circulation. We were convinced, however, that the Government and the burghers would not, in the excitement of the moment, believe that we had not

invited Dr. Jameson in, and there was no course open to us but
to prepare to defend ourselves if attacked, and at the same time
to spare no effort to effect a peaceful settlement. It became
necessary to form some organization for the protection of the
town and the maintenance of order, since in the excitement caused
by the news of Dr. Jameson's coming serious disturbances would
be likely to occur, and it was evident that the Government organization could not deal with the people without serious risks of
conflict. The Reform Committee was formed on Monday night,
the 30th December, and it was intended to include such men of
influence as cared to associate themselves with the movement.
The object with which it was formed is best shown in its first
notice, namely,—

"Notice is hereby given that this Committee adheres to the
National Union manifesto, and reiterates its desire to maintain
the independence of the Republic. The fact that rumours are in
course of circulation to the effect that a force has crossed the
Bechuanaland border renders it necessary to take active steps
for the defence of Johannesburg and the preservation of order.
The Committee earnestly desire that the inhabitants should
refrain from taking any action which can be construed as an
overt act of hostility against the Government; by order of the
Committee, J. Percy Fitzpatrick, Secretary."

The evidence taken at the preliminary examination shows that
order was maintained by this Committee during a time of intense
excitement, and through the action of the Committee no aggressive steps whatever were taken against the Government, but,
on the contrary, the property of the Government was protected,
and its officials were not interfered with. It is our firm belief
that had no such Committee been formed the intense excitement
caused by Dr. Jameson's entry would have brought about utter
chaos in Johannesburg. It has been alleged that we armed
natives. This is absolutely untrue, and is disposed of by the
fact that during the crisis upwards of 20,000 white men applied
to us for arms, and were unable to get them. On Tuesday morning, the 31st December, we hoisted the flag of the Z.A.R., and
every man bound himself to maintain the independence of the
Republic. On the same day the Government withdrew its police
voluntarily from the town, and we preserved perfect order. During
the evening of the same day, Messrs. Marais and Malan presented

themselves as delegates from the Executive Council. They came (to use their own words) to offer us the olive branch, and they told us that if we would send a deputation to Pretoria to meet a Commission appointed by the Government, we would obtain "practically all we asked in the manifesto." Our deputation met the Government Commission, consisting of Chief Justice Kotze, Judge Ameshoff, and Mr. Kock, member of the Executive. On our behalf our deputation frankly avowed knowledge of Jameson's presence on the border, and of his intention, by arrangement with us, to assist us in case of extremity. With the full knowledge of this arrangement—with the knowledge that we were in arms and agitating for our rights, the Government Commission handed to us a resolution of the Executive Council, of which the following is the purport: "Sir Hercules Robinson has offered his services with a view to a peaceful settlement. The Government of the South African Republic has accepted his offer. Pending his arrival, no hostile steps will be taken against Johannesburg, provided Johannesburg take no hostile action against the Government. In terms of a certain proclamation recently issued by the President, the grievances will be earnestly considered." We parted in perfect good faith with the Government, believing it to be their desire, as it was ours, to avert bloodshed, and believing it to be their intention to give us the redress which was implied in the "earnest consideration of grievances." There can be no stronger evidence of our earnest endeavour to repair what we regarded as a mistake by Dr. Jameson than the offer which our deputation, authorized by resolution of the Committee, laid before the Government Commission, "If the Government will permit Dr Jameson to come to Johannesburg unmolested, the Committee will guarantee with their persons, if necessary, that he will leave again peacefully as soon as possible." We faithfully carried out the agreement that we should commit no act of hostility against the Government; we ceased all active operations for the defence of the town against any attack, and we did everything in our power to prevent any collision with the burghers, an attempt in which our efforts were happily successful. On the telegraphic advice of the result of the interview of the deputation with the Government Commission, we despatched Mr. Lace, a member of our Committee, as an escort to the courier carrying the High Commissioner's despatch to Dr. Jameson, in order to assure our selves that the despatch would reach its destination. On the following Saturday, January 4, the High Commissioner arrived in Pretoria. On Monday, the 6th, the following telegram was sent to us :—

"Pretoria, 6th January, 1896.—From H.M. Agent to Reform Committee, Johannesburg.—I am directed to inform you that the High Commissioner met the President, the Executive, and the Judges to-day. The President announced the decision of the Government to be that Johannesburg must lay down its arms unconditionally, as a condition precedent to a discussion and consideration of grievances. The High Commissioner endeavoured to obtain some indication of the steps which would be taken in the event of disarmament, but without success, it being intimated that the Government had nothing more to say on this subject than had already been embodied in the President's proclamation. The High Commissioner enquired whether any decision had been come to as regards the disposal of the prisoners, and received a reply in the negative. The President said that as his burghers to the number of 8,000 had been collected, and could not be asked to remain indefinitely, he must request a reply, yes or no, to this ultimatum within twenty-four hours.—J. DE WET, Her Majesty's Agent."

On the following day Sir Jacobus de Wet met us in Committee, and handed us the following wire from the High Commissioner :—

"High Commissioner, Pretoria, to Sir Jacobus de Wet, Johannesburg.—Received, Johannesburg, 7.36 a.m., 7th January, 1896. Urgent.—You should inform the Johannesburg people that I consider that if they lay down their arms they will be acting loyally and honourably, and that if they do not comply with the request they forfeit all claims to sympathy from Her Majesty's Government and from British subjects throughout the world, as the lives of Jameson and prisoners are practically in their hands."

On this, and assurances given in the Executive Council resolution, we laid down our arms on the 6th, 7th, and 8th January. On the 9th we were arrested and have since been under arrest in Pretoria—a period of three and a half months. We admit responsibility for the action taken by us. We practically avowed it at the time of the negotiations with the Government, when we were informed that the services of the High Commissioner had been accepted with a view to a peaceful settlement. We submit that we kept faith in every detail in the arrangement. We did all that was humanly possible to protect both the State and Dr. Jameson from the consequences of his action ; that we have committed no breach of the law which was not known to the Government at the time ; and that the earnest consideration of our grievances was promised. We can now only put the bare facts before the Court, and submit to the judgment that may be passed upon us.

(Signed) LIONEL PHILLIPS,
FRANCIS RHODES,
GEORGE FARRAR.

PRETORIA, 24*th April*, 1896.

I entirely concur with the above statement.

—JOHN HAYS HAMMOND.

PRETORIA, 27*th April*, 1896.

STATEMENT HANDED IN BY THE REMAINDER OF THE COMMITTEE

"We have heard the statement made by Mr. Lionel Phillips, and we fully agree with what he has said as regards the objects of the Reform Committee. We have worked with these gentlemen, and the only object all had in view was to use their utmost endeavours to avert bloodshed, but at the same time to endeavour to obtain the redress of what we considered very serious grievances."

APPENDIX IV

THE CONVENTION OF LONDON (1884).
(CRITICAL CLAUSES.)

ARTICLE I. (defines Boundaries).

Art. II.—The Government of the South African Republic will strictly adhere to the boundaries defined in the first Article of this Convention, and will do its utmost to prevent any of its inhabitants from making any encroachments upon lands beyond the said boundaries. The Government of the South African Republic will appoint Commissioners upon the eastern and western borders whose duty it will be strictly to guard against irregularities and all trespassing over the boundaries. Her Majesty's Government will, if necessary, appoint Commissioners in the native territories outside the eastern and western borders of the South African Republic to maintain order and prevent encroachments.

Her Majesty's Government and the Government of the South African Republic will each appoint a person to proceed together to beacon off the amended south-west boundary as described in Article I. of this Convention ; and the President of the Orange Free State shall be requested to appoint a referee to whom the said persons shall refer any questions on which they may disagree respecting the interpretation of the said Article, and the decision of such referee thereon shall be final. The arrangement already made, under the terms of Article XIX. of the Convention of Pretoria of the 3rd August, 1881, between the owners of the farms Grootfontein and Valleifontein on the one hand, and the Barolong authorities on the other, by which a fair share of the water supply of the said farms shall be allowed to flow undisturbed to the said Barolongs, shall continue in force.

Art. III.—If a British officer is appointed to reside at Pretoria or elsewhere within the South African Republic to discharge functions analagous to those of a Consular officer, he will receive the protection and assistance of the Republic.

Art. IV.—The South African Republic will conclude no Treaty or engagement with any State or nation other than the Orange Free State, nor with any native tribe to the eastward or westward of the Republic, until the same has been approved by Her Majesty the Queen. Such approval shall be considered to have been granted if Her Majesty's Government shall not, within six months after receiving a copy of such Treaty (which shall be delivered to them immediately upon its completion), have notified that the conclusion of such Treaty is in conflict with the interests of Great Britain, or of any of Her Majesty's Possessions in South Africa.

Arts. V. and VI. (deal with State financial liabilities).

Art. VII.—All persons who held property in the Transvaal on the 8th day of August, 1881, and still hold the same, will continue to enjoy the rights of property which they have enjoyed since the 12th April, 1877. No person who has remained loyal to Her Majesty during the late hostilities shall suffer any molestation by reason of his loyalty; or be liable to any criminal prosecution or civil action for any part taken in connection with such hostilities; and all such persons will have full liberty to reside in the country, with enjoyment of all civil rights and protection for their persons and property.

Art. VIII.—The South African Republic renews the declaration made in the Sand River Convention, and in the Convention of Pretoria, that no slavery or apprenticeship partaking of slavery, will be tolerated by the Government of the said Republic.

Art. IX.—There will continue to be complete freedom of religion and protection from molestation for all denominations, provided the same be not inconsistent with morality and good order; and no disability shall attach to any person in regard to rights of property by reason of the religious opinions which he holds.

Art. X. (is about graves of British soldiers in Transvaal).

Art. XI.—All grants or titles issued at any time by the Transvaal Government in respect of land outside the boundary of the South African Republic, as defined in Article I., shall be considered invalid and of no effect, except in so far as any such grant or title relates to land that falls within the boundary of the South African Republic; and all persons holding any such grant so considered invalid and of no effect will receive from the Government of the South African Republic such compensation, either in land or money, as the Volksraad shall determine. In all cases in which any Native Chiefs or other authorities outside the said boundaries have received any adequate consideration from the Government of the South African Republic for land excluded from the Transvaal by the first Article of this Convention, or where permanent improvements have been made on the land, the High Commissioner will recover from the native authorities fair compensation for the loss of the land thus excluded, or of the permanent improvements thereon.

Art. XII.—The independence of the Swazis, within the boundary line of Swaziland, as indicated in the first Article of this Convention, will be fully recognised.

Art. XIII.—Except in pursuance of any treaty or engagement made as provided in Article IV. of this Convention, no other or higher duties shall be imposed on the importation into the South African Republic of any article coming from any part of Her Majesty's dominions than are or may be imposed on the like article coming from any other place or country; nor will any prohibition be maintained or imposed on the importation into the South African Republic of any article coming from any part of Her Majesty's dominions which shall not equally extend to the like article coming from any other place or country. And in like manner the same treatment shall be given to any article coming to Great Britain from the South African Republic as to the like article coming from any other place or country. These provisions do not preclude the consideration of special arrangements as to import duties and commercial relations between the South African Republic and any of Her Majesty's Colonies and Possessions.

Art. XIV.—All persons, other than natives, conforming themselves to the laws of the South African Republic, (*a*) will have full liberty, with their families, to enter, travel, or reside in any part of the South African Republic; (*b*) they will be entitled to hire or possess houses, manufactories, warehouses, shops, and premises; (*c*) they may carry on their commerce either in person or by any agents whom they may think fit to employ; (*d*) they will not be subject, in respect of their persons or property, or in respect of their commerce or industry, to any taxes, whether general or local, other than those which are or may be imposed upon citizens of the said Republic.

APPENDICES

Art. XV.—(Makes some exemptions from compulsory military service, completed as regards all British subjects by Lord Loch's 1894 arrangement).

Art. XVI.—(Extradition).

Arts. XVII., XVIII.—(Pre-retrocession debts and other contracts).

Art. XIX.—The Government of the South African Republic will engage faithfully to fulfil the assurances given, in accordance with the laws of the South African Republic, to the natives at the Pretoria Pitso by the Royal Commission in the presence of the Triumvirate and with their entire assent, (1) as to the freedom of the natives to buy or otherwise acquire land under certain conditions; (2) as to the appointment of a commission to mark out native locations; (3) as to the access of the natives to the courts of law; and (4) as to their being allowed to move freely within the country, or to leave it for any legal purpose, under a pass system.

Art. XX.—(Ratification provision).

Signed in duplicate in London this 27th day of February, 1884.

(Signed) HERCULES ROBINSON.
(Signed) S. J. P. KRUGER.
(Signed) S. J. DU TOIT.
(Signed) M. J. SMIT.

APPENDIX V

CECIL RHODES AND HIS POLICY

As Sketched by the Author in 1889-90

(Extract from "In Afrikanderland.")

. . . "THERE lies before me another curious illustration of the efforts which, in the anti-English period after the Transvaal war, the Government of the Republic repeatedly made, but made in vain, to conclude arrangements with the Matabele King. This is a copy of a letter which was sent by General Joubert to Lobengula nine years ago. It was given to me by Mr. Selous, the eponymous hero of the "Selous Road" to Fort Salisbury, the Nimrod of South Africa, the English Pathfinder whose unerring skill has since guided the pioneers of Mashonaland safely to their goal through the trackless bush. It had never before been published, this strange State paper, and Mr. Selous had become possessed of it as follows: On one of the adventurous hunting expeditions which have chequered the last twenty years of Mr. Selous' life, the young Englishman happened to be up at the King's kraal when the letter arrived. It was couched in Dutch, and the messenger could not translate it. At Lobengula's request Mr. Selous took the letter down to his wagon, and there wrote out the very translation which he showed me in manuscript. The letter is dated "Marico, S.A.R., March 9, 1882," and addressed to "the great ruler, the chief Lobengula, son of Umziligaze, the great King of the Matabele nation." "Now you must have heard," it runs, "that the English took away our country, the Transvaal, or, as they say, annexed it. We then talked nicely for four years, and begged for our country. But no; when an Englishman once has your property in his hands, then is he like to an ape that has its hands full of pumpkin-seeds. If you don't beat him to death, he will never let go. And thus all our nice talk for four years did not help us at all. Then the English commenced to arrest us, because we were dissatisfied, and that caused the shooting and fighting. Then the English first found that it would be better to give us back our country. . . . And we will now once more live in friendship with Lobengula, as we lived in friendship with Umziligaze; and such must be our friendship that so long as there is one Boer and one Matabele living these must remain friends." After a hopeful allusion to the time "when the stink which the Englishman brought with him is blown away altogether," this unique document of diplomacy closes with the signature of "The Commandant-General of the S.A. Republic, for the Government and Administration, P. J. Joubert."

. . . "In truth, Mr. Rhodes will only be striking the last, winning stroke in a battle which he has been fighting ever since 82–'83—since the time of the filibustering "Republics" of Stellaland and Goshen, the expedition of Sir Charles Warren, and the proclamation of Bechuanaland as a protectorate with Crown colony for base. It was an open eye to the north which made the Government of the Transvaal turn a blind eye on the west to the irregularities of the overflow into Bechuanaland. That overflow would have locked the Republic with German territory, built a Boer wall, as it were, across the continent of Africa, and so fenced us off once and for all from direct expansion towards the interior of the continent. In the firm and timely settlement which checkmated that design Mr. Rhodes had a hand, and struck the keynote of his policy ever since towards the Boer pioneer. "Keep your land titles," he said in effect to the adventurers who called themselves the "Republic of Stellaland"—"keep your titles, but write them in English instead of Dutch." On the one hand he realized that everything must be done with and through the Dutch; on the other, he already regarded Bechuanaland as the English high road to Zambesia.

"The story of how Paul Kruger was outflanked takes us back to the "Railway Question." . . . Oom Paul would not hear of the Kimberley line being carried forward to the Transvaal goldfields, which were then regarded as its goal. He must first see the completion of the Delagoa Bay railway—not to say the Greek Kalends, or the coming of the Coqigrues. For a time, no doubt, President Kruger simply pleaded precedence for the Delagoa Bay line as a means of delaying altogether the advent of the iron horse. Then he seems to have conceived the idea of Pretoria as a railway capital, the centre of a grand trunk system which would throw out an arm not only to Delagoa Bay and to each of the colonial ports, but northward, *viâ* the north-eastern gold deposits of the Transvaal, to the land of Ophir.

"But while Oom Paul, like the marketer in the fable, was deliberating on the giddy wealth that his crockery ought to bring him in, the pick of the basket was spilt before his eyes. Just when Cape Colony as a whole is beginning to feel heartily sick of being played off against Natal, when even the Dutch farmer of the "Paarl party" is stung with the suspicion that he has been cheaply humbugged by Oom Paul's promises of a favouring tariff—at this psychological moment enters on the scene Mr. Rhodes with his concession and Charter. "Kruger will not let us take the Kimberley line into his country? Very well, says the Kimberley Diamond King, then we will take it round him and beyond, on the way to the richer Transvaal of the Zambesi. What is more, here is my Company ready, for a consideration, to undertake the job." A three-cornered bargain between the Imperial Government, the Colonial Government, and the Company is soon arranged; so much land for taking the line to Vryburg (where it now is),[1] so much more for taking it to Mafeking, hitherto the *ultima Thule* of South African traders—terms on which the Cape Government should raise a loan, and on which it can eventually take over the railway. What does this mean? It means that instead of young Cape Colony seeking careers in the Transvaal, young South Africa, the Transvaal included, will have to seek careers in the great interior under the flag of Mr. Rhodes. . . . Cape Town will have its pull at whatever milk and honey may be flowing in Matabeleland proper, through that thin strip of territory which was saved from Boer clutches in 1885 as the neck of the bottle. But strategically, in any case, the railway has done its work. It has given into Cape keeping the key to the land of Ophir. Oom Paul has let a pawn be pushed past him, and the pawn, by all the rules of chess, has made itself a queen.

"You see at once how the situation has been revolutionized. Suppose for a moment that in the long struggle for ascendency in Matabeleland, Boer, and not British, had won the day. Suppose, in other words, that instead of a Transvaal pent in between the Vaal and the Limpopo, and already overrun with English or English-speaking men, we had now to deal with a Transvaal

---

[1] It is to reach Buluwayo this year.—Feb., 1897.

larger than Great Britain, France, Austria, and Italy put together, its boundaries marching on the west with German territory, and on the east with Portuguese, while to the north the Boer pioneer might stand, as the Englishman stands now, and look across the Zambesi to a vista which it will be for future history to limit. Then, indeed, the Transvaal might well call itself the "South African Republic"; and on what a vantage-ground would it take its stand when the time comes to make terms for the confederation of the future! At present every community of English and Colonial miners that we plant on Transvaal soil is as a great piece of blotting-paper laid over so much of the map, soaking up the script which marks it alien to England. Within the Republic this absorbent power has well nigh done its work. But if, by a sort of fissiparous birth, a new and a larger Transvaal could suddenly appear clinging to the side of the old, that work would be more than half undone. As it is, the Boer will multiply and spread side by side with the Englishman and the English Afrikander; but he will do so under the English flag. Among the members of the United South Africa of the future the two premier States have changed places. The dream of a Boer hegemony has melted away. With the gold of Ophir to put into the scale against the gold of the Transvaal, and a territory encircling the two Dutch Republics as the sea washes a peninsula, we hold the balance in our hands. Once again the South African centre of gravity has been moved along its wonted line from Cape Town to Kimberley, from Kimberley to Johannesburg, from Johannesburg to Matabeleland. John Bull's "John Company" has brought in a new world to redress the balance of the old.

* * * * *

"'Il n'y a pas un homme nécessaire.' That philosophical apophthegm, like the historical one which says that the moment makes the man, not the man the moment, is only half true. There is no indispensable man—no, not if you mean indispensable to a hemisphere, to an epoch, to a time or an interest large enough to count in the eternal sum of things. But when you come down to such trifles as the interest of the British Empire in a particular century in a particular quarter of the globe, it is different. From such a point of view as this Mr. Rhodes has been for some years a Necessary Man in South Africa. Of course, the better work he does, the less indispensable will he become every day, as is the fate of necessary men. But I think my nickname will serve him for some time yet. He is still the one common denominator to all the fractions—the Colonial Imperialist, the Federal Home Ruler, the English Afrikander, the man who can so carry the Union Jack that Dutch Boer will go forward under its folds shoulder to shoulder with Cape Colonist, with Natalian, with Englishman. He alone at the Cape seems able to strike out of his native energy heat enough to bring to the fusing-point those divergent elements—divergent in a low temperature—" Empire and Self-government."

"Cecil John Rhodes, the founder and moving spirit of the British South Africa Company, the amalgamator and moving spirit of the De Beers Diamond Mining Company, and the Prime Minister of Cape Colony, is only thirty-eight. A year ago, when Sir Gordon Sprigg resigned office, and Mr. Hofmeyr declined it, and Mr. Rhodes formed a Ministry in twenty-four hours, he had to play for a time yet another part. Forced to add the cares of a grown colony to those of an empire in the making, Mr. Rhodes at first stickled to be "Prime Minister without portfolio." But, an hour before the new Government met Parliament, the Speaker (by an error since corrected) ruled the arrangement unconstitutional; and Mr. Rhodes found himself pitchforked into the Commissionership of Crown Lands and Works. It boasts as much detail as most of the Cape Departments; but Mr. Rhodes, thus cornered, buckled to his Lands and Works with a will, and never flagged for the rest of the session.

"But a mere pluralist is not "Necessary" as such. Even if Mr. Rhodes' offices were more multiplied and more responsible than all that I have named, they would hardly do more than hint, on the face of them, how much this gentleman of large designs would be missed. The faithful reader who has followed through its intricacies the story of the English in Ophir will understand how completely the whole gigantic enterprise has pivoted on Mr. Rhodes. A corporation, as Professor Seeley has said of the old John Company, can neither catch a fever nor be killed in battle. But the fortunes of a corporation can largely be bound up with the life of a man who, though he stands as big as Saul and is as ruddy as David, was hardly expected some thirteen years ago to outlive the voyage to the Cape. Certainly you would not guess it now; and Mr. Rhodes tells a humorous story of the discomfiture of a certain worthy doctor who had pronounced doom on him in those youthful days. "*You* the same Rhodes, sir? Impossible! According to my books you have been a corpse these ten years. Here is the entry . . . tuberculosis . . . recovery impossible." "Impossible" is a word wanting in Mr. Rhodes' dictionary.

"Cecil Rhodes was only fifteen—a delicate and rather dull lad, "privately educated"—when he sailed for the Cape under such gloomy auspices. His father, for twenty years rector of Bishop Stortford, had a family of six boys. Four of them turned soldiers, and one of them, now with Lord Harris in Bombay, has been through the Soudan. Probably Cecil was the last of the brothers that any one would have picked out for the great career. He began as a planter in Natal, but abandoned cotton for diamonds in the early seventies. At Kimberley he put a few thousands (as many as he could get) into old De Beers shares, and claims, and lands. When the mines fell on evil days he saw that he could unite them into a Golconda; did so, and made himself a millionaire.

"That is an old story, told in an earlier chapter. The curious thing is that even while he was in the first flush of excitement over mining and money-making, the young man determined to send himself to college. Five years he spent hovering between the iron shanties of Kimberley and the grey towers of Oriel. He discovered a new use for the Long Vacation. At Oxford the young colonist and his friend Maguire were the most popular men in a jovial hunting set. Rhodes "kept the drag," but got his pass, and found time withal to go north and study pumping machinery. To-day his *entourage* finds in him that strange hybrid —an Afrikander and a Diamond King under the old-world spell of a university in the old country. I suspect Oriel and Oxford enter largely into his patriotism; and a new Oriel and a new Oxford, nestling under the shadow of Table Mountain, are more than mere accessories in his dream of a United South Africa. At twenty-eight the member for the Diamond constituency was what we should call Chancellor of the Exchequer in the brief Scanlen Ministry. The office served his purposes and ours better than appeared at the time. It saved him from being stabbed along with Gordon at Khartoum. Gordon had met Rhodes at the Cape at the time of the Basuto trouble. There was a robust faith in "God's Englishmen," if nothing else, common to the two men; and Gordon took a liking for the young colonist—though he did once flame out at him Gordonesquely: "You are one of those men who will never approve of anything not organized by yourself." From this liking sprang the invitation to come and join Gordon on his mission to Khartoum, which the Treasurer-Generalship happily debarred. From this point, for the last five or six years, Mr. Rhodes has divided with Mr. Hofmeyr the underlying forces of Cape politics. He has done more than any other man for the racial, if not yet for the political, union of South Africa. We have seen him in these pages peace-making in Bechuanaland (in 1884-1885), or at Blignaut's Pont (last year), where he helped the High Commissioner to strike the Swaziland Convention with President Kruger. He was the first to grasp and to popularize what I have called, for want of a better word, the New Afrikanderism—the conception of Imperial progress made through and for the colony, of Colonial progress made through and for the Dutch, and not merely for the mother country in the one field, and the mother country's scions in the other. All that he has done has been done in touch with the Bond and the Paarl, hand in glove with the "Parnell of the Dutch." Some say Rhodes is using Hofmeyr—some say Hofmeyr is using Rhodes. In either case the result is that we see a Dutch majority in Cape Colony following an English Premier while he takes away the north from their Dutch cousins of the Transvaal Republic, tells these cousins, "As rivals you are stopped, but we want you as helpers," and calls on all South Africa to join in developing the new empire under the British flag.

"The Dutch know that if Imperialism meant, as it once did mean in South Africa and elsewhere, the Divine right of Downing Street, the subordination of the sentiments and interests of an embryo nation in the New World to the convenience of a clique of official failures and place-hunters in the Old, in that moment Rhodes the Imperialist would yield to Rhodes the Republican, and the Presidency of the independent United States of South Africa would be the goal of his ambition. Incapable by temperament of the narrow provincialism which regards the position of a Colonial Switzerland under a guarantee of the Powers as a grander prospect than enfranchisement of the Empire, Mr. Rhodes would yet accept that prospect unhesitatingly as the alternative to complete Home Rule. Unity, with complete local self-government of the units—it is hard to say which of the two conditions appeals more to Mr. Rhodes where both are attained. It is not hard, if it were a case of one without the other, to say which Mr. Rhodes would choose.

"The princely gift to the Irish Nationalist exchequer, a few years ago, while it witnessed the intensity of this feeling, defined it precisely. The declaration by Mr. Parnell which Mr. Rhodes thought worth £10,000 was an acceptance by the Home Rule dictator of the Colonial, or so called federal, reading of Home Rule. As long as Mr. Parnell was Mr. Parnell, and held by that, Mr. Rhodes would have held by him—the English passion for the finer personal ethics in a politician being a northern exotic which languishes at the Cape. But an Ireland under Separatist Home Rule Mr. Rhodes would fight against as hard as the most fanatical Unionist in the three kingdoms. "Your Bill, sir," he insisted to Mr. Gladstone in one of his stout, outspoken talks, "your Bill of 1886 would have created a taxed Republic. If I were an Irishman, and it had passed, I would have started a crusade for Representation or Separation the very next day!"

"Mr. Rhodes is an opportunist, yes: in the same sense as Mr. Gladstone, or Sir Henry Parkes, or the late Sir John Macdonald. The morality of the thing all hangs on the quality and steadfastness of the central idea. Here is a man who spends his time in persuading a great many other men that they all really want the same thing as each other and as himself—a man who one day is in close conference with Unionist aristocrats in a directors' boardroom, the next with Home Rule Radicals in the lobby, to-day lunching with a journalist at an hotel, to-morrow dining with Her Majesty at Windsor Castle; equally at home in a parley at the Foreign Office and at a Dutch dinner in the Paarl. To political purists and doctrinaires at one pole, to political cynics and men of the world at the other, such a man is bound to seem something of a humbug. All things to all men can hardly be one thing to himself. The taste for managing men is as dangerous as dram-drinking. I can easily believe what Cape gossip says, that Mr. Rhodes has been hard put to it sometimes to cheat that modern understudy of the political conscience—the shorthand reporter. You may accept the most flattering version of the famous ten years' work of Mr. Parnell (also in his day a Necessary Man) without affecting to acquit him of having somewhere fibbed to somebody. But the extreme cynical view of Mr. Rhodes, like the too vaulting ambition and cupidity which it would ascribe to him, o'erleaps itself altogether. I once listened patiently to a detailed dissection of Mr. Rhodes by one who had "seen through" him, in which the only doubt was whether the poor man's politics are a stalking-horse for his finance or his finance for his politics; the one thing past doubt being the dark, and deep, and devilish nature of both. Not even genius was left—only the City swindler's vulgar art of "squaring the circle." Patiently I listened, until in due course the all-sufficient explanation was applied to Mr. Parnell's famous cheque. Then I breathed again. The touchstone of one supreme anachronism and absurdity sufficed for all the rest. A "man of the world" may believe that Mr. Rhodes, who at least is not a fool, sunk £10,000 in buying a parliamentary support which at any time would be valueless for an object which at that time he demonstrably meant to obtain by extra-parliamentary means. Not so anybody who knows anything about politics here and at the Cape.

"The fact is that Mr. Rhodes, like the rest of us, is a bundle of inconsistencies, at once headstrong and politic, keen and lazy, cynical and enthusiastic. With all his finance and his finesse, he can be bluff almost to brutality. Up to a certain point he is patience itself; no delay fatigues him, no objection proves too great for his accommodating skill. "Now, sir," says he, "you want this; I want that; will not so-and-so serve the turn of both of us?" But once pass that point, and you might as well try to move the rock of Cashel. About the time of the Kimberley amalgamation he came to Europe to raise a large sum of money, and wasted his time in the ante-chamber of a very high and mighty financier. At last the despot of the *bourses* said that he would consider the matter, and give Mr. Rhodes an answer in a few days. Now the matter had been well considered already, and this was *blague*. "Sir," said young Mr. Rhodes quietly and simply, "I will call again in half an hour. If you are not ready with your answer then, I shall go elsewhere." Mr. Rhodes had not to go elsewhere. First impressions, again, from the heavy build and step, the sauntering manner, and something dreamy in the prominent grey eyes, notwithstanding the masterful chin to the contrary, would put Mr. Rhodes down as a lazy man. A different tale is told, not merely by the work he has done, but by his way of doing it. Friends have queer reminiscences of the amalgamation years—the years of infinite plotting and plodding which built up "De Beers' Consolidated." "We would be riding out together, chatting indifferently," said one, "when suddenly Rhodes would wake up, as it were, and exclaim, pointing with his whip, 'We must have that property.' The rest of the ride would be a brown study. A week later I would hear that the property was bought." "In the middle of the night," said another and more intimate friend, "Rhodes would jump out of bed, come round to me, and wake me up. He would say, 'I've just hit on an idea,' and then he would unfold the solution of some knotty problem that had been worrying us for weeks." "Rhodes does half his business in the street," a third observer told me. "He pulls out his cheque-book, and settles a big transaction while other people would be passing the time of day." I have heard Mr. Rhodes defined as a cynic whose one formula for success was "Find the man's price." If you read price in a large enough sense, I am not disposed to dispute that, nor to deny that even when the price is of the most sordid quality, Mr. Rhodes will often use the man for ends worthy a better instrument. But if he is a cynic, he is also an enthusiast, and he presses the former's quality into the latter's service. Money, either to hoard or to spend, he does not care for. Power is his idol: creative power, efficient energy, control over men and things in the mass. In the British Empire he recognises the most perfect and far-reaching machine for this purpose which the world has yet seen, and the Empire, accordingly, is his religion. "Sentiment," he once said to me, when I objected that some idea or other, on which he laid stress, was "mere sentiment," "sentiment rules half the world." We have seen what is the sentiment which rules Mr. Rhodes. "The brother who eats a whole country for his dinner," as he was described at Lobengula's kraal, is a vivid embodiment of the earth-hunger which has set in among the nations, and which in Mr. Rhodes' countrymen at least is more than a mere instinct for idle land-grabbing. "The time is coming," says Mr. Rhodes again, "when every square mile of the earth's surface will be valuable;" much more, then, every territory where men of the dominant white race can thrive, and work, and dig power out of the earth. For some millionaires it is enough to run a yacht. Mr. Rhodes' hobby is running an Empire. He has that inclusiveness of mind, that passion for the

x

grand scale, for generalizing and combining in the gross, which goes to make Newtons, and Napoleons, and Darwins, and Bismarcks—each in his own field of thought or action. He is always thinking of the next move but one; he is the general who carries the whole line of battle in his head. When he was in England, nominally absorbed in the "Manica Question," he was really as full of Canada as of the Cape. No doubt the tariff crisis in the American Continent, taken in its Imperial bearing, was a much bigger matter than a wrangle with a tottering Power on the East Coast of Africa. But Mr. Rhodes, at least, might have been excused for not seeing that. The same sense of true perspective serves him as to the relation of names and things. So long as he governs, who will may reign. The opposition of the Pungwe short cut and the Kimberley Railway opposes the Managing Director of the Chartered Company to the Premier of the Cape; the opposition of the new Wesselton Mine and the De Beers monopoly opposes the Premier of the Cape to the Managing Director of De Beers. To-day all these persons are one—Mr. Cecil John Rhodes. Within the year that may become impossible; then Mr. Rhodes, without a moment's doubt, will resign the Premiership.

"The personal charm which Mr. Rhodes seems able to exercise over men of the most various temperaments has nothing to do with that "sugar-doodling" which somebody defined as the secret of the same knack in Laurence Oliphant. He is brusquely frank. With Mr. Gladstone we have seen him. Lord Salisbury bears almost plaintive witness to his "considerable force of character." Sir William Harcourt he provoked to that amusing parody of his views on the Native Question and Imperial Zollverein : "Reasonable man, Mr. Rhodes—so easily satisfied ! All he asks us is to give up free trade and restore slavery."[1] He has had many a brush with those "Little England" Liberals who see the town-pump of Ballymahooly so out of focus that it dwarfs nations and continents. "You make it very hard for us colonists to be Liberals," is a phrase of his. But *brusquerie* and *bonhomie* go together. A man in the mines at Kimberley told me a pleasant tale of a *rencontre* of his, when new to Kimberley, with the Diamond King incognito. In talk with an unknown visitor, who seemed

---

[1] I owe this story to the *Review of Reviews*.

RHODES IN '90]

anxious to learn, my man held forth with the dogmatism of the practical worker on some point or other in which Rhodes was at fault—" this Rhodes, who thinks he knows all about it, I suppose." The inquisitive visitor turned out to be "this Rhodes" himself— but both parties profited by the meeting. In conversation Mr. Rhodes is no show talker. But he has a zest, a grip, a strong sense, a straightforward heartiness, which are simply irresistible. You feel that he has read (for a business man) much, thought for himself, and knows just what he means. As a public speaker he is much the same. His manner is awkward, his tone colloquial. He is no more an orator than Lord Hartington, but he has Mr. Healy's knack of shoving the gist of the matter into some blunt phrase. His tastes are simple to a fault. He cares not a pin what he eats and drinks, so there be enough of it, or wherewithal he shall be clothed, so there be not too much of it. The Premier's is the dowdiest hat in the House of Assembly. He lives in chambers and at the club. His unconventionality shocks the sticklers. They were opening an extension of the Cape Town suburban railway the other day—an extension at the edge of one of those tempting blue bights which fret the Cape peninsula. Suddenly the central figure of the ceremonies was missed—and descried a short way off, stalking out of the water to rejoin his clothes. Lastly, Mr. Rhodes is still an unappropriated match, and not, so friends declare, a "marrying man"; which is a pity, for the man would be none the worse for a few more feminine traits about him.

"Such, as well as I can sketch him, is the Colonial statesman who has lately burst upon the public consciousness as in some vague sense "the coming man"; who a few months ago carried London before him; whose "amalgamating" quality sufficed to bring together round the same table men in society and politics who had not met before for years; whose praises as an Imperialist were sung in chorus by wiseacres who used to shake heads at him as an Afrikander. They have realized at last that he is the one in spite of the other. Perhaps some day they will realize that he is the one *because* of the other, and both for the same reasons.

"One day, some six years ago, Mr. Rhodes, then busy with the amalgamation of the Diamond Mines, was looking at a map of Africa hung in the office of a Kimberley merchant. After gazing intently at it for some time, he placed his hand over a great slice of Southern and Central Africa, right across the continent; and, turning to a friend at his side, "There," said Mr. Rhodes, "all that British! That is my dream." "I give you ten years," returned the friend—who told me the story himself on the very scene of the incident. More than half the allotted term has passed, and more than half Mr. Rhodes' dream is already accomplished. It is of good omen for the rest.

"It suggests that the Necessary Man may crown and complete his work in South Africa while he is yet in the prime of life. That we shall then have a larger use for this Englishman, none can doubt who believes that the problem of reconciling central unity with local self-government is the problem on which our future as a factor in the world's history depends."

www.ingramcontent.com/pod-product-compliance
Lightning Source LLC
Chambersburg PA
CBHW031859220426
43663CB00006B/690